ALSO BY TOM VANDERBILT

You May Also Like

Traffic

Survival City

BEGINNERS

BEGINNERS

THE JOY AND TRANSFORMATIVE POWER
OF LIFELONG LEARNING

TOM VANDERBILT

ALFRED A. KNOPF   NEW YORK   2021

THIS IS A BORZOI BOOK
PUBLISHED BY ALFRED A. KNOPF

Portions of this work previously appeared, in different form, as
"Learning Chess at 40" in *Nautilus*, Issue 36 (nautil.us) on May 5,
2016, and "My Family Vacation Swimming in the Open Sea" in
Outside (outsideonline.com) on July 2, 2019.

Library of Congress Cataloging-in-Publication Data
Names: Vanderbilt, Tom, author.
Title: Beginners : the joy and transformative power of lifelong
learning / Tom Vanderbilt.
Description: New York : Alfred A. Knopf, 2021. | Includes
bibliographical references.
Identifiers: LCCN 2019057320 (print) | LCCN 2019057321 (ebook)
| ISBN 9781524732165 (hardcover) | ISBN 9781524711849 (open
market) | ISBN 9781524732172 (ebook)
Subjects: LCSH: Self-actualization (Psychology) | Self-managed
learning.
Classification: LCC BF637.S4 V375 2020 (print) | LCC BF637.S4
(ebook) | DDC 646.7—dc23
LC record available at https://lccn.loc.gov/2019057320
LC ebook record available at https://lccn.loc.gov/2019057321

Jacket illustration and design by Tyler Comrie

Manufactured in the United States of America
First Edition

To my father,
for picking up the piano,
and sticking with it

You must become a beginner.

—RAINER MARIA RILKE

CONTENTS

BEGINNERS

THE OPENING GAMBIT

One Sunday morning in a crowded room in New York City, I sat down to a chessboard with my heartbeat elevated and my stomach on the boil.

My opponent and I shook hands, as is the custom. Apart from stating our names, which we duly jotted in our notation pads, we exchanged no words. While I set the time on the clock—twenty-five minutes for each player—he methodically centered each piece on its square.

Nonchalantly, as if to appear faintly bored, I did the same. I tried to arrange my pieces even *more* symmetrically, as if seizing some minute advantage (a ploy undermined by momentary panic that I'd incorrectly placed the bishop and knight). An expectant hush fell about the room as we waited for the tournament director to give the start signal.

As we sat, I tried to size my opponent up. He idly rolled a pencil between his fingers. His eyes drifted to the neighboring tables. I peered at him with what I hoped looked like remorseless pity. I was trying to project as much feral menace as one could while sitting in a library chair. I wanted to channel a feeling that had been described to me by Dylan Loeb McClain, the former chess columnist for

The New York Times, when, in 1995, he'd played the then world champion, Garry Kasparov, in an exhibition game.

"I didn't feel like he wanted to beat me," McClain said. "I felt like he wanted to reach across the board and strangle me." He intuited that Kasparov, hunched like an angry bear and channeling "unbelievable psychic ferocity," would not be happy gaining some minor positional advantage, or even simply winning. Something "more personal, more disturbing" seemed to be driving him.

This is a common sensation in the world of chess. "I like the moment when I break a man's ego," the mercurial champion Bobby Fischer once put it.

I looked again at my opponent. Could I, through tactical finesse and the withering power of my merciless gaze, slowly dismantle the core of his being?

Just then, a woman appeared at his side, bearing a small carton of chocolate milk. She kissed him on the head, said, "Good luck," and flashed me an owlish smile. Ryan, my opponent, was eight years old. With admirable composure, and an occasional sniffle, he dispatched me somewhere after the thirtieth move. I congratulated him, and as I went to inform the tournament director of the result, I saw him in the hallway, ego intact, proudly relaying the news to his mother.

Ryan and I were among those gathered for a Sunday morning "Rated Beginner Open" at New York City's Marshall Chess Club. Occupying several floors of a historic town house on one of Greenwich Village's most handsome blocks, the Marshall is a delightful anachronism, a relic of the days when any number of chess teams, collegiate and otherwise, battled across the region, their exploits recorded in the sports sections of newspapers.

That it exists here today, nestled amid some of the most expensive real estate in the country, is only thanks to a plot twist worthy of Dickens.

In 1931, at the height of the Depression, a group of wealthy benefactors, chess enthusiasts all, bought the building on behalf of the club's namesake, Frank Marshall. A grandmaster and U.S. champion who'd once operated an oceanfront chess emporium in Atlantic City—where he sometimes played passersby for money—Marshall had for decades piloted his eponymous club through a number of iconic Manhattan locales, from Keens Chophouse to the Chelsea Hotel. The Marshall now had a home for life.

The place has lost a bit of its old-school luster—there are no longer jacketed waiters to serve coffee or tea—but playing chess at the Marshall today, you still feel you're in some Gilded Age temple to the Game of Kings. History envelops you: busts of famous grandmasters; vintage photographs of team champions; the very table that Magnus Carlsen, the current world champion, sweated over as he defended his title against Sergey Karjakin in 2016.

The Marshall is no museum, though. Entering the place on a weekend, during a big tournament, is like walking into a human-powered data center: rows and rows of processors, silently calculating, thrumming with intensity, generating heat and a persistent tang of nervous perspiration.

The Sunday Beginners tournament was strictly small stakes, for players rated under 1200, or having no rating at all. Most grandmasters have ratings above 2500; I had the newbie rating of 100.

My day had started promisingly. Against my first opponent, John, a gray-haired man with the look and quiet gravity of a scholar, I'd initially fallen behind on "material," as pieces are called in chess. As the game drew on, he tried to press his advantage. And yet I kept fighting, finding inventive obstacles to his victory. To each of these he would respond with a small, tired sigh. I could feel his discomfort, and with each sigh I seemed to grow in strength.

Then, with my own king nearly surrounded, I spotted the chance for a checkmate. I just needed him to not see it. There is an old expression in chess that the winner is the player who makes the next-to-last mistake. And indeed, my opponent played offense when he needed to be playing defense, moving a pawn toward what he assumed was my demise. As I slid my rook into position, trapping his king along the "A file" (the first vertical row on a chessboard), a slow, queasy realization spread across his face.

My next opponent, Eric, was a serviceman on leave from Afghanistan, where he spent a lot of downtime playing online chess. He knew he'd be coming through New York on a visit stateside and had dedicated time for a Marshall pilgrimage. He looked a bit like the actor Woody Harrelson: buzz cut, grizzled, with a thousand-yard stare. Our match was tense and close fought, until he captured one of my rooks with a bishop pin. After I resigned, he looked relieved and said I had played much better than my rating would indicate—the first words he had uttered.

That morning's grouping, everyone from U.S. Army Rangers to AARP members to fidgety kids, was typical of the Marshall's Beginners tournament. The age range at the Marshall must have spanned six decades, but we were all, in the eyes of chess, beginners.

There is a wonderful purity to chess's rating system, which renders distinctions like age largely irrelevant. Chess is one of the few skilled endeavors in which children can acquire a proficiency on par with adults—or above. There are twelve-year-olds who will innocently skin you alive.

There was one child in the Sunday tournament at the Marshall in whom I had a particular interest: my own daughter. We weren't paired against each other—though that moment would come—and we took very different paths that morning. She placed near the top and collected a check for eighty-four dollars, money that was immediately plowed into Beanie Babies and glitter putty at the corner toy shop.

And as I heard her gleefully report to her grandparents on the phone, later that day, "My dad finished, like, fortieth." Out of fifty-one.

What had I gotten myself into?

*

One day a number of years ago, I was deep into a game of holiday checkers with my daughter, then almost four, in the small library of a beachfront town. Her eye drifted to a nearby table, where a black-and-white board bristled with far more interesting figures (many a future chess master has been innocently drawn in by "horses" and "castles"). "What's *that*?" she asked. "Chess," I replied. "Can we play?" she pleaded. I nodded absently.

There was just one problem: I didn't know how. I dimly remembered having learned the basic moves as a kid, but chess had never stuck. This fact vaguely haunted me through my life. I would see an idle board in a hotel lobby, or a puzzle in a weekend newspaper supplement, and feel a pang.

I had picked up a general *awareness* of chess. I knew the names Fischer and Kasparov. I knew that the game had enchanted historical luminaries like Marcel Duchamp and Vladimir Nabokov. I knew the cliché about grandmasters being able to look a dozen moves ahead. I knew that chess, like classical music, was shorthand in movies for genius—often of the evil variety. But I knew chess the way I "knew" the Japanese language: what it looks like, what it sounds like, its *Japaneseness*, without actually comprehending it.

I decided I'd learn the game, if only to be able to teach my daughter. Learning the basic moves was easy enough. It took a few hours, hunched over my smartphone at kids' birthday parties or waiting in line at Trader Joe's, to get a feel for the basic moves. Soon, I was playing, and sometimes even beating, the weakest computer opponents (the ones with catastrophic blunders abundantly programmed in). Yet it soon became apparent that I had little concept of the larger strategies.

I didn't want to try to teach what I knew only poorly. And yet how to learn? The number of chess books was dauntingly huge. Sure, there was *Chess for Dummies*. But beyond that, the chess literature was enormous. It was filled with algebraic-looking thickets of chess notation, a quasi-language that itself had to be learned.

And the books were achingly specific: for example, *A Complete Guide to Playing 3 Nc3 Against the French Defence*. That's right: an *entire* book devoted to the permutations of a *single* move—a move that, I should add, has been regularly played for a century. Yet people were still figuring out, one hundred years and many chess books later, 288 pages of new things to say about it.

A well-traveled fact one hears early in chess is that after only three moves there are more possible game variations than there are atoms in the universe. And, indeed, I felt cosmically stupefied as I tried to figure out how to boil down this exponentially complex game to someone whose favorite show was *Curious George*.

So I did what any self-respecting modern parent does: I hired a coach. The twist was that I wanted someone to teach my daughter and me at the same time.

Through some internet sleuthing, I'd found Simon Rudowski, a Brooklyn-based Polish émigré. He had an air of old-world formality, and a hint of tough-love sternness, that lent what I thought was an appropriate gravity to the task. When playing, he would move pieces with an emphatic, almost operatic flair. Simon, vegetarian, thin and hyperalert, preferred that the house be quiet, save for classical music playing quietly in the background. There were cups of tea and my wife's fresh-baked pastries, which she had served to him during the first lesson out of politeness.

This meant-to-be-occasional treat had soon hardened, and even intensified, into an almost comic ritual. "We need to make pastries for Simon," she would urgently announce the morning of the lesson (store-bought cookies would only be nibbled at, in a subtle sign of displeasure). The music, along with the refreshments and the intrinsic elegance of the board and pieces, turned our house, or so I liked to imagine, into a sort of feverish, caffeinated Viennese salon, filled with the heady ferment of chess theory.

*

Although it scarcely occurred to me at the time, my daughter and I were also embarking on a cognitive experiment, with a sample size of two: We were two novices, attempting to learn a new skill.

We were starting from the same point, but separated by some four decades. So far, in her young life, I'd been the expert—in knowing what words meant or how to ride a bike—but now we were on curiously equal footing, at least in theory. Would one of us get better faster? Would we learn in the same way? What were our respective strengths and weaknesses? Who would prevail in the end?

I soon stopped attending the lessons. My presence, for one, seemed distracting; I was getting between her and her teacher. Also, in the beginning at least, she was picking it up much more slowly. Simon and I would sometimes grin at each other, secret confidants, when she was on the verge of discovering a difficult move on a crowded board.

I drifted to the background. I regularly played online, struggled through YouTube videos that analyzed tournament matches, and leafed through books like *Bent Larsen's Best Games*. And then my daughter and I, each armed for battle in our own way, would come together, at the kitchen table, over the chessboard.

Early on, I seemed to be doing better with the game, if only because I was more serious about it. I had an attention span, I had decades of experience with other games, I had my adult pride. When we played, she would sometimes flag in her concentration, and to keep her spirits up, I would commit disastrous blunders and hope she would see them. In the larger chess world, I was a patzer—a hopelessly bumbling novice—but around my house at least I felt like a sage, benevolent elder statesman.

Week by week, though, she improved. She would calmly explain to me some hidden intricacy in a puzzle, or tell me why the online game I was certain I was going to win was actually likely to end in a draw. She'd learned strategies and rules of thumb that were new to me. She'd started playing in tournaments: at first, small gatherings in the basement of the local library and, eventually, the big citywide competitions. She collected trophies and landed fairly high up on the list of the country's top one hundred female players for her age. I suddenly had to work to beat her, and sometimes could not.

One reason, in retrospect, was obvious. Where I was just playing online game after online game, hoping to get better through sheer exposure—attributing wins to my talent and losses to bad luck—she was being drilled in opening theory and endgame tactics by Simon. When she lost a game, she would have to analyze, in painstaking detail, why she lost. Importantly, this often took longer than the actual match.

In the eyes of the psychologist Anders Ericsson, the man behind the now-familiar, often-misunderstood ten-thousand-hour rule, she was engaging in "deliberate practice."

I, on the other hand, was settling for "mindless repetition," trying to get better through brute force, without tangible goals. I was trying, in a way, to play like Alpha-Zero, DeepMind's celebrated artificial intelligence engine. Given no more than the basic rules of chess, AlphaZero had mastered the game after playing itself forty-four million times.* It learned as it went along the whole way through, without the aid of a coach, becoming the most formidable opponent in the world.

But I didn't have that much time or that much brainpower. "If you want to improve in chess," wrote Ericsson, "you don't do it by playing chess. You do it with solitary study of the grandmasters' games." In my crowded life, it was usually easier to play a five-minute blitz game while riding the subway.

In any case, my attention had largely shifted to her. She was the talent to be nurtured; she was winning the trophies. Her improvement was more important than mine. I had become the archetypal Chess Dad, waiting through the typical five or six hours of a scholastic tournament.

The experience is a bit like being stranded in a second-tier airport during a flight delay. You try to find a comfortable place to kill time, but you end up with the dust bunnies on the power-waxed tile floor, on some win-

---

* In terms of Ericsson's formulation, assuming an average time of ninety minutes per chess match, this would entail some *sixty-six million hours* of experience for a human.

dowless lower level of a school, huddled near an electrical outlet to keep your devices alive. You graze Goldfish crackers scavenged from the parent-run concession stand and breathe stale air. You try to work, but you are hopelessly jittery and distracted.

Waiting for my daughter to return from a match, anxious about the result, I'd glance down the hall every few minutes, my senses so attuned that I could tell within a millisecond's glance whether she'd won or lost. Each scenario—a bounding, smiling run or a stoop-shouldered shuffle often accompanied by tears—had the tendency to break my heart.

During those moments of tears, I would sometimes wonder why I was putting her—and, to be honest, me—through it all. What had started as a simple, playful exploration had become something more serious. But to what end? I'd mostly bought into the societal image that equates chess with intelligence and academic success, even though I knew, rationally, that the evidence was inconclusive. The studies were typically small, often filled with motivated chess players fully aware they were being studied, and often undertaken by chess organizations themselves. There was a big "direction of causality" problem: Did chess make kids smarter, or did smarter kids gravitate to chess? If chess were so tied to intelligence, one might think better chess players would be generally smarter than lesser players or non-chess players. Again, there's no strong evidence.

Still, I tried to convince myself that there were tangible positives. I thought that chess, "as a way to teach thinking," as one educator put it, was a useful proxy for the rigors of school—concentrating, solving, memorizing, applying—dressed up in a game.

As for those tear-inducing losses, I imagined that chess tournaments, with their poignant, mostly meaningless

results, might be a good place to rehearse the larger challenges of life. And maybe the results weren't so meaningless. Three times out of four, by my rough estimation, she
was playing a boy. Despite efforts at change, an attitude
of gender superiority persists in chess. Male players' ratings tend to be higher, which may simply be, it's been suggested, a statistical artifact of there being so many more
male players.

But there's something more to the story. A study
looking at scholastic chess tournaments found that when
female players played male players, they seemed to under-
perform. As the researchers wrote, "*Girls lose to boys at a rate
that cannot be explained in terms of initial ratings strength.*"
The reason, they hypothesized, is the phenomenon of
"stereotype threat": Female players were battling not only
male opponents but the perception that they weren't as
good. What's more, female players who didn't do as well
as their rating would predict played in fewer tournaments
the next year—an effect not seen in boys.

Life was going to be full of these vicious cycles, I
reasoned. Let us tackle them head-on, right now. And,
undoubtedly, my proudest moment as Chess Dad was
when, at a big tournament, I overheard a boy telling his
compatriots, all wearing the purple T-shirts of the elite
Hunter College Elementary School chess squad, to "watch
out for the girl in the pink bunny shirt."

*

When my daughter first began competing in scholastic
tournaments, I would chat up other parents. Sometimes,
I'd ask if they played chess themselves. Usually, the reply
was an apologetic shrug and a smile.

When I volunteered that I was learning to play,
the tone was cheerily patronizing: *Good luck with that!* I

thought, "If this game is so good for kids, why are adults ignoring it?" Seeing someone playing *Angry Birds*, I wanted to tap them on the shoulder and say, "Why are you having your kids do chess while you do that? This is the Game of Kings! There are chess games recorded from the fifteenth century!"

At chess tournaments, I saw a dynamic that was all too familiar from the world of children's activities: kids doing the activity, adults like me staring into their smartphones. Sure, we parents had work to do, work that we allowed to spill into weekends, work that helped pay for the lessons our kids were enjoying (or enduring).

But I also wondered if we, in our constant chaperoning of these lessons, were imparting a subtle lesson: that learning was for the young.

Strolling down the hall during one tournament, I looked into a classroom and saw a group of parents, with what I took to be an instructor. *They were playing chess!* Just then, as if on cue, a group of kids passed me, peering in on the same scene. "Why are adults learning chess?" one asked, in a vaguely mocking tone, to the collective amusement of the group. They marched on while I slowly died in front of a cheery bulletin board.

I was tired of sitting on the sidelines. I wanted in. And that is how I got a membership card from the U.S. Chess Federation and started joining my daughter, not at the scholastic tournaments—where I would have cut an odd figure—but at the Marshall.

Early on, I was nervous, even though I really had nothing to lose, save my pride. "A master can sometimes play badly," as one grandmaster put it, "a fan never!" And fan I was: the somber rituals, the pulse-pounding encounters, the tense atmosphere. It was three hours of sustained concentration and intense thinking, with my phone turned off. It felt like a gym for the brain.

The most striking thing was how hard it was to play against people. Playing online, at home, you were just moving pixels. In a real-life tournament, you were sitting across from a human, in all their humanness: their eyes, their scent, their body language, the strange sounds emanating from their deepest inner recesses.

This was an early lesson in learning: It is *context dependent*. You want to get good at online blitz? Play lots of online blitz. You want to get good at chess tournaments? Play at chess tournaments, against warm bodies.

And you never knew who was going to sit across from you on any given Sunday. I played—to a draw—a young girl with blue-framed eyeglasses who had the disconcerting, perhaps involuntary, habit of commenting under her breath on my moves as I made them ("thank you for bringing my king into the endgame"). There was the older man with shaking hands who set a towering, sloshing twenty-four-ounce cup of hot coffee on the table as he sat down to play me, drawing alarmed looks from the neighboring players, positioned mere inches away; rattled, I nearly threw the game away and only salvaged a draw because my opponent was unsettled by his dwindling clock. I sent an earnest kid in a charter school uniform to his doom—it took more work than I would have liked—and felt obliged to tell his father, who was watching a movie on his smartphone, how well his son had played. I checkmated a lank-haired, somewhat eccentric man I had seen there on many occasions, wondering, a bit darkly, how long he had dwelled in the "Beginners" section. I was paired against my daughter, who coolly delivered a back-rank checkmate, trapping my helpless king on the last row.

I was nearing fifty and getting beat by kids. I loved it.

CHAPTER ONE

A BEGINNER'S GUIDE TO BEING A BEGINNER

A man . . . progresses in all things by
making a fool of himself.*

—GEORGE BERNARD SHAW

BEGIN, AGAIN: A MANIFESTO

Beginners is a book for anyone who ever started out, who
was unsure, who was afraid to ask a question in a roomful
of people who all seemed as if they knew what they were
doing. It's for anyone who had to be shown the ropes,
however many times, who didn't know what they were
doing but did it anyway. It's for anyone who entered a race
they weren't even sure they could finish. It's a catalog of
errors, a celebration of awkwardness. To paraphrase the
movie *Repo Man*, it's about spending your life not avoiding
tense situations but getting *into* tense situations.

It's a handbook for the clueless, a first-aid kit for the
crushed ego, a survival guide for coping with this most
painful, most poignant stage: the awkward, self-conscious,
exhilarating dawning of the novice. It's not a "how to do"

---

* Apologies for the archaic gender slant of this quotation. As you will see, a
majority of the fearless beginners I met have been women.

book as much as a "*why* to do" book. It's less about making you better at something than making you feel better as you try to learn. It's about small acts of reinvention, at any age, that can make life seem magical. It's about learning new things, one of which might be *you*.

*

For me, it had all begun with the chess experiment. Something had been awakened in me, thanks, ultimately, to my daughter.

Becoming a first-time parent is one of the more fundamental experiences of being a beginner. You sail into the process having chatted with friends and maybe read a few books, and on day one you're on the bunny hill of life.

"Perhaps you think that you can know what it's like to have a child, even though you've never had one, because you can read or listen to the testimony of what it was like for others," writes the Yale University professor of philosophy L. A. Paul. "You are wrong."

It is, she writes, "an epistemically unique" experience. Meaning: You don't know shit.

You barely know how to hold this breathing, blinking thing. You struggle to interpret its actions. You lie awake grappling with weird decision trees—forward- or rear-facing car seats? You wrestle with strollers. Life becomes a constant process of racing to the internet to watch YouTube videos (a subject I'll revisit later in the book). You find yourself talking to strange new people—those heretofore ghostly figures you would pass on the street known as parents—swapping information as you rapidly scramble toward some kind of expertise.

Being a good parent, like any learning process, requires thoughtful practice. Novice parents, to the extent that there's any research on the subject, can certainly be found wanting. In one study, novice parents shown a sample household environment failed to identify *half* the child hazards that were present. Even something as basic as the way you speak to your young child can be done in a way that will ultimately make them more verbally proficient.

Beginner parents also become beginner *teachers*. And because we no longer remember, or have much access to, how we ourselves learned something, we may not be the best instructors. Playing catch with my daughter, I struggled to give more compelling instructions than "Throw the ball to me." Could I write out instructions? That wouldn't really do. Step one: Take ball. Step two: Throw ball. Maybe I could use metaphor or imagery, often so effective in sports instruction? *Imagine that you're throwing the ball. To me.*

We have to learn how to teach. Sometimes we have to relearn what we are trying to teach. I made the mistake—as I now firmly believe it to be—of having put my daughter, at age three, on a bike with training wheels. She began happily riding around the park, until she took a corner too fast and tipped over.

Rather than teaching the actual skill needed in riding a bicycle, training wheels simply impart misplaced confidence. Such "errorless learning" may make the learner feel better, but it eliminates the huge part of learning that comes from mistakes. Like water wings in swimming, training wheels take away from the actual feeling of riding a bike.

So I took off the training wheels, stripped the pedals, and, presto, it was a "balance bike." She had some wobbles, but those wobbles were more instructive than her seemingly steadier performance on the training wheels. A few weeks later, with a starting push from me, she was off.

Like any parent, I suddenly found myself surrounded, in a way I could scarcely remember, by the process of learning. It wasn't just the chess. There was piano. Soccer. Tae kwon do. Choir. Skateboarding. Intro to Coding. Track and field. Indoor climbing. Not all of these things would "stick," but it scarcely seemed to matter. They're kids. They're exploring. We should let them try as many things as possible. It's good for them.

But something began to gnaw at me. As I became the full-time supervisor of my daughter's learning career, as I sat in any number of waiting areas while she improved, I wondered, what new skills had *I* learned?

Each of us, of course, is constantly learning new things, in endless, small ways. "As adults," write the authors of *The Scientist in the Crib*, "we at least sometimes retain our childlike ability to learn." You just rented a car at the airport? Take a minute to learn the new cockpit configuration. You're walking on a sidewalk that's not usually covered in ice, or going down an unfamiliar set of wooden stairs in your socks? You've just subtly recalibrated your proprioception—that "sixth sense" of your body in the world—or you fell. Just switched from Android to iPhone? You're going to have to retrain your fingers.

Had I, though, acquired any more substantial skills? In my job as a journalist, I am constantly learning new *information*. I am a "perpetual novice," constantly helicoptering into some world I barely know of (nuclear waste, watchmaking) and meeting the key players, soaking up the terminology, reading the weird trade magazines—did you know the world of shipping pallets has *two* leading journals?—and otherwise geeking out. I still puff with pride when someone says, "You've really done your homework." And then it's on to the next thing.

I am brimming with *declarative knowledge*, or what is called "knowing that." I have a lot of "knowing that"; hell, I was on *Jeopardy!* (I lost, to someone who knew more of "that.")

But what about *procedural knowledge*, or "knowing how"? I was a quick study when it came to facts, but what had I actually learned to *do* lately? Compared with my daughter, I seemed to be coasting along on my professional plateau, fixed firmly in my comfort zone of competence.

This was brought home to me when, one day, her school featured a "Talent Day," in which parents were asked to demonstrate some skill in front of a room of twenty-five first graders. I racked my brain. What talent did I have? I didn't think the kids would be dazzled by the grace of my prose under deadline. I am, on the other hand, a pretty mean whistler. Or should I take them outside for a crack parallel-parking demonstration?

A thought began to emerge: I would try to learn, along with chess, a number of skills at once. Rather than just sitting on the sidelines while my daughter learned, I would join her—sometimes, as with chess, in the very same pursuit. This is a strangely novel notion. Type "learn with your child" into Google, and you get a lot of results on how to improve *their* learning. You are a foregone conclusion.

But what did I want to try to learn? Seeking inspiration, I posted an inquiry online: "What new tricks should this old dog learn?"

The first response came quickly: "Have you tried writing classes?"

Was the universe trying to tell me something?

*

In my quest to acquire skills, I had some rough criteria mapped out. First, I had to be a beginner in the activity. There were things I had done a bit of, and certainly wouldn't mind getting better in (making pizza, fixing my bike), but I wanted real novelty.

Second, they had to be things I could learn in New York City. That semester at "gelato university" in Italy, suggested by a friend, was out (a decision not made easily), as was the mountain climbing course in Alaska.* Luckily, in a city of nine million, if you can imagine it, someone is teaching it.

The skills, furthermore, should not be too difficult or time-consuming. Learning Mandarin or how to fly a plane was out. Last, they should be things I actually really wanted to learn—not things that I felt I *should* learn.

The suggestion came several times to take coding classes. Coding is a fine enterprise, but I wanted to spend less, not more, time in front of a screen. I wasn't necessarily looking for skills that represented some kind of professional development, as worthy as that endeavor is. I had a job; I wasn't looking for another, or anything that much felt like work. More than looking to make myself more marketable to employers, I wanted to make myself more marketable to *me*.

I wanted the skills to be substantial. There are plenty of micro-skills out there—building a fire, driving a manual transmission—that are totally worthwhile and we're all constantly tackling. I am all in favor of this "micro-mastery," as it's been called: Learning little things can embolden you to learn bigger things. But most of these skills are easily achievable. I wanted things that you never finished learning.

And I wanted to stick to a small number of skills. There were all sorts of people on the internet who had

---

* One can, of course, learn to make gelato in New York City, or climb in indoor gyms, but that somehow didn't sound as exciting.

embarked on self-reported quests to pick up one new skill every month, or every week, or every day; one guy had the beginner's hubris to play Magnus Carlsen after a month of learning chess. This is the Magnus who routinely defeats people who have been playing chess *every day of their lives since age five.* Not surprisingly,* the would-be challenger was handily dispatched.

I applauded the bravado spirit of such endeavors, and thought there were things I could certainly learn from them, but I wasn't looking for bucket-list items to tick off. I wasn't interested in rapidly "hacking" skills, Silicon Valley–style, so I could boast about them on social media and move on to the next one. I wanted things I could grow into slowly, taking time to appreciate the skill and how it is learned, to measure its impact upon my life. Why not just *one* skill? you might be asking. I worried about picking something I would not like. Because I was interested in the starting stages of things, tackling more skills simply meant I would be a beginner more often.

I eventually settled on a group of pursuits I'd long wanted to learn. In addition to chess, I chose singing, surfing, drawing, and *making* (in this case, a wedding ring to replace the ones I'd lose surfing). Oh, and juggling—as much for the thing itself as for the brain research that's been done around it, which offers a fascinating window onto learning. There were all sorts of tempting things— free diving, improv theater—I put on a possible to-do list for the future.

I didn't think I was going to master any of these things. I didn't have a spare ten thousand hours—the suggested baseline of deliberate practice required to achieve mastery in a field—for anything; I'd be lucky to have *a hundred*

---

* As Martin Amis has argued about chess, "Nowhere in sport, perhaps nowhere in human activity, is the gap between the tryer and the expert so astronomical."

hours for any one skill. In place of mastery, I was hoping for distributed competence.

In trying to bolster my "life résumé," I was, in some ways, trying to reach back into the past, to try to learn things that had eluded me. We often use our children as proxies for this. Under what's called "symbolic self-completion theory," parents are often suspected of trying to vanquish their own failed ambitions via their children's accomplishments.

But I was trying to use my own accomplishments to "compensate," as Jung put it, for what was unfulfilled in my past life. Sometimes, these just happened to coincide with my daughter's accomplishments. I was wary, and perhaps guilty, of trying to create my own "mini-me"—a process psychologists call enmeshment—at the expense of my daughter's own self. I wanted us to have some shared learning experiences, but not wholly overlapping ones. She urged me to learn the popular game *Magic: The Gathering*, for instance—as a former *Dungeons & Dragons* nerd, I thought it looked pretty fun—but I invented excuses. I wanted her to have her own domains in which I was the clueless adult.

I also sensed I was preparing for the future. As a somewhat older father, I wanted to make sure I would be in fighting trim—physically and mentally—for what I hoped would be many years of shared adventures with my daughter. Climbing life's little learning curves together would, I hoped, not only bring us closer but keep me feeling younger.

I knew that I would struggle. That I would fall. But I felt it would be good for me. I would have beginner's mind; I would have beginner's *body*. My brain and muscles would forge new paths.

And I had a feeling it would be good for my daughter, too. In one fascinating experiment, researchers demonstrated, to different infant subjects, the act of retrieving a toy from a container. One adult model struggled with the process, while another adult did it quickly. The infants who saw the adult struggle tried *harder* when it was their turn to try to retrieve the toy. The ones who saw the adult do it more easily didn't want to try as much.

In learning along with our children, by tackling things together as beginners, sharing the pratfalls and little triumphs, we can actually teach them one of the most valuable lessons of all: Just because you're not immediately good at something does not mean you won't eventually get it.

THE JOY AND PAIN OF STARTING OUT

No one is born a master. We are all, at one time or another, beginners.

Being a beginner is hard. It feels better to be good at something than to be bad. People in various domains give beginners special, not complimentary names. In surfing, you're a "kook." In cycling, a "fred." In chess, a "patzer." In the military, you're a "boot" (supposedly for your freshly shined footwear*). Or simply: "noob" or "rookie" or "greenhorn." The word "novice" itself? "Beginner monk."

Beginners ask the same obvious questions, suffer from the same misconceptions, make the same mistakes. Every field has its nervous beginners. Beginner archers grip the bow too hard and aim too long. Beginner auto mechanics spill oil, snap lug nuts, strip Phillips head screws. Novice sailors run over their dinghy lines, get hair and jewelry

---

* Although it also has been suggested as an acronym for "beginning of one's tour."

tangled in jib sheets, and forget "how much deep and shallow water look the same."

In chess, novices, like Tolstoy's happy families, are all alike: They move their pawns too much, they bring out the queen too early, they trade pieces too readily,* they move without seeming to consider the motives for their opponent's last move. And they lose. Except when, sometimes, they beat other beginners, often from pure dumb beginner's luck.

Beginners fall down, slip up, and get hurt. It's the rookies getting woozy and dehydrated in 10K races. In snowboarding, the majority of injuries are suffered by novices. In equestrian sports, novices are eight times more likely than professionals to get hurt. In skydiving, an endeavor with particularly high consequences for error, beginner jumpers are up to twelve times more likely to be injured than someone who has jumped *at least once.*

For all the bumps and bruises, the gaffes and blunders, what I'm going to try to show you here, across the course of this book, is that being a beginner can be a wonderful thing. I hope to reveal to you something that I've become convinced of: that there is magic to the early stages.

In the beginnings of a love affair, we are in what has been called an "extreme neurobiological state": The brain is jacked on a supersized hyper-caffeinated energy drink of dopamine and stress hormones (the good kind). Our language often reverts to a fragile, childlike babble, as if we were born anew. It will all eventually calm down.

Learning a new skill is curiously similar. Your brain is in a state of hyperawareness, bathing in novelty, and

---

* AlphaGo Zero, the artificial intelligence engine developed by DeepMind to teach itself the strategy game Go, was seen, early in its learning process, to focus "greedily on capturing stones, *much like a human beginner.*" David Silver et al., "Mastering the Game of Go Without Human Knowledge," *Nature*, Oct. 19, 2017, 354–59.

almost overwhelmed as it tries to understand why the three-point shot you just unleashed and thought was perfect was actually an air ball (these moments are dubbed prediction errors).

As you plunge into learning some art or skill, the world around you appears new and bursting with infinite horizons. Each day brims with new discoveries as you take your tentative first steps, slowly pushing the bounds of exploration. You make mistakes, but even these are empowering, because they are *mistakes you have never made before*.

You're freed from the worries of "impostor syndrome"—that anxiety of not being the expert you're cracked up to be—because no one actually expects you to be any good. You're liberated from expectation, from the weight of the past. In Zen Buddhism, this state is referred to as beginner's mind. Your mind is ready for anything, open to everything. "In the beginner's mind there are many possibilities," writes Shunryu Suzuki. "In the expert's mind there are few."

This will not be comfortable. Like a Zen pilgrimage, being a beginner means undertaking a journey of not knowing. Not only will you not know; you will not even *know* what you don't know. You will feel as if everyone were looking at you, waiting for you to make a mistake, like those loudly advertised "student drivers" you see on the road. You will wear a scarlet *B*.

As you learn new things, however, you will learn new things about yourself. You seem to make progress by leaps and bounds. You can sense exactly *how* you are improving. The novelist Norman Rush described love as like entering a series of new rooms, and each time, even though you've done this sort of thing before, you're surprised. "You never intend to go from one room onward to the next—it just happens. You notice a door, you go through, and you're delighted again." That's what learning feels like, especially in these early stages.

You should cherish this moment: The gains you make early will far exceed those you make later.

The meaning of a "steep learning curve" is often misconstrued as something that's dauntingly hard. A skill may or may not be difficult to learn, but the steepness of the learning curve is actually just a graphical representation of time versus progress. *A steep learning curve means you're climbing faster.* And the steepest learning curves come right away.

*

A few years ago, I took my daughter snowboarding. At nearly fifty years old, I was entirely new to the sport, as was she. On the drive to the mountain, I tried to approach it with the spirit of beginner's mind. I had no expectations about the activity. I might hate it, or it might be my new favorite thing. It didn't matter if I was good at it or not; I would simply try to embrace the experience. I had no goals other than avoiding the hospital. I just wanted to enter a new "room." In all this I think I was in sync with my daughter, who had little more in mind than having fun.

After a few hours, and more than a few falls and scrapes on the icy slopes, something had happened. I had become a *snowboarder.* A bad snowboarder, to be sure, and everyone will tell you snowboarding is easier early but gets harder (with skiing, it's the opposite).

But a metamorphosis had happened: I went from a person who had never been on a snowboard in his life to one who had successfully ridden one down a large hill, if not yet a mountain. I'd sailed up the learning curve, and it's unlikely I'll ever see such a single jump in snowboarding improvement again. "Hold on to this," I thought.

For most of us, the beginner stage is something to be gotten through as quickly as possible, like a socially awkward skin condition. But I want to suggest that even if we're only passing through, we should pay particular attention to this moment. For once it goes, it's hard to get back.

Think of a time when you first visited a new, distant place, one with which you were barely familiar. Upon arrival, you were alive to every novelty. *The smell of the food in the street! The curious traffic signs! The sound of the call to prayer!* Flushed from the comfort of your usual surrounds, forced to learn new rituals and ways to communicate, you gained sensory superpowers. You paid attention to everything because you didn't even know what you needed to know to get by. After a few days, as you became more expert in the place, what seemed strange began to become familiar. You began noticing less. You became safer in your knowledge. Your behavior became more automatic. The burst of neural activity you experienced at the outset subsided.

As a sometime travel writer, I have a strategy: Take the most notes on the first day. That's when you see the most. In the clumsily self-conscious early stages of skill learning, it can be hard to remember to take note of your surroundings. But *progress will come.* Just enjoy the moment; take it all in.

THE BEGINNERS' ADVANTAGE

Even as your skills and knowledge progress, there is a potential value to holding on to that beginner's mind.

In what's come to be known as the Dunning-Kruger

effect, the psychologists David Dunning and Justin Kruger famously showed that on various cognitive tests the people who did the worst were also the ones who most "grossly overestimated" their actual performance. They were "unskilled and unaware of it."

This can certainly be a stumbling block for beginners. But additional research later showed the only thing worse than hardly knowing anything was knowing *a little bit more.* This pattern appears in the real world: Doctors learning a spinal surgery technique committed the most errors not on the first or second try but on the *fifteenth;* pilot errors, meanwhile, seem to peak not in the earliest stages but at around eight hundred hours of flight time.

I'm not suggesting experts have much to fear from beginners. Experts, who tend to be "skilled, and aware of it," are much more efficient in their problem-solving processes, more efficient in their movement (the best chess players, for example, tend also to be the best speed chess players). They can draw upon more experience, more finely honed reflexes. Beginner chess players will waste time considering a huge range of possible moves, while grandmasters zero in on the most relevant options (even if they then spend a lot of time calculating which of those moves are best).

And yet, sometimes, the "habits of the expert," as the Zen master Suzuki called it, can be an obstacle— particularly when new solutions are demanded. With all their experience, experts can come to see what they expect to see. Chess experts can become so entranced by a move they remember from a previous game that they miss a more optimal move on a different part of the board.

Or consider an experiment involving a group of London taxi drivers, an oft-studied class with super-proficient navigational skills. They were asked to plan a route in a fictitious town whose layout they'd just learned. They did this quite well—much better than people who didn't drive taxis. But when they were asked to plan a route in a new, fictitious area that was grafted onto the London they knew, their performance suffered. The London they knew—the "overlearned" London—was getting in the way.

This tendency for people to default to the familiar, even in the face of a more optimal novel solution, has been termed the *Einstellung* effect (after a German word that means "set").

In the famous "candle problem," people are asked to attach a candle to the wall using nothing more than a box of matches and a box of tacks. People struggle to solve it because they get hung up on the "functional fixedness" of the box as a *container* for tacks, not as a theoretical *shelf* for the candle. There is one group, it turns out, that tends to do pretty well on the candle problem: five-year-olds.

Why? The researchers who found this suggest that younger children have a more fluid "conception of function" than older children or adults. They are less hung up on things being *for* something, and more able to view them simply as things to be used in all sorts of ways. Small wonder they conquer new technology so handily; *everything* is new for them.

Children, in a very real sense, have beginners' minds, open to wider possibilities. They see the world with fresher eyes, are less burdened with preconception and past experience, and are less guided by what they know to be true. They are more likely to pick up details that adults might discard as irrelevant. Because they're less concerned with being wrong or looking foolish, children often ask questions that adults won't ask.

Take the curious case, reported in *The New York Times*, of a funeral home that had accidentally placed the wrong body in a casket.

At the funeral, the grieving adults had noted how

the deceased, a beloved relative who had died of cancer, looked strangely different from the woman they remembered. But they all found ways to explain the difference. The chemo had changed her hair. Time on a respirator had changed the way she looked. The adults, used to living in an ordered, rational world, did not consider the possibility of such a colossal mistake. They used all their knowledge and wisdom to deceive themselves. It took a ten-year-old boy among them to raise the preposterous suggestion,* only later confirmed to be the startling truth: The body before them was not their relative.

No one wants to stay a beginner. We all want to get better. But even as our skills improve, and our knowledge and experience grow, what I hope to encourage throughout this book is the preservation, even cultivation, of that spirit of the novice: the naïve optimism, the hypervigilant alertness that comes with novelty and insecurity, the willingness to look foolish, and the permission to ask obvious questions—the unencumbered *beginner's mind.*

What the chess master Benjamin Blumenfeld advised a century ago applies as much to life as to chess: "Before you make your move, look at the position like if you were a beginner."

YOU'RE NEVER TOO OLD TO BE A BEGINNER
(TERMS AND CONDITIONS MAY APPLY)

Being a beginner can be hard at any age, but it gets harder as you get older.

For children, it's practically their job to be beginners. Their brains and bodies are built for doing, failing,

---

* The episode brings to mind, of course, Hans Christian Andersen's famous tale "The Emperor's New Clothes."

and doing again. We applaud virtually anything they do, because they are trying.

Parents know well the phenomenon of "toddler helping," in which the child wants to, say, help "clean" the kitchen, an act that itself usually requires a second, more thorough cleaning by the parent. We allow it because the extra cleaning feels better than telling them they can't do something.

With adults, it's more complicated. The phrase "adult beginner" has an air of gentle pity. It reeks of obligatory retraining seminars and uncomfortable chairs. It implies the learning of something that you should have perhaps already learned.

There is safety in sticking with what we're already good at. "It's hard to be old and bad at something," as a friend, returning to hockey after many decades, put it. We can be so put off by being a beginner that we forget we were once beginners in all sorts of things, until we were not.

Even children sometimes prefer to dwell in this cocoon of competence. When one of my daughter's friends turned down an invitation to go snowboarding, his father explained, a bit sheepishly, "He kind of only likes to do things he's good at." I wanted to shout, *How does he know? He's only gone once!*

Adult beginners face their own kind of "stereotype threat," the one that says it's harder to learn when you're older. There's a pernicious, goading little voice: *You've started too late. Why bother?* One day, at her swim lesson, I was impressed to see my daughter "flip turn" at the end of the lane while doing a backstroke. This is not something I can do. "How'd you learn to do that?" I asked. "You have to be a kid," she responded matter-of-factly.

As I was finding out, this kind of idea is deeply ingrained

in chess.* There seems to be a relation between the age at which you first learned the game and your later success in tournaments. This idea is so pervasive that Magnus Carlsen, the current number one, is held as a fascinating outlier. "At five years old," one account marvels, "an age by which any aspiring grandmaster should at least have made a start— Magnus Carlsen showed little interest in chess."

Sitting down against younger opponents, I tried to keep in mind a bit of advice gleaned from Stephen Moss's book *The Rookie:* Just face them the way you would anyone else.

This could be hard. The way they played just threw me. In the face of my agonized dithering, they would launch fast, brute-force attacks—sometimes effective, sometimes foolhardy. "Children just kind of go for it," Daniel King, the English grandmaster and chess commentator, told me. "That kind of confidence can be very disconcerting for the opponent."

Young children, for example, have been shown to be faster and more accurate at tests involving "probabilistic sequence learning"—the sort in which people must guess which triggers will lead to what events (for example, if you press button A, event X will happen).

After age twelve, this ability begins to decline. As researchers suggest, people start relying more on "internal models" of cognition and reasoning, instead of what they see right in front of them. In other words, they overthink things. In chess games, where my adult opponents often seemed to battle unseen internal demons, the kids just seemed to twitch out a series of moves.

---

* The "Elo rating" that every player gets as a measure of their skill actually comes from a study done on age and expertise in chess published in the *Journal of Gerontology.*

I was buying into the stereotype threat. If I lost to an adult, I would chalk it up to my own stupid errors; if I lost to a child, I would suddenly imagine them as some incipient genius against whom I never had a chance.

When I asked Simon, our chess coach, about what it was like to teach adult chess beginners versus child chess beginners, he thought for a moment and said, "Adults need to explain to themselves why they play what they play." Kids, he said, "don't do that." He compared it to languages. "Beginner adults learn the rules of grammar and pronunciation and use those to put sentences together. Little kids learn languages by talking."

The analogy goes deeper than we might think.

My daughter was, in effect, learning chess like a *first* language, whereas I was learning it like a second language. Even more important, she was learning it young. Language is one of those endeavors (like music, and perhaps chess) that seems to flourish best if learned during a so-called sensitive period in which, as one researcher described it, "neural systems are particularly responsive to relevant stimuli, and are more susceptible to change when stimulated."

By contrast, because I am an adult, expert speaker of English, my brain may be so "tuned" to the sounds of my native language that it is harder for me to take on new grammar. What I know already gets in the way of what I want to learn. Kids, by knowing less, can actually learn more (the cognitive scientist Elissa Newport calls it the "less is more hypothesis").

Harder does not mean impossible. "Sensitive" periods are not "critical" periods, and the science, in any case, is not conclusive. The skill of having perfect pitch, for example, which not only is exceedingly rare but has long been thought to be impossible outside a narrow band of childhood, can, as research from the University of Chicago has shown, be trained—if to not quite as high a level as those possessing "true" perfect pitch—in some adults.

Kids often make more progress simply because they are *kids*, with lives built largely around learning, having few other responsibilities, and with eager parents to cheer them on. They are also motivated: If you were dropped into an entirely new setting, the way infants are, and found that you couldn't communicate, *you'd* probably learn pretty quickly.

*

When my daughter and I began sitting down to the chessboard, it was clear that something very different was going on in our heads.

My daughter's brain, like a chessboard at the beginning of a game, was still full of infinite possibility, bristling with countless synapses that had yet to be "pruned." The average seven-year-old has a brain that's almost fully formed, but with a "synaptic density"—or number of "wires" that connect neurons—more than one-third higher than the adult mean. She was, in a sense, still making sense of the world, and as she did, those synapses closed. It's like deleting lesser-used applications from one's computer to help optimize overall performance.

What was happening in my brain-as-chessboard, by contrast, seemed more like a cagey, defensive middle-game battle in which I was trying to hold on to pieces in the face of a closing denouement. I'd had this process described to me, in unsettling terms, by Denise Park, the director of research at the University of Texas's Center for Vital Longevity, as we sat one afternoon in a conference room in her Dallas lab.

"As you get older, you actually see clear degradation of the brain, even in healthy people," she told me. "Your front cortex gets smaller, your hippocampus—the seat of memory—shrinks." My brain volume was atrophying annually, my cortical thickness waning each year. From age twenty onward, in a normal lifetime, we lose about one neuron per second. As you read this sentence, say goodbye to two more!

No wonder that as I plotted a move against my daughter, I seemed to be putting more thought into it. Young adults, Park notes, will show activations in specific parts of the brain during a cognitive test; older adults, meanwhile, will show much broader activation.

Aha! Chalk up one for the olds! But, wait, this broader activation is not necessarily a good thing. The reason, Park argues, is that the aging brain is "compensating" for its various shortcomings by building "scaffolds" that connect a wider range of areas in the brain. We become less efficient, using more brain to get the same result. Using more brain means that different areas "overlap," which can cause "interference"; simply put, you're trying to learn a new skill, but the memory of a different skill is getting in the way.

Younger people also show more "modulation," meaning that when mental tasks get more challenging, they can quickly ramp up their mental energy. Older people can barely modulate at all. "Their brain is stuck at one speed," Park said.

Not surprisingly, overall firepower degrades. As the work of the psychologist Timothy Salthouse has revealed, cognitive tests on speed, reasoning, and memory show age-related declines that are "fairly large," "linear," and, most alarming, "clearly apparent before age 50."

To put the aging brain into perspective, consider that a seventy-five-year-old needs to do only *half* as well as a twenty-one-year-old on an IQ test to get the *same* score.

I was playing against a stacked deck. It was even worse

for my seventy-something father, who, inspired by his granddaughter—and wanting to bond with her—had also taken up chess again, many decades after last playing. In a family tournament, the results seemed drearily predictable: her, me, him.

This general pattern is replicated in the literature. In one study, Neil Charness, a professor of psychology at Florida State University who has long studied chess and performance, had players of various ability try to assess when a check was threatened in a match. The more skilled the player, the quicker they spotted the threat. No surprise there. But no matter what the skill, the *older* the player was, the slower they were to spot the threat.

If playing chess as you get older is harder, *learning* chess will be harder still. Charness, in another study, had subjects of various ages and experience levels learn a novel word-processing program. Age didn't matter so much for those who had word-processing experience.

With novices, there was a striking discrepancy. They all took more time to learn than those who had experience—as you would expect—but the older the novice, the longer it took them to learn.

"If you're talking about two novices," Charness said, when I asked him about my daughter, me, and chess, "your daughter would probably pick things up about twice as fast as you could."

*

I fought back. I still had plenty of pieces to play with. The volume of white matter in my brain—all those nerve fibers that enable learning and are changed by it—was, statistically, about to begin declining. But I still had *plasticity*, that superpower-like ability of the brain to rapidly change itself in the face of new challenges.

Take a bunch of forty- to sixty-year-olds, as one study did, and have them practice a golf swing for thirty days. Their brains will become more efficient at handling the task, and they'll have a better swing. We don't lose our ability to get better.

I tried to ratchet up my chess brain. I did puzzles. I clicked through endgames on Chessable, a website that used "spaced repetition" and other proven learning techniques. I played games of 960, where the pieces are randomly scattered, to shake myself up. To help me make faster moves in the thirty-minute games, I played five-minute blitz games. To help me get faster in blitz, I played rounds of one-minute "bullet chess." To get faster at bullet, I tried the truly terrifying "hyper-bullet chess," lasting all of fifteen seconds. To get faster at hyper-bullet? I would need quantum entanglement.

I had other things in my corner. People who study aging and the brain like to talk about two forms of cognitive ability: "fluid" and "crystallized" intelligence. Fluid intelligence helps you think on your feet and solve new problems. Crystallized intelligence is what a person already knows—wisdom, memories, metacognition. Fluid intelligence is generally seen to favor the young, while the crystallized variety is rewarded by age (though there are many exceptions).

In life, they complement each other. And in a game like chess, both had their roles: A player might draw upon fluid intelligence to quickly calculate a novel position, but crystallized intelligence could help one avoid a poor strategy deployed in a previous game.

Like most children her age, my daughter was all fluid. She had not memorized a huge repertoire of games. Nor did she think much of higher-level strategies: *Hmmm . . . I think I'll go with the Rubenstein variation to the French defense.* When children play chess, notes the psychologist

Dianne Horgan, they often rely on simple heuristics and "satisficing": They choose the first good-looking move and don't spend much time fretting in retrospect if it was good. Early on, my daughter would make a rapid-fire move, and I'd invariably ask, "Do you want to take a little more time?" She rarely did.

My daughter had a lightning-fast CPU, fresh off the shelf. I had a garage-sale hard drive teeming with decades of old files. Who had the edge? One advantage I had, Charness had assured me, was that I had a lot of experience with learning itself. I could attack the process more efficiently.

But having a big, lumbering hard drive means it takes longer to search for and retrieve files. I was running out of storage, and some of my pathways were corrupted. You've no doubt found, as you've gotten older, that you sometimes struggle to retrieve the name of a film or a person. *Of course you do!* It's because you've seen thousands of films and met thousands of people. Try implanting five decades of raw data into a kid and let's see how *they* do.

The linguist Michael Ramscar argues that some of what looks like cognitive decline in laboratory tests is actually just a function of learning. He has shown that when you ask younger and older subjects to memorize bunches of word pairs like "baby-cries" and "obey-eagle," older adults do worse at the pairs like "obey-eagle." In a test result, this looks bad.

But older adults, he maintains, have simply learned that over time we tend to hear words like "baby" and "cries" in the same sentence and tend *not* to hear "obey" closely linked to "eagle." That latter phrase seems less important, so our brains don't waste effort encoding it to memory. That seems smart, not a sign of cognitive decline.

All of this brings us back to beginner's mind. My daughter was on a pilgrimage of "not knowing." She'd not yet decided which words always go with each other. Her brain was taking it all in, while mine was encumbered by what it already knew and thus more resistant to change, less open.

Because of what I already knew, I was less likely to see "transfer" in the learning of chess to anything else. Children don't yet have as fixed an idea of what the skills or information they're learning is *for*, so they may make wider use of it.

Where my daughter's brain was hungrily forming new neural connections, mine could probably have used a few new ones. "You don't want to be pruning; you want to be growing," Park told me. My daughter's brain was trying to efficiently tame the chaos. "For older adults," Park said, "there's not nearly *enough* chaos."

I wondered what I could do about that.

WHY EVEN EXPERTS SHOULD BECOME
BEGINNERS ONCE IN A WHILE

You may, by now, be rightly asking, What if I'm not a parent? What if I'm not older? What if I already know how to sing or draw? What if I'm not in the throes of a midlife crisis? And, most pressingly, why should I bother learning a bunch of things that aren't relevant to my career? Why dabble in mere hobbies when I'm scrambling to keep up with the demands of a rapidly changing workplace?

First, I might suggest that it's not at all clear that learning something like singing or drawing actually *won't* help you in your job—even if it's not immediately obvious how. Learning has been proposed as an effective response to stress at one's job; by enlarging one's sense of self, and perhaps equipping us with new capabilities, learning becomes a "stress buffer."

Maybe that's one reason why, as an analysis at University College London found, students who studied both science and arts—a relative rarity—were much more likely to later assume leadership roles. When we expand the self, we can see more. As David Epstein notes in *Range*, Nobel laureates, compared with other scientists, "are at least twenty-two times more likely to partake as an amateur actor, dancer, magician, or other type of performer."

I doubt any of them woke up one day and thought, "Hmmm, what my neurobiology career really needs is for me to learn the tango." But maybe, in taking on those new pursuits as a beginner, they could think, again, like children: freed from preconceptions, unburdened by expectation, less categorical in their outlook. They could push beyond their domains, beyond themselves. And they could have fun—never to be underestimated as an agent of learning and discovery.

To take one example, Claude Shannon, the brilliant MIT polymath who helped invent the digital world in which we live today, plunged into all kinds of pursuits, from juggling to poetry to designing the first wearable computer. "Time and time again," notes his biographer, "he pursued projects that might have caused others embarrassment, engaged questions that seemed trivial or minor, then managed to wring breakthroughs out of them."

Regularly stepping out of our comfort zones, at this historical moment, just feels like life practice. The fast pace of technological change turns us all, in a sense, into "perpetual novices," always on the upward slope of learning, our knowledge constantly requiring upgrades, like our phones. Few of us can channel our undivided attention into a lifelong craft; even if we keep the same job, the required skills change. The more willing we are to be brave beginners, the better. As Ravi Kumar, president of the IT giant Infosys, describes it, "You have to learn to learn, learn to unlearn, and learn to re-learn."

Second, it's just good for you. I don't mean only the things themselves—like singing and surfing—are good for you, although they are, in ways I'll return to. I mean that skill learning *itself* is good for you.

It scarcely matters what—tying nautical knots or throwing pottery. Learning something new and challenging, particularly with a group, has proven benefits for the "novelty-seeking machine" that is the brain. Because novelty itself seems to trigger learning, learning various new things at once might be even better. A study that had adults aged fifty-eight to eighty-six simultaneously take multiple classes—ranging from Spanish to music composition to painting—found that after just a few months the learners had improved not only at Spanish or painting but on a battery of cognitive tests. They'd rolled back the odometers in their brains by some thirty years, doing better on the tests than a control group who took no classes. They'd changed in other ways, too: They felt more confident, they were pleasantly surprised by their work, and they kept getting together after the study ended.

Skill learning seems to be *additive;* it's not only about the skill. A study that looked at young children who had taken swimming lessons found benefits beyond swimming. The swimmers were better at a number of other physical tests, like grasping or hand-eye coordination, than nonswimmers. They also did better on reading and mathematical reasoning tests than nonswimmers, even accounting for factors like socioeconomic status.

Many of these studies or recommendations are oriented toward children. Chess, for example, is held up as a way to improve children's focus and concentration, to strengthen their problem-solving skills, to bolster their creative thinking.

But I've become convinced that whenever something is touted as being good for children, it's *even better* for adults, in part because we assume we no longer need all those benefits an activity is said to provide.

And yet what better remedy for the widespread affliction of "smartphone addiction" than two hours of burning your eyes and brain into sixty-four squares on a board, trying to analyze an almost infinite variety of moves and countermoves?

*

What I'm talking about goes beyond scores on standardized tests. There are any number of reasons to learn a new skill, above and beyond the huge reward of the skill itself.

There's that feeling of growth, that sense you've just become someone new, which you can't help excitedly telling people about (recalling the old joke: How can you tell someone's a triathlete? They tell *you*). In the course of my learning, I met people for whom learning some new skill was instrumental to reclaiming their identity in the wake of a dissolved marriage, or redefining their life after some large setback.

This sense of "self-expansion" can apply to couples as well. Research suggests that couples who undertake novel and challenging activities together recapture some of the "initial exhilaration" of when they first met, and the positive feelings they experience—from, say, taking a dance class—get transferred to the relationship itself.

There's a feeling of growth too in the new people you're exposed to, some of whom may become friends— something that itself gets more difficult later in life. You're meeting people who are like-minded in their desire to learn new things, in their willingness to appear foolish. In psychology, this is called openness to experience. It's one of the so-called Big Five personality traits—along with extraversion, conscientiousness, neuroticism, and agreeableness—that are said to define us. It's also come to be increasingly linked with longevity. The exact reasons are still unclear, but psychologists theorize that openness entails a "cognitive and behavioral flexibility" that's useful in addressing the challenges of later life.

Learning new skills also changes the way you think, or the way you see the world. Learning to sing changes the way you listen to music, while learning to draw is a striking tutorial on the human visual system. Learning to weld is a crash course in physics and metallurgy. You learn to surf and suddenly you find yourself interested in tide tables and storm systems and the hydrodynamics of waves. Your world got bigger because you did.

Last, if humans seem to crave novelty, and novelty helps us learn, one thing learning does is equip us with how to better handle *future* novelty. "More than any other animal, we human beings depend on our ability to learn," observes Alison Gopnik. "Our large brain and powerful learning abilities evolved, most of all, to deal with change." We're always flipping between small moments of incompetence and mastery. Sometimes, we cautiously try to work out how we're going to do something new. Sometimes, we read a book or look for an instructional video. Sometimes, we just have to plunge in.

THE LIMITS TO MASTERY

With so many pots on the boil—so many skills to try to acquire—I knew I was running the risk of being labeled a "dilettante."

In fact, that's the very thing I was hoping to become.

That word, which has an almost entirely pejorative

meaning today as a hopelessly superficial dabbler, is derived from the Italian *dilettare*, which means "to delight." As the art historian Bruce Redford notes, "dilettante"—one who exhibits delight—entered English with the formation of the Society of Dilettanti, an eighteenth-century group of Englishmen who had returned from the grand tour brimming with enthusiasm for Continental art and culture. As the process of acquiring knowledge gradually became more specialized, Redford notes, the meaning of the word shifted. By the time George Eliot wrote *Middlemarch* in the early 1870s, the word had become an insult.

A gulf was opening. Unless you were a professional, you were a mere dilettante, or an "amateur." And what did *this* loaded word originally signify? "To love," derived from the French *aimer*. With the increasing specialization of knowledge, and professionalization of everyday life, suddenly being delighted by something, or loving something, was seen as vaguely disreputable.

We live in an age of high performance, in which everyone is supposed to be constantly maximizing their potential, living their "best life." Social media has made everything from marriage proposals to this morning's breakfast into exquisitely choreographed, unsubtly competitive rituals. The ethos of work—"the long arm of the job," as one scholar put it—pervades our leisure, to the extent that we even have any.

Everything must be *for* something. I tell someone I'm going on an eighty-mile bike ride, and they ask, "What are you training for?" I want to answer, "I don't know . . . life?" "What is admired is success, achievement, the quality of performance," writes the psychologist Mihaly Csikszentmihalyi, "rather than the quality of experience."

But what if we don't want to become virtuoso musicians or renowned artists? What if we only want to dabble in these things, to see if they might subtly change our outlook on the world or even, as we try to learn them, change *us*? What if we just want to enjoy them?

The idea of undertaking new pursuits, ones that you may never be very good at, seems perverse in this age of single-minded peak performance. George Leonard, in his book *Mastery*, warns of the "Dabbler," "who loves the rituals involved in getting started." The dabbler, warns Leonard, "might think of himself as an adventurer, a connoisseur of novelty, but he's probably closer to being what Carl Jung calls the *puer aeternus*, the eternal kid." Guilty as charged!

Psychologists have noted, over the past several decades, a rise in self-reported perfectionism, marked by overly harsh self-evaluations and a societal pressure to constantly appear at one's best—a potentially harmful offshoot, they suggest, of society's becoming more individualistic and competitive. We "overvalue performance," as one psychologist put it, "and undervalue the self." We're afraid of being just okay at things.

This is a trap. "For to permit yourself to do only that which you are good at," writes the legal scholar Tim Wu, "is to be trapped in a cage whose bars are not steel but self-judgment."

One way to view liberty, as George Orwell reminded us, is the right "to do what you like in your spare time." You should be able to choose your amusements, he wrote, "not have them chosen for you from above." Letting someone else's ideas about performance stop you from trying something means relinquishing your freedom.

Our confidence has been so shaken by this cult of expertise and performance that when we don't perceive ourselves to be experts in something, we're almost expected to outsource the task to someone who does.

With something like chess, this might not be a bad idea. But this happens even for things we probably know how to do or could easily learn ourselves. My in-box, for a time, overflowed with classes aimed at my daughter. There were "learn to ride" workshops, in which "experienced instructors" teach kids how to ride . . . a bike. This filled me with sudden doubt: Was my technique—giving her a push and yelling, "Pedal!"—not good enough? "Leave it to the pros," runs a department store advertisement for a "shoe-tying clinic" aimed at children. I'm a firm believer in expert coaching, but *it's a shoelace!* And yet, even here, insecurity creeps in. As ever, the internet is there to undermine your authority. "You've Been Tying Your Shoes Wrong Your Entire Life," declares a typical article.

I'm not opposed to mastery. Who wouldn't like to be among the very best?

But mastery can become a closed system. About a decade ago, I took up road cycling. It was just what my life needed at the time: It gave me fitness, a spirit of adventure, a new and non-work-related social circle.

You may not think there's a learning curve to riding a bike as an adult, but then you find yourself packed tightly in a peloton, riding a few inches off someone's back wheel, or bombing down a hill at fifty miles per hour on a plastic bike wearing little more than pajamas. I made all sorts of beginner mistakes, and I was lucky not to get seriously hurt.

But the mistakes began to fall away. I got better. I got faster. I started racing. I got upgraded. I tried to act "pro." This all felt great. Cycling became my "jam," a key part of my identity. With some five thousand hours on the bike, I gained a fair amount of mastery.

The more I put into cycling, however, the more it seemed to require—more training hours, harder efforts, more expensive equipment. What had made my life feel richer was becoming a major time suck. On the bike, I was having less fun. The faster groups I was riding with took a masochistic pleasure in not stopping for coffee and a snack. Too much of the talk was about monastic, faddish nutrition regimens. I seemed to spend as much time staring at the bike computer on my handlebars as whatever scenery was around me. It all suddenly started to feel like work—performance reviews, peer pressure, deadlines, a single-minded focus on results. I began to feel a bit trapped in an identity, a set of expectations.

As I began branching out into my new pursuits, I felt a kind of liberation (I still love cycling, by the way; we just needed to start seeing other people). After he was fired from Apple, Steve Jobs wrote, "the heaviness of being successful was replaced by the lightness of being a beginner again, less sure about everything." He soon enjoyed an intensely creative period.

I'm not suggesting you quit your job. What I am saying is that even the things you love doing can begin to restrict you.

I wasn't looking to learn new things because I lacked fulfillment in my job or because I wanted to "recharge" myself *for* my job—two of the supposed functions of leisure. In fact, I love my job. I love my job so much I never really saw the need for much *besides* my job.

As Winston Churchill wrote in his small, delightful book *Painting as a Pastime*, "It may well be that those whose work is their pleasure are those who most need the means of banishing it at intervals from their minds."

We are assured that this single-minded focus is a good thing: "I'm following my passion." Whoever said it had to be *one* passion? What new passions might be out there that you've yet to discover?

*

When we're young, we're generally given free rein to try any number of things, without worrying whether we're good at them. We're all invited to sing in the school choir, to paint and draw, to try our hand at a staggering variety of sports. Over time—and seemingly ever earlier these days—specialization creeps in, and suddenly one is an "art kid" or a "theater kid" or a "math kid," on a path toward being an artist, an actor, or a mathematician.

We want to believe in the prodigy, the natural. Never mind that, as the author of a study of successful pianists argued, for much of the time these future masters were developing, "it would have been impossible to predict the pianists' eventual accomplishments." Learners need time and space, the author suggests, to appreciate "small signs of growth," to try their hand at techniques without being initially concerned whether they're getting them right. And if the pianists—or their parents—had pushed for such perfection from the outset, it's unlikely they'd have been as successful.

While still young, we start being told—and start telling ourselves—what we "can't" do. Children's participation in sports, for example, is said to be on the decline. Many children said that they didn't think they were good enough to participate; others, citing overly rigorous practice schedules or the stress of competitive pressure, said it simply wasn't fun—the main reason they were interested in the first place. Like footprints in a wet sidewalk, once these steps harden, changing direction becomes difficult.

But I would guess that like phantom limbs, those early attempts at things, even if underdeveloped, never leave us. Most of us probably sing a bit every day, if poorly, in the shower or the car. If asked, I could most likely re-create on a piece of paper the intricate war scenes—tanks and fortifications and entire squads of soldiers—I sketched out on Mead spiral-bound notebooks as a kid. The desire is there, maybe even a bit of the ability.

But that's as far as we're likely to take it. Sure, we could learn to sing or learn to draw. But who has the time? Why risk the embarrassment and polite condescension? Shouldn't we specialize in those things we know we're good at? We ask ourselves the question of the prototypical pragmatic parents when they hear of their offspring's choice of an "artsy" college major: What are you going to do with *that*?

The point is this: You do not yet know. Nor should you.

THERE'S NEVER BEEN A BETTER TIME TO BE A BEGINNER

We live in what might justifiably be called a golden age of learning.

Each of us has, at our fingertips, access to a vast amount of recorded information. The rise of the internet has also spawned a massive increase in the amount of learning opportunities. Online institutions like Khan Academy offer the promise to "learn almost anything— for free." Coursera's smartphone app gives a way to "fit learning into your commute, coffee break, or other quiet moments in your day." "Learn from anywhere," promises Skillshare. "Tomorrow is for the taking."

Bolstered by new understanding of the methods for effective learning, programs like Duolingo, meanwhile, promise to compress a semester's worth of language classes into thirty-four hours of online instruction. In chess, players' chess ratings as a whole have been rising because they can learn from (and play) better opponents, human or otherwise, on online platforms or take Skype lessons from international masters.

YouTube contains a vast constellation of instructional videos—more than 135 million, last time someone
checked—everything from how to make your own knife to
how to cook seal meat. You can learn how to do a backflip
or fly a 747. You can learn how to boil water or change toi-
let paper rolls (those are the cheeky ones). Stories abound
of people—often kids—achieving impressive proficiency
in everything from opera singing to dubstep dancing to
Olympic sports by simply copying what they'd seen in
YouTube videos. As a man arrested for performing illegal cosmetic surgery put it, "Pretty close to anything you
want to learn you can learn it off YouTube for free."

YouTube pedagogy has swept through—and virtually helped create—fields like competitive cubing (that
is, Rubik's), where solve times have plummeted, aided
largely by widespread transmission of techniques. There
is, to an extent unparalleled in history, the promise that
anyone, anywhere in the world, without cost or travel or
the embarrassment of public failure, can learn just about
anything.

But there's also been a proliferation of ways to learn
in person. Sites like CourseHorse and ClassPass provide
a marketplace for lessons (an online version of the post-
ers for guitar and Spanish lessons that have long adorned
coffee-shop bulletin boards). Maker spaces like Portland's
ADX and Chicago's Lost Arts give people the space and
tools to let them play around with serious machines and
ask their neighbors for advice. Charles Adler, who co-
founded Kickstarter before opening Lost Arts, told me the
name comes not from looking back to the past but from
the chance to "lose yourself in self-discovery."

He'd been motivated by the experience of trying to
build furniture to house his DJ equipment. He had an
idea but like many novices struggled to get to the next
step. "What I needed was temporary access to tools," he

told me, "and a mentor to provide some guidance." He couldn't find what he needed, so he created it.

In my own neighborhood, there are outfits like the Brooklyn Brainery, which offers inexpensive crowdsourced learning, with classes ranging from Intro to Batik to Biotechnology Crash Course. England's How To Academy promises a similar range: "Whether you want to build a bicycle in a morning, make a movie in a weekend, or start an on-line business, we have the expert who will help you make it happen."

You may be thinking, "Not everyone has the money, or, even more important, the time, to learn new things." It's true that coaches and classes can be expensive; on the other hand, they sometimes cost less than a meal. And online many are free. It may not be the most effective way to learn, but on a cost basis it can't be beat.

When it comes to time, I'd wager you could make a fair bit of progress in any skill in the time you might devote to one Netflix series. Time-use data show, despite our constant claims to be increasingly busy, that we largely have as much leisure time as we ever did. But our smartphones, for one, suck up hours a day and make us *feel* busier.

Overscheduled parents among you may protest that your hands are too full taking care of your children to learn something new. Why not learn something together? There's any number of skills—playing guitar, making bread, origami—where adults may be as initially clueless as their kids. Skill learning brings you closer on various levels and gives you a fascinating window onto your child's growth.

And this can happen in the most unlikely of places. When my daughter began playing the popular video game *Fortnite*, my first instinct was to be the detached, cautious parent, strictly concerned with monitoring her playing

time. But then, intrigued by the complexity of the game
and the passion it seemed to spark, I started joining the
ferocious squad campaigns that sprang up among her and
her friends. As a *Fortnite* "bot," or beginner—so labeled
by my plainly attired avatar—I had a lot to learn. "Grab
the legendary assault rifle!" one of her friends would shout
through the headpiece. "Head for Slurpy Swamp!"

The sheer range of stimuli was overwhelming; no
wonder action video games are said to increase your perceptual abilities. I was overwhelmed, and as I pleaded for
my teammates' patience, I suddenly realized the roles had
been reversed. Usually I was the one walking my daughter
through some math workbook, trying not to get frustrated
when she struggled with something that seemed obvious to me. Now I was in her place, as some ten-year-old
incredulously demanded to know why I wasn't building a
protective wall as a battle raged (uh, because I didn't know
how).

Your child can become, temporarily, the teacher of
you, and few things solidify learning better than teaching.

Sometimes, playing a game of online chess and facing
a thorny endgame, I'll ask my daughter for suggestions.
She'll stride over, puffing up with newfound authority, and
examine the board. I show her my idea. "You don't want to
trade pieces so early," she'll scoff, before magnanimously
offering a better move. Being a kid, she shrewdly barters
this advice for more *Fortnite* time.

Learning with your kid can also help solve a perpetual
issue of busy parents: child care. When I first told my wife
about the project behind this book, I could practically *hear*
the calculations going behind her unblinking eyes: "Uh,
who's going to be the parent here while you're off learning
to sing and surf?" It was a fair point. Being a dilettante was
one thing; being a deadbeat was another.

But she soon found, to her pleasant surprise, that my and my daughter's shared interest in surfing or chess translated into whole days where we'd be off at some beach or chess tourney. After such outings, my wife would gleefully report that she'd devoured an entire book while still in her pajamas, or had gone for a long, contemplative walk. These gifts are far better for a busy parent than what can be bought.

This co-learning can help turn potential sources of friction—like allocating leisure time—into win-wins. What might have been Daddy trying to sneak out for a quick surf session suddenly became a cherished family ritual. When my daughter joined a youth track and field club, I started using the time I'd otherwise be waiting for her to actually run myself. My philosophy was this: *If you have to take 'em, join 'em.* In all this, I was inadvertently helping overcome a potentially harmful dynamic that's been observed in a number of studies: Fathers spend less time with daughters than with sons, particularly in so-called achievement time—the things that help develop children's "human capital."

*

You may also be thinking, "It's too late." Nonsense: We learn until we die. Progress can be had at any age. Even the studies that look for signs of cognitive decline warn of the phenomenon of practice effects, which can throw off results. Practice effects occur when subjects' performance improves when they're exposed to the same test twice. This may be a methodological problem for psychologists, but for the rest of us it's wonderful news: *We get better.*

"I still insist that I can get better as I go along," the singer Tony Bennett said in 2016, at the age of ninety. Having achieved basically everything one could achieve as a singer, he had recently started to learn jazz piano (he'd picked up painting decades earlier). He wanted to get a better sense of it. What better way to appreciate something than to try it yourself, however initially clumsily?

The adult brain, once believed to be hopelessly "fixed and immutable," is now thought capable of much greater plasticity than ever before. At the same time, as life expectancy has increased in the United States and elsewhere, the "creative aging" movement has tried to promote the "productive and creative potential" of older adults.

When I met with Denise Park in Dallas, she was in the midst of a long-term effort, called the Dallas Lifespan Brain Study. In one part of the project, a group of older adults took classes in digital photography or quilting, while another group simply met and socialized. The subjects who took the classes had larger improvements in a variety of cognitive areas, ranging from episodic memory to processing speed.

It's not that learning by yourself is bad, or that simply socializing is mind-numbing, but learning *with* people just seems to hit some sweet spot in the human brain. It helped, Park said, that in the activities chosen, "everyone could proceed at their own rate, and it wasn't obvious if you were doing it badly." Learners were motivated by the presence of other learners and challenged by the instructors.

"People were just seeing progress that they didn't believe they could make," Park said.

*

I can't promise that *Beginners* will make you great at anything or that it will help you learn a specific skill. But, beyond being a guinea pig in the laboratory of lifelong learning, I will bring you the work of neuroscientists, expert coaches, scholars who study the acquisition of motor skills—among others—in the hopes that you might get more out of the things you do learn.

You may even learn from my own efforts—and not-so-occasional failures. Research suggests we can actually learn more by watching others who are closer to our skill levels perform the same task—mistakes and all—than by watching the flawless perfection of experts, who often can't really explain how they do what they do, or much remember what it was like to be where you are.

As I spend time in rehearsal studios, in surf camps, in art schools, and at the workbenches of craftsmen, I only hope that in my struggles and small accomplishments you may see truths you've encountered in your own journeys, reflected in some new light, or even that you might be encouraged to pick up something you have long wanted to tackle.

Beginners of the world, unite! You can only get better.

CHAPTER TWO

LEARNING HOW
TO LEARN

What Infants Can Teach Us About Being Good Beginners

BUILT TO SPILL:

INFANTS AS LEARNING MACHINES

As I readied to plunge into the world of beginnerdom, I thought it made sense to start with the most absolute beginners of all: infants.

They come screaming into a world of bright light, a barrage of sounds and smells, the sudden shocking tug of gravity. They are equipped with the barest capacities to do anything. If they could make it, I thought, so could I. One spring morning, I headed to one of the country's best places to understand infant behavior, luckily just a subway ride away: the Infant Action Lab, on the fourth floor of New York University's Center for Neural Science.

There, I watched a gregarious fifteen-month-old named Lily as she gamely adjusted to the fact that her body weight had just increased 15 percent. With her tiny, cherubic face knotted in puzzlement, she steadfastly plodded on an instrumented, pressure-sensitive mat toward her smiling and cajoling mother, who offered a handful of Cheerios. Call it one small step for science, one huge leap for a hungry baby.

Lily was outfitted with a snowsuit in which most of the stuffing had been ripped out and replaced by weights. She was not, as it might have looked, doing some baby boot camp. The purpose, as Jennifer Rachwani, a researcher in the lab, explained to me, was to understand how infants respond when a "cost" is added to walking. How does the extra weight affect the way infants walk? Does it change their willingness to walk toward a toy, or toward their mother?

The suit had been tweaked to Goldilocks perfection: You had to change it in just the right way to get babies to change their behavior. When the weights were placed entirely around the ankles, for instance, instead of distributed throughout the suit, babies just sat down.

At the aptly named Action Lab, which looks like a day-care center nestled into the groves of academe— padded walls, stain-resistant carpeting, a smattering of toys—infants clamber down steep ramps, wobble toward steep drop-offs, stagger across open chasms on adjustable walkways, and endlessly cavort. They do this under the watchful eyes of researchers, who sit, in another room, over notebooks and desk salads, carefully monitoring video screens.

The point of all this infant parkour—don't worry, no one gets hurt—is to understand how infants go about acquiring one of life's biggest skill sets: mobility. When do they learn to crawl or walk? How do they do it, and what do they choose to do with their newfound skills?

Karen Adolph, the lab's director, whose soothing voice belies a sharp sense of humor, has learned, after many years of observation, a lot about how infants get around. Each hour, the average toddler (from twelve to nineteen months) travels the length of some eight football fields, taking some twenty-four hundred steps. That's more than the average *adult* in America. Some 30 percent of each hour is dedicated to moving. Infant walking is spread across some 160 separate "bouts," some no more than a step or two. They zigzag, they retrace their steps, they sometimes, as Adolph noted, "take multiple steps on the same foot." Even though it only makes walking harder, new walkers will often carry things—some thirty-eight times per hour.

Before they can walk, they are hardly immobile, of course. They "drag, pull, hoist and propel their bodies," as Adolph described. They crawl in all manner of ways. Roughly one-fifth of them will "bum shuffle"—yes, that's the official term.

The long-standing hypothesis was that infants were always walking *to* something: a friendly caregiver, an alluring toy. And sometimes they are. But as research at the Action Lab has shown, the majority of walking instances don't really seem pointed toward an obvious destination. Infants walk in place, stop in the middle of nowhere, and often seem to stumble into interesting objects or destinations by happenstance. Eye-tracking software reveals that they're rarely looking toward some goal as they begin to walk.

Curiously, as one experiment showed, an empty room prompted infants to walk just as much as a room dotted with interesting toys. Mobility seems its own reward.

Some 2.6 million steps, or about six months, later, by Adolph's estimate, infants will become proficient walkers (they don't reach "adultlike" fluency until they're between five and seven). Along the way, they will have toppled over—a lot. Infants fall an average of seventeen times an hour. Novice walkers, who struggle to regain balance with nearly every step, tottering with a Frankenstein-like gait that is wider than it is long, can take up to thirty tumbles an hour. One unlucky subject of Adolph's hit the deck almost *seventy* times in one hour.

Most of these are "good falls." Babies are engineered to hit the ground. "They are loose-muscled; they are fat," Adolph said. "They are bouncy and soft." Like a modern car, they have crumple zones and air bags to diminish the physics of impact. "I could show you some beautiful videos of baby falls," she told me, excitedly, in her office. "They're really hypnotic. When they fall, it's like a graceful leaf."

Babies, in Adolph's eyes, are the ultimate beginners. The most mundane things, like sitting, are completely new and challenging to them. Sitting requires many weeks of practice and constant calibration; even when sitting still, infants are subtly swaying, like Thanksgiving parade floats, as they work to perfect balance.

Luckily, they exist in a perfect learning environment. "They have everything going for them," Adolph said. "They're highly motivated to learn things and be part of the world. There's almost nothing to dissuade them." Unlike adults, they do not receive negative feedback for their errors—their mistakes, if anything, may only generate more lavish parental attention—and they rarely get hurt.

Their ability to be *bad*, and have everyone be okay with that, is a crucial part of how they get good. Infants are learning machines, relentlessly curious and engineered with errors in mind. They take fourteen thousand steps a day with a failure rate that would be deeply discouraging—maybe even catastrophic—for adult beginners trying to learn a skill.

"We're not bouncy, hypotonic, and fat," Adolph said. "Our bones are brittle now; falling has much worse consequences."

And yet we fall. Workplace falls cost some seventy billion dollars in the United States alone, according to the Occupational Safety and Health Administration. One way to prevent them is to make the environment safer. But can we *teach* people not to fall?

As we know from infants, learning not to fall involves falling. So how can you do that safely? A "slip simulator," used by companies like UPS, puts trainees, held upright by a harness, on a surface that is randomly "perturbed." Rather than listening to a lecture on workplace falls, employees learn "kinetically," that is, by practicing, with their bodies, how to avoid falling. The technology has been credited with reducing the subsequent number of falls where it's been deployed.

One of the problems of older age, when falls can be so dangerous, is that we've tried to get through life falling as little as possible. And so we're out of practice. We're rookies just at the moment the stakes couldn't be higher. Hence the rise of "adult parkour" and other "learning to fall" classes for seniors, which teach not only fall avoidance but the best way *to* fall. It's as if we were beginners again, reaching back to our earliest selves, looking for courage.

Without an ability to take so many falls, would babies ever learn to walk? Would *we* so resolutely keep trying to learn something that seemed so elusive?

BABY STEPS: WALKING IS LEARNING

The high failure rate of novice walkers raises an interesting question. As Adolph writes, "Why would expert crawlers abandon a presumably stable, quadrupedal posture that took months to master in order to move in a precarious, upright posture where falling is rampant?"

The larger question of why children give up well-honed existing skills to clumsily take on new ones, she adds, isn't really known. Maybe they simply want to do what these larger people around them are doing.

Even with bad walking, however, there's an immediate payoff. This is something we should pay heed to as adult beginners as we ponder whether to leave our cozy enclaves of ability and strike out into the failure-prone landscape of skill learning.

"Infants are faster in the first week of horrible walking," said Adolph, "than they are in their twenty-one weeks of crawling." The babies are now covering three times the distance they did before. "All of a sudden your kid is leaving your sight," she said, "and running to the kitchen and pulling something down."

And though they are falling a lot as novice walkers, it turns out they were actually falling just as much (when adjusted for the amount of activity) when they were crawling.

So why *not* walk? There are all sorts of benefits to this new skill. It frees up their hands. It allows them to see more (crawling infants look mostly at the ground). It helps them gain "social agency." It gives them a measure of control over their environment. Parents even talk differently to walking infants than they do to crawling infants; perhaps not surprisingly, they start saying the word "no" more often.

For infants, mobility isn't just something to be learned. It's learning itself. Infants who are carried, for instance, learn less about their environments than infants who propel themselves. "Perceptual information doesn't come for free," as Adolph put it. "You have to *do* something."

Walking skill, says Adolph, comes more with experience than with age—the more steps, the better the walker. A well-traveled eleven-month-old tops a reluctant sixteen-month-old. The milestones aren't as neat as you might think. Some infants walk much earlier or later; some infants skip crawling; some start walking, only to resume crawling a few days later.

My own daughter, to the dismay of my wife and me—cue panicked googling—waited until she'd been on the planet for seventeen months to start walking. Perhaps she figured crawling was all the mobility she needed for our cozy Brooklyn apartment. Still, as anxious parents, we were ready, if she wasn't.

Walking used to be regarded as just another "milestone," a stage of "neuromuscular adaptation" that just magically happened. But babies *learn* to walk; just because we don't "teach" them to walk doesn't mean they're not learning. Infants in day care, Adolph told me, tend to walk sooner ("if you don't get that toy, someone else is going to get to it first"). In certain cultures, walking is enthusiastically practiced and emphasized—the way a Western parent might bombard a kid with Mozart or sight words—the result being infants who are walking before they're a year old.

The impulse is there, after all. Infants constantly move their legs even before they are born. When you hold a baby so that its feet are just touching a surface, they start to march, rather comically. The newborn "stepping reflex" usually disappears by around eight weeks. This proto-walking soon gets "unlearned" by infants because, as the leading theory goes, their legs get too heavy during a subsequent growth spurt to make it worth their while.

In the early 1970s, the psychologist Philip Zelazo, wondering if the gesture could be preserved, started giving his son, then several months old, daily training sessions in newborn stepping.

As a result of this constant movement, Zelazo reported, his son began walking at seven and a half months, well ahead of the norm. That son became a developmental psychologist himself, and as Adolph joked, "Every time I see him, at a conference, I'm kind of checking out his walking." Prodigy or not, he doesn't seem to walk with any noticeable panache.

In other cultures, such as the Aché of Paraguay, an indigenous foraging society that's often on the move through dense and dangerous forests, children are carried almost constantly; they traditionally don't begin to walk until they are between twenty-three and twenty-five months.

Does delayed walking hurt them?

"Not in the long term," Adolph said. "Those Aché Indians are using machetes and climbing palm trees by age eight."

The majority of scientific studies seem to have concluded that kids who hit motor-skills milestones early aren't any better at them later. My late-walking daughter has grown into a highly athletic tween. There's a lesson here for beginners of all ages: Each of us might begin to acquire a skill according to a slightly different schedule, but over time—and assuming we put in the same amount of practice—we essentially catch up with each other.

*

As much as learning any one skill, infants seem to be "learning to learn." The phrase comes from the prominent developmental psychologist Harry Harlow. In trials with monkeys, Harlow found that the more tests (or "learning sets") he gave them, the better they seemed to do. They were learning how to process new information faster.

Similarly, in a series of experiments at the Action Lab, infants were exposed to a variety of novel situations, like an opportunity to descend a steep slope. A striking pattern was observed. Infants looking at a daunting thirty-six-degree decline would, as knowing crawlers, avoid it, or at least approach it cautiously, slowly figuring out one of the many ways they might make it down. New *walkers,* however, would blithely plunge down slopes or toddle off cliffs—usually into the rescuing arms of a trained experimenter.

"Novice walkers will attempt *huge* drop-offs," Adolph said. "These babies behave as if they have no clues about the limits of their own abilities." It's not as if they were blind to the precipice itself, Adolph said, or its seeming risk. "We've done experiments where the mom tells them, 'No! Look at that slope!' And the kid just goes, 'I don't know why you're yelling; it looks good to me.'" She slapped her hands together and said, "Splat!"

"It's not like babies don't consider it," Adolph said. "They just don't know."

But shouldn't infants have learned about the difficulty of the slope, and its potential risks, from their crawling? What about all that learning how to learn stuff? On the face of it, it seems puzzling, even to Adolph. "Are they just not cognitively developed enough to make the linkage? Are they so intent on learning that they wipe the slate clean?"

Infants learn how to learn, Adolph has suggested, within the boundaries of the same "problem space." Crawling is one problem. Walking is another problem altogether. Information gathering is different (eyesight, for example, is suddenly elevated). The muscles involved are different, the motions are different, the balance requirements are different. There's no evidence that any crawling skills "transfer" to walking.

And the baby, as Adolph pointed out, now has a different body. Babies grow in astonishing episodic bursts; they've been reported to wake up almost an inch taller than when they went to sleep. Their head can grow nearly a third of an inch in circumference overnight.

Whatever worked for the crawling infant is not going to work for the walking infant. "You learn to move,"

Adolph said, "with the body you have." So they have to learn all over again—beginners once more—and, as Adolph has noted, "the process is no faster the second or third time around."

But wouldn't it be useful to preserve all that hard-fought knowledge? She shook her head. Babies, she said, do not want to learn "fixed associations," nor should they. "Why should I learn that a fifteen-centimeter drop-off is risky?" Adolph said. "Next week, I'm a better walker, and I'm taller." It's no longer so risky.

In other words, they're learning for today's world, not yesterday's. That world constantly changes, so babies must constantly change their solutions to problems.

Curiously, they often don't seem to learn much from the many mistakes they make. In one case, a baby in one of Adolph's studies fell down a set of stairs at home and was taken to the emergency room. A few days later, the baby was back in the lab and immediately plunging headfirst down steep slopes.

Wouldn't it be *good* to learn a healthy fear of sudden drops? "You don't want a baby to learn 'don't do this, you're going to fall,' " Adolph told me, "because they're going to fall all the time." So if they fall, they don't analyze; they just get back up. "If you're a baby, what are you supposed to learn from these falls?" Adolph asked. *"You don't want the baby to learn to stop trying."*

Babies are constantly facing a new normal. Hard-and-fast rules about what works and what doesn't will be of little use. "For babies," Adolph said, "most of the time they're doing things they've never done before."

As the ultimate beginners, they need a kind of learning—learning how to learn—that is flexible, that is powered by exploration, that can allow them to adapt to novel situations, that accepts plentiful errors, often without any seeming cause, as part of the process. They experience fall after fall, until, slowly, their brain and body figure out how to stop falling, in all sorts of situations.

Infants live what might be called the beginner's creed: If you don't learn to fail, you'll fail to learn.

*

As fellow beginners, we can take away some other important lessons from infants (after all, you were once one yourself). Before we head into the world of adults learning new things, let us consider these:

1. We all have latent abilities that can be unlocked. After eight weeks or so, newborns lose the "stepping" impulse they are born with. Or do they? Put them in water, and they start marching again. It was there all along, they just had to decide—or be encouraged—to use it.

2. Skills take time. Infants spend roughly a third of their day for six solid months practicing walking (and don't truly perfect it until several years later). Think of that the next time you fret about your tennis serve or your ability to paint clouds during that hour per week you spend on an activity. They're called baby steps for a reason.

3. Failure is an essential part of learning. We tend to remember the milestone achievements (for example, the day the baby first began to walk) and forget the many, many falls that came first. Behind every highlight reel is a huge B-roll of mistakes.

4. Change up your practice. One of the key findings in the science of learning in the last few decades is the benefit of what's known as variable practice.

When we practice a variety of skills, rather than long, monotonous drills in the same skill, we often do worse during the practice session but better in the long run. Because we have to work harder to remember the different exercises, and the ways we solved them, we perform them better.

Infants, intentionally or not, adopt this approach in learning to walk. Rather than repeating, drill-like, long, straight paths, they take truly random walks, filled with stops, starts, different patterns and motions, across a large variety of surfaces and environments. They never take the same walk twice.

This is a good thing. You don't want to teach an infant one "proper" way to walk, which they then must repeat in lockstep. When it comes to learning, *variability* is the key. What might look like clumsiness or randomness can simply be beginners exploring a range of possible solutions, which seems to help promote faster learning.

5. Your progress may not be linear. Learning happens in fits and starts. Stages are only rough benchmarks. Development does not always march uniformly in one direction. Infants may learn to walk, then briefly revert to crawling.

Progress is often "U shaped," meaning kids (and adults) can get worse before they get better. Children beginning to learn grammatical rules, for instance, often eagerly "overapply" their new (but still incomplete) knowledge. Where they were properly calling them "feet," they now speak of "foots." They are, roughly speaking, getting ahead of themselves for a moment, developmentally, but they will catch up.

6. Skills rarely "transfer." Infant crawlers don't seem to carry much of what they've learned as crawlers into walking. This isn't so unusual. Skill learning, at any age, tends to be very specific. You might think that people who stayed comfortably upright on a wobbly platform in a lab test would also do well on a ladder-climbing test—because both skills involve balance. But more than half a century of research has found very little correlation among skills.

Being good at one skill rarely gives you an automatic leg up in another.

7. Always be on the edge of the impossible. Young children, Adolph has noted, seem to learn best "when operating near the limits of their current skill level." In that "zone of proximal development"—between what they can currently do and what they are trying to do—they'll look for any assist they can get. Remember: If it feels easy, you're probably not learning.

8. Learning skills helps open new worlds. Infants who learn to walk can suddenly go more places and do more things. This is a lesson we should carry through life.

9. Goals are good, but keep your eyes open for opportunity. Infants learning to walk don't seem motivated by specific goals; instead, they simply move and encounter interesting things by accident. As the developmental psychologist Esther Thelen—who accidentally found her career by taking a class as a "bored housewife" looking to expand her interests "beyond Jell-O cubes and *Sesame Street*"—observed, we should take inspiration from "the improvising infant" and remember that "part of life should be taking advantage of opportunities that come along."

As you try to learn something, you shouldn't lose sight of all the interesting little detours along the way. Learning to walk may be less the goal than simply unlocking all the good things and places walking gets you to.

Now let's try to learn something.

CHAPTER THREE

UNLEARNING TO SING

I don't sing because I'm happy, I'm happy because I sing.

—WILLIAM JAMES

WE'RE ALL BORN TO SING

When was the last time you sang?

If you're like most, probably not that long ago. I'm not talking about a solo recital at Carnegie Hall but any incidental singing: morning crooning in the shower, the murmured half hum as you briskly walked to the train, the up-tempo Hall and Oates song emanating from the fluorescent heavens of the grocery store that lodged itself in your head.

And let's not forget the car, which is nothing short of a private acoustic chamber.* "Driving with background music," one researcher speculated, "might be *the* most prevalent music behaviour ever taken on by the human species."

Which makes the car, almost by default, our most reliable venue for singing, particularly in private or semi-private (one study—seemingly plucked from my own

---

* To take just one measure, it has been reported that the majority of queries on Shazam, the app that recognizes a song that is playing, happen at speeds of over thirty kilometers per hour.

life—reported a number of instances of children "forcefully requesting" a parent to stop singing along to music in the car). "Car-aoke" is so endemic it's been investigated as a possible source of driving distraction.

Our desire to sing, and indeed our larger love of music, seem, from an evolutionary standpoint, "very strange," suggests Steven Mithen, an archaeologist and author of *The Singing Neanderthals*. Other than sex and food, he maintains, there are few things besides music to which people "are so compulsively drawn."

Singing *is* good for us; it can boost our immune function, endorphins, and oxytocin (the so-called cuddle hormone). It improves respiratory function and can reduce the risk of sudden cardiac arrest. By activating the crucial bundle of fibers, known as the vagus nerve, that helps the brain regulate heart rate, blood pressure, digestion, and many bodily functions, it may even counter depression.

Could something that brings us such pleasure, that we partake in so regularly, that seems so beneficial to our bodies, not be without some design?

The human capacity for music, Mithen suggests, is "embedded in the human genome." Long before we had language, we were messing around with pitch and rhythm. This was a way to talk to one another and also to express emotions and forge social connections (interestingly, the oxytocin boost that singing provides also helps us to bond with others). When language arrived to take over the day-to-day workload of interpersonal communication, Mithen suggests, singing could focus on all the feel-good emotions-and-connections stuff.

When we sing, we're singing a very old song. It can certainly feel that way when, as a new parent, you're holding your infant in your arms, staring into their eyes, and, not really knowing what else to do with this little wriggling preliterate bundle of joy, you make harmonically pleasing, heretofore unexpressed, cooing sounds. Or you just sing.

It's what babies do, after all, long before they speak their first word. You might sing a nonsense song or something entirely random (we regularly treated our daughter to renditions of the cowboy lullaby "My Little Buckaroo"). You just feel the need to do it, as if some primal door has been opened and this long-lost language, this back channel to the heart, one that you wouldn't normally use with your friends or even your spouse, flickers to life.

Without anyone telling us to do so, we sing to infants in a special way, one that feels warmly instinctual. In one study of "infant-directed singing," when mothers sang a song to their baby, and then sang the same song without the baby present, people listening to recordings of the two songs could tell when the baby was present, even when the song was in an unfamiliar language.

One reason is pitch. Mothers and fathers sing higher to infants than they normally do—women seem to raise their pitch even more—and infants like it when they do (presumably because it's less threatening). Simply raising the voice of a *stranger* by half an octave was, in one study, enough to get infants' attention. And we can raise our pitch by smiling, which makes us look friendlier.

Babies not only enjoy singing; they virtually *demand* it: Infants prefer mothers' singing over mothers' speech. Babies like it when fathers sing as well. In one study, infants actually preferred the dads' tunes. Not because the fathers had better pipes, but because most infant singing is done by moms. Infants were drawn to male singing for the sheer novelty of it.*

---

* The researchers also noted that fathers' performances tended to be more self-conscious than mothers': "For example, they tended to 'ham' for the microphone, as if performing for a listening audience that went beyond their infant (or themselves)."

I could relate. As a new father, I found I was a beginner again in many ways, scrambling to acquire all sorts of curious skill sets. I knew how to sing—who does not?—but as I made my way through dimly remembered lullabies, I felt as if I were dusting off some vestigial skill.

Being a beginner, however, meant I had a certain freedom, because I'd not yet acquired the burden of expertise and expectation. A father singing to his eight-pound daughter? *How cute!* It didn't matter if I knew all the words or hit every note. We were just two amateurs, my daughter and I, speaking in this ancient language, our eyes locked and our bodies afloat in a river of uplifting hormones, each of us the most forgiving audience we could ever have.

Singing these gentle songs, in this higher pitch, I suddenly felt as if a weight were being lifted from me, and I remember wondering, why don't I do this more often?

I don't consider myself a natural vocal talent, or even particularly musical. Whatever music theory I learned early in school is mostly lost to me. I can't really play any instruments. I'm not a natural performer; apart from a thankfully forgotten, pre-smartphone outing at a friend's bachelor party, I hadn't even dipped into karaoke.

But I did enjoy singing around the house, in the shower, in the car. My wife had occasionally told me I had a "nice voice," but, she carefully allowed, it *was* sometimes off-key. It was better, she said, when I wasn't overly self-conscious about it.

But how could you not be self-conscious about this act that derives entirely from one's self, that seems to so powerfully express that self? "It's so good to hear your voice," we say on a long-distance telephone call, when we really mean "it's so good to hear *you*." Parenthood had put me back, however briefly, into a world of singing, but it suddenly occurred to me I'd been discreetly and aimlessly singing my entire life—to a song on the radio, along with a band at a concert.

What would happen if I tried to go about it in a more purposeful way?

BEGINNERS WELCOME

I decided I needed a teacher. While there are countless books on vocal technique, many with good insights, these seemed aimed at people who mostly knew what they were doing.

The internet, too, is filled with instructional videos, a sea of people guiding you through heavy metal screams or Broadway belting, but these can be of decidedly mixed quality. Like books, they have a key weakness: There's no one, except your own inexpert self, to tell you if you're doing things right.

"Sing as if no one were listening," goes the refrain. I agree with the spirit, but if you want to get better, having another set of ears is invaluable.

Luckily, living in New York City, I had access to a wealth of musical talent. An online search revealed what seemed to be hundreds of teachers in Brooklyn alone. The bulletin boards in my local shops bristled with flyers from voice coaches making bold, seemingly life-altering promises: "Find the voice you never knew you had!"

One day, I was reading a profile of the actor Ethan Hawke, who lives in my neighborhood. Hawke was promoting his new film, *Born to Be Blue*, a biopic of the celebrated, notorious jazz trumpeter and vocalist Chet Baker. With interest, I read that Hawke had decided to record his own vocal tracks for the film, taking an intensive crash course in singing with a voice teacher in Brooklyn.

I'm a longtime fan of Baker's, particularly his singing. In college, I dragged non-jazz-loving friends to see Bruce Weber's reverent 1988 film, *Let's Get Lost*. When my wife and I began seriously dating, she was struck by the way I would constantly warble a track from *Chet Baker Sings*, "Like Someone in Love" (in the way that fledgling couples often attach songs to their heady courtship). People have even said, at various times in my life, that I *looked* a bit like Baker. It seemed kismet.

What's more, Baker is arguably a perfect spirit guide for an insecure, would-be singer, because he himself was so technically challenged. He struggled to stay in tune, took endless takes, was said to sound flat and without sentiment, and was famously conflicted over what one biographer called his "androgynously sweet tenor." Critics, even at the peak of Baker's powers and renown, were harsh. One described "an anemic voice which sounds like a boiled owl trying for out-of-reach high notes."

Many others, including myself, *felt* something in that imperfection and seeming flatness, an emotional poignancy that, real or not, left an indelible impression. There are, after all, plenty of singers who are technically spot-on—and utterly forgettable. "Eighty percent of singing is how you sell the song," one voice expert told me, "rather than the brilliance of the instrument."

Some internet sleuthing led me to Hawke's teacher, Danielle Amedeo. From her website, which bore the magic words "Beginners Welcome," I learned she lived just down the street.

A week later, we met at a nearby café. Amedeo, thirty-eight, with her first child due in a few months (she warned me her maternity leave would interrupt our lessons), studied theater and sang at NYU and, following a nine-year stint in the corporate world, began teaching full-time. Half her students were musical theater students, Broadway hopefuls. The other half were all sorts of people: actors looking to improve their vocal delivery, aspiring singers trying to refine their craft, novices like me.

With brightly inquisitive eyes, perched with the good posture and actorly poise that reflects a life of performing, she listened, nodding sympathetically, as I laid out my hopes and fears in a nervous stammer.

Am I just too old? What if I just can't land on the proper notes? What if we discover I just don't have a good voice?

She smiled at this last question, as if she'd heard it often before. A small number of people, she said, might *physically* struggle with producing accurate notes. They should see a doctor before seeing her. Luckily, she found "no reason for concern" in mine.

But, I pressed her, what if I could hit the notes but didn't like the *sound*?

"Someone will come to me and say, 'This is my voice, this is what I've been doing my whole life, and I don't like it—is this the only voice I have?'" But, she argued, we're only tapping into a small portion of what our voice can be. Anatomy gives us a vocal default setting, but imitation, habit, and intention give us *our* voice. "People believe it's a feature, like having blue eyes," she said. "But it's very much related to use and habit, and it's a skill that can be learned."

This learning would take place across the whole body. While singing is a motor skill, it's unique in that most of what happens is invisible to the singer. "When you're looking at a skilled athlete, you can see what they're doing," she said. "With singing it's all hidden." Even if you hold a golf club poorly, you can at least see your hands. You can't see your cricothyroid or thyroarytenoid muscles doing the wrong thing as you tackle "My Way."

Because we can't easily control the individual muscles and other anatomical bits involved in good singing technique, vocal pedagogy relies heavily on metaphor and imagery. To coax certain sounds, singers are invited to imagine birds landing on branches or balls held aloft by fountains of air.

Whatever my voice was, Danielle insisted I was using only a fraction of its potential. "We can open it up, expand it, make it richer," she said. As a near fifty-something, I wasn't going to be able to do certain things as easily as when I was a teenager, but unless there was a long history of misuse, it didn't mean I'd be less capable of singing.

"You should walk into this completely open and think of it as a joyful experience," she said. She wanted me to emphasize only of exploration, not limits. "We tend to start that way, and the limits we place on ourselves mentally tend to create physical limits on ourselves."

*

Let me rephrase the question I asked a bit earlier: When was the last time you sang *to* someone, or in *front* of someone, or *with* people?

I would hazard a guess that unless you're a musician or sing in church, you could count on one hand the times you can remember singing in public in the last year.

When I asked my wife this question, she paused, then said, "Well, there was that time we sang Christmas carols around the piano at Tina's party in Rye." That was nearly *ten* years ago, I reminded her. My wife is someone who, upon hearing some obscure hymn, can instantly begin to sing along, the result of many Sundays spent in church as a child. Now, because she sings so infrequently, what happened a decade ago looms in her memory as a recent event.

It's hard to escape the feeling that singing has greatly declined in public life.

A few years ago, I was in St. Croix, in the U.S. Virgin Islands, tagging along as a journalist with a team from Google Maps. One night, over beers at a local restaurant, we noticed a piano in the corner. One of the team, it turned out, was trying to learn the instrument. Early on, he'd set for himself the eminently practical task of learning one whole song so he could provide instant entertainment at gatherings. The song was Journey's "Don't Stop Believin'," a crowd-pleaser if ever there was one.

I imagine you know it. I certainly thought I did. But a funny thing happened: Once we got past the opening verse, things began to fall apart, and we were all frantically looking to each other for lyric prompts as we fumbled our way through. We thought we knew how to sing the song, but we knew only how to sing *along* with it. There's a difference.

Something else happened: A teenage girl got up from her family's nearby table and began filming us—who knows whose social media feed we populated that day? What would once have been an everyday occurrence now seemed worthy of documenting, like the spotting of some rare animal.

Singing is more present than ever, thanks to the seemingly nonstop soundtrack of recorded music in the world. But as a thing you do with others, in a non-jokey way, it has faded, in ways that can't be precisely measured but are intuitively felt.

"There was such a lot of singing in the villages then," says an elderly English horseman, reflecting back to the early twentieth century, in Ronald Blythe's *Akenfield*, his classic account of a small English town.* "Boys sang in the fields, and at night we all met at the Forge and sang. The chapels were full of singing. When the first war came, it was singing, singing all the time."

---

* Blythe's book, while fictionalized, is based on extensive oral interviews.

But like cursive handwriting or map reading, the skill and practice of communal singing have seen a slow, palpable decline.

Why do we sing less? One reason is that the arrival of recorded music, radio, and then television meant people no longer had to produce their own musical entertainment, whether alone or communally. Music went from "lean in" to "lean back."

Everyone had access to the world's greatest singing talent, right in their living room. Why hang with the amateurs when you had the professionals at ear's length? This also implied, unfortunately, that one's *own* singing might begin to pale in comparison. We began to develop a national vocal insecurity complex whose underlying message was this: If you weren't *really* good at singing, why bother?

Singing declined for other reasons, such as the fact that church attendance has been broadly in retreat. But here too we find that sinister idea: We're just not good enough. Even in the most flourishing churches, choirs have been shrinking. Why? "Our culture of performance and expertise," maintains one Lutheran pastor. "We don't sing anywhere else in our lives the way we once did. I grew up singing in home, in school and church every week. Now, people think they are not good enough to sing."

Singing has come to occupy a curious place in our lives. It's a furtive, almost shameful activity that few of us feel confident doing in front of anyone.

When scientists at the University of California at San Francisco wanted to investigate what parts of the brain were activated under conditions of embarrassment, they needed a go-to embarrassing activity. So they asked people to sing "My Girl" by the Temptations. For most, watching oneself sing elicits a "considerable embarrassment reaction," said one of the researchers. It's little surprise that

karaoke bars, one of our few strongholds of public singing, are fueled by heavy doses of alcohol and ironic humor.

On the other hand, we've lifted singing into an almost
ethereal art form, one beyond the reach of most mortals.
We say, "Oh, I can't sing," as if it were a medical condition, a fixed state.

"We mythologize and romanticize singing and singers," suggests the musician Tracey Thorn, "seeming to
hold it up as a skill both more difficult and rarer than it
actually is." Between the tuneless hordes on one side and
the elite cadre of vocal acrobats on the other, there isn't
much middle ground for just-all-right singers.

And, in truth, people often aren't very good. When
academics have inquired into how well people sing, the
results are not encouraging. The title of one paper—
"Imprecise Singing Is Widespread"—tells you pretty
much all you need to know. The litmus-test song is usually "Happy Birthday." No wonder: According to *Guinness
World Records*, it's the most familiar song in the English
language.

But how well do we know it? "Listening to any gathering of people singing 'Happy Birthday,'" one pair of
exasperated researchers observed, "makes one wonder if
everyone learns it accurately in the first place." As they do
with most songs, people usually sing it too quickly. Maybe
they just want to get it over with.

You might take a bit of comfort in that "Happy Birthday" isn't actually the easiest of songs. "It begins on the
dominant," writes Steven Demorest, a professor of music
at Northwestern University, "and spans an octave with a
number of intervallic leaps of different lengths." Which
means that several times singers must make sizable jumps
from lower notes to higher notes, and landing with precision can take practice.

There is something deeply ironic in the idea that the

song we all must sing—the song that very well may be the last song you sang in front of someone—is, as Demorest says, "quite challenging."* Maybe people were better singers back in the late nineteenth century when a pair of Kentucky schoolteachers penned that particular ditty.

IF WE WERE BORN TO SING, WHY DO WE FIND IT SO HARD?

For our first lesson, in the makeshift studio (that is, bedroom) of her ground-floor Brooklyn Heights duplex, Amedeo had asked me to bring a song to perform. Given what had led me here, I chose "Time After Time," the jazz standard written by Sammy Cahn and Jule Styne, a number 16 hit for Frank Sinatra in 1947. Chet Baker recorded it a decade later, in a much sparer, almost wistful version.

This was the rendition I was most familiar with—almost too familiar. Before the lesson I'd been listening heavily to it and singing along. When Amedeo, seated at her digital piano, began to play and sing a few notes, all of which sounded musically correct, I could only think, "That's not Chet."

I'd so associated the song with Baker's version that I could barely hear what Amedeo was playing. "It sounds kind of . . . different than I'm used to," I said. After experimenting with the timing, she turned to me and said, "Let me just hear you go. I'm going to plunk out some notes."

"TIME—" I croaked, followed by the first of a series of coughs. Anxiety, unhelpfully for singing, often manifests itself in the throat.

---

* For Americans, the national anthem, penned by Francis Scott Key, is another song that *is* more commonly sung, at sporting events and the like, and is also famously challenging.

"Drink your water, take your time," she counseled.

"From the top!" I joked, and then, without even realizing she was no longer accompanying me on piano (because, she later told me, I had changed key halfway through and the piano was just confusing me), I was into the song, churning along until the end, a "big finish" octave jump, as the singer emphatically reaffirms his earlier thoughts with a dramatic, drawn-out flourish: "*And TIIIIIIIMMMME after time / You'll hear me say that I'm / So lucky to be loving you.*"

I careened through this line with the control of a snake on ice, and on the word "lucky" my voice trailed upward in a dying screech.

Several things seemed to happen at once. Amedeo was clapping and exclaimed, "Well done for getting through that!" I was bathed in sweat. She urged me to stick my face in the nearby air conditioner. I tried to blame it on the humid New York day, but like the persistent cough I'd suddenly developed, it was almost certainly a psychosomatic reaction to this prospect of suddenly having to sing, by myself, before a relative stranger, into a room, without the recorded presence of Chet Baker in my own ears.

This may sound obvious or even naïve to the non-novice, but there is something deeply transformative about sending your voice, *as music*, unaccompanied by the radio or someone else, into a room. You're not only hearing the song as you've never quite heard it; you are hearing your voice as you've never quite heard it.

Singing along to recorded music gives you all kinds of cover. People often don't sing as accurately when singing along to recorded music, research has shown, precisely because they don't have to. Someone else is picking up the slack.

When your voice is out there, alone, filling up space, you suddenly realize how strange it is, this thing that dwells inside you but only comes to life when it leaves you. Whatever technical limitations were there before, but were covered up in your radio sing-alongs, are now nakedly present.

But there's something more profound going on.

You feel as if *you* were now out there, exposed and emotionally vulnerable. I was opening myself in strange ways at the very same moment I was displaying my incompetence, which made the experience immensely more powerful than, say, snowboarding, which I'd recently tried for the first time.

There, I was just bumbling with everyone else on the novice slope, a puppet pulled by the strings of gravity and inexperience. Here, as a person not accustomed to freely offering up his emotions or his singing voice, I felt as if I'd just extracted an essential organ and handed it, still dripping, to Danielle.

Like most people, you've probably been surprised and displeased by the sound of your own voice on a recording. The usual explanation is that when we hear our own voices, we're hearing more than the voice that leaves our mouth. We're also hearing an inner voice, transmitted through vibrations in our bones, resonating in our internal acoustical chambers.

This homegrown hi-fi system convinces us that our voice sounds deeper and richer than it actually is.* But thanks to various filtering devices in our bodies and brains, as the MIT researcher Rébecca Kleinberger notes, we largely screen ourselves out. "You hear your voice," as she put it, "but your brain actually never listens to the sound of your voice."

---

* You can get a sense of how you sound to the outside world via a neat trick, suggested by the vocal coach Chris Beatty: Take two folders or magazines, and hold them up, perpendicular, against the front of your ears. Take turns saying things with and without the folders.

When we really do listen, it can be unsettling, and not just for reasons of sound quality. When we have this "voice confrontation," as the psychologists Philip Holzman and Clyde Rousey described it, we may suddenly realize how much our voice is *saying:* We hear ourselves expressing things about ourselves we didn't realize we were expressing, or didn't even want to be expressing.

Our unseen, humble larynx, after all, contains "the highest ratio of nerve fibers to muscle fibers of any functional system." Our voice—this turbulent gust of air bouncing around our inner cavities and streaming into the world—speaks volumes about us, everything from our health to our physical characteristics to our desirability as a mate. From just a fleeting utterance of the word "hello," one study showed, listeners were able to form consistent impressions of the speaker's personality. Imagine what a whole song reveals.

"You sounded really lovely!" Amedeo said. Listening later to the recording, I'd say she was erring on the side of encouragement. "You said it's something you've used all your life, just for fun, and that's clearly there for you," she said. "Can you tell me what went well?"

"Um," I stammered, still flustered, "there was a bit of quavering. The timing seemed off. I felt like I needed to *sing* more, rather than just passively sounding the words."

She looked at me expectantly. "Was there anything you *liked* about it?"

"And those high notes," I continued, in my vein of self-flagellation. "Ugh!"

I'd made the error, common to beginners, of fixating on the idea of a "high" note as something just that—vertically high. "A singer will do all sorts of physical things to try to achieve that, like lift their head up, tighten the shoulders and neck, look up to the sky, picturing the note up here and reaching for it," she said.

None of these things were ultimately productive for hitting a high note; they were habits that would have to be undone.

I was also trying to hit the notes using my "chest voice," the lower register, typically used in speech. It's named "chest voice" because that's where you feel it, but it's actually made by muscles in your throat.

As a presumed baritone, I knew that method was simply beyond my range for the notes in question—at least for now. To avoid potentially damaging strain, I needed to tackle the notes in the lighter "head voice." This is felt more—you guessed it—in the head (falsetto, depending on whom you listen to, is either a weaker head voice or not a head voice at all). There too is a "mixed" register, which could combine the lightness of the head voice with the more substantial resonance of the chest voice.

Baker, a tenor, had a clear, seemingly effortless head voice, one that doesn't often come easily to men. I took comfort in the idea that Hawke, Amedeo's other would-be Baker acolyte, hardly had an easy time of it. "He really had to learn to use a different part of his voice," she said.

"You already have a bit of access to that, which is interesting," she said. My ears perked up. "From your speaking voice, I would have thought you were a baritone. But you have some really lovely high notes there, which most men do not have right off the bat."

I felt a weird flush of pride, as if I were suddenly in some kind of competitive sing-off for the soul of Chet Baker. Take that, Hawke! I had *access*.

THE ROOTS OF VOCAL INSECURITY

Why do so many of us—myself included—seem to be mediocre singers?

Before we get to that, you may be wondering about your own singing ability. I would urge you to take the online test that Steven Demorest helped create.* It's based on pitch accuracy, the easiest-to-measure, most fundamental variable in singing quality. No matter your score, remember one thing: It can be *improved*.

Demorest has an idea why so many of us are poor singers, and it has little to do with innate talent. He's tested the singing abilities of groups of various ages and found a striking pattern: From kindergarten to the sixth grade, children show a clear improvement.

But when he's tested college students, they're basically equivalent to the kindergartners. Why do they regress?

Demorest thinks most of them simply stop singing as much. Singing, like all music education, typically becomes an "elective" after sixth grade. All music participation drops, but particularly singing. Maybe because, unlike violin or piano, parents don't equate it with academic achievement (for the record, a study at Canada's Royal Conservatory found that voice students had a higher average IQ than piano students).

Early on, kids seem to sing all the time; what parent has not wept on a preschool carpet as their kids sweetly pipe "I Wanna Linger"? There is singing at assemblies, not by "choirs," but by entire classes (and more weeping). Households with young children ring with song; to this day, when I hear the song "1234," by the singer Feist, I instinctively launch into her version from *Sesame Street*. I have a clear memory of donning a blue "Union cap" in a third-grade historical pageant and marching across the stage, singing, "As the caissons go rolling along!" It was the last time I used the word "caissons" and the last time I could remember singing onstage. A subtle, profound shift

* Found at Seattle Singing Accuracy Protocol, ssap.music.northwestern.edu.

happens as children age. They begin to acquire a "musical self-concept." They begin to think they "have it" or they don't.

The key word here is "think": As research by Demorest and others has found, there's not a strong relationship between children's self-perception of their singing skill and their *actual* singing skill. As they say, "Fake it till you make it." But self-perception *does* influence future participation in music. "Disbelief in one's capabilities," writes the psychologist Albert Bandura, "creates its own behavioral validation."

And so kids get sorted into two categories: the musical and the nonmusical, singers and non-singers. "My colleagues are part of the problem," says Demorest of fellow music teachers. "They view teaching singing to someone who's not going to be good enough to do it in front of somebody as giving them false hope or wasting their time, rather than providing someone with instruction because they want it."

When I told Demorest that my daughter, then seven, had passed an audition for a local choir—something I'd been reflexively proud of—he drew a sharp breath. "I question whether or not we should be auditioning seven-year-olds who want to sing."

When he was running the after-school choir of his daughter's elementary school, he recalled, there were two girls who "really could not sing accurately." He left them in. He tried to give them a bit of instruction, but didn't want to make them feel self-conscious. "Both of those girls," he told me, "ended up singing choir in middle school and high school." They got better.

We often interrupt people at the beginner stage, forgetting that talent can take time.

Not surprisingly, children come to view musical ability, even more than athletic prowess, as a function of innate talent. We say someone *has* a good voice; we don't say they worked hard to get (and keep) that voice.

But many of us mostly stop singing, and then, finding ourselves as adults not particularly proud of our singing ability, we listen with admiration to proficient singers and, suddenly impressed by this massive gulf in ability, reach for quasi-mystical explanations of their gifts. It makes us feel better about our own perceived inadequacies to employ categorical explanations: We are musical, or not.

You've probably heard someone in your life—maybe even yourself—declare themselves tone-deaf. In fact, congenital amusia, as the condition is known, is exceedingly rare, much rarer than the number of people who report suffering from it. Most of us could notice, for example, if a single note is changed in a popular song, as one experiment did.

The widespread use of the phrase "tone deafness" obscures the real problem, as Sean Hutchins, director of research at Canada's Royal Conservatory, told me. We're incredibly sensitive listeners when it comes to pitch. The problem is not *perceiving* correct notes,* Hutchins says, but *producing* them. We tend to overlook the fact that singing, while being, yes, an amazingly expressive conveyor of emotion and a sonorous delight, is primarily a motor skill. It's a matter of coordinating muscles to achieve a desired outcome, really no different from archery or pitching a fastball.

It's also just like any other musical skill.† "Nobody

---

* An interesting exception here is the famed *American Idol* contestant William Hung, who was widely reported to be "off-key" and "tuneless." As various observers have noted, his pitch accuracy was actually spot-on. Whatever dissonance those listeners were feeling came from something besides musical pitch.

† Even though people often make a distinction *between* musicians and singers. For example, the U.S. Bureau of Labor Statistics has an employment category called "Musicians and Singers." On its website, it features information on "how to become a musician or singer," as if the two things were mutually exclusive.

expects adults who haven't picked up their trumpet since fifth grade to play with any skill," Demorest argues, "but we think that we either 'have' or 'don't have' a singing voice."

We find ourselves in a vicious cycle: The reason we're not so good at singing is that we don't do it so much. We don't do it so much because we think we're not so good.

And as a result, from those magical days of early childhood, when children and parents are largely communicating through this musical language, reaching for infrequently accessed sounds—we use a much wider vocal range with singing than with speech—we slowly revert to a life of harmonic monotony, where speech is firmly on one side and singing on the other, where singers are on one side and non-singers are on the other.

We lose our voice.

UNLEARNING TO SING

Going into it, I imagined learning to sing would be exactly like that first afternoon in Amedeo's studio: I would sing songs, my teacher would listen and point out problems, and then I'd try to sing them again, better. It would prove to be both much simpler than that and much more profound.

The first thing needed was basic tuning of the instrument. And what an instrument it is!

When we speak or sing, we push air up toward the larynx. When that stream encounters the "vocal folds"— the preferred term for "vocal cords"—it pushes them open and, rushing through the coin-sized, V-shaped glottis, closes them again. It's like the way a balloon sputters as you let out air. Stretch the balloon—or the cords—and the pitch gets higher.

This happens faster than an eyeblink: about 120 times per second for the average male, 210 times for the average female. A soprano hitting a fearsome F6 in an operatic aria will have folds vibrating nearly *1,400* times per second. Weirdly, whispering usually puts more strain on the vocal folds than speaking.

If the rush of air ended at the vocal folds, it would sound a mere buzz, like a raspy duck call. Our vocalizations pick up their personality as they flow, turbulently, into the "resonant chamber" of our vocal tract—the larynx, the pharynx, the mouth. When you are truly resonant, your *face* vibrates. The bulk of that air, however, never reaches our lips. The job of good singing is to get it there.

Through this complex orchestration of muscles, we become vocal powerhouses. As Ingo Titze, who directs the National Center for Voice and Speech, has pointed out, with our two humble "strings" humans can cover a musical range for which the piano requires eighty-eight. Some people can go *beyond* the piano. "Think of how many different things you can do with your voice," the Royal Conservatory's Hutchins said to me. "Compare that to your cat or dog." We can imitate both; they can't imitate anything.

Astonishingly, we're doing this with a mechanism whose primary purpose is not in fact speaking or singing but helping to prevent food or other objects from accidentally entering the airway. Like two tiny trapdoors, the vocal folds snap shut when we swallow—to keep things from "going down the wrong pipe" and into the lungs.

Only later in our evolution did we "learn" to sing with this same apparatus. Maybe that's why, as one team of neuroscientists has suggested, we sometimes struggle with producing accurate tones: We simply don't have as much neural control over our larynx as we do over our mouth. We can usually *whistle* more accurately than we can sing.

As I struggled with "Time After Time," I felt like what the Japanese call a tone idiot. More than simply learning how to produce consistent notes, I needed to work on another key singing skill: listening. Danielle designated an octave on the piano, running from C3 to C4, with C3 being 1 and C4 being 8. It was a simplified version of solfège, or what we know as do-re-mi.

These eight notes would become a kind of major-scale comfort zone for me over the next months. She'd play simple patterns, like 1-2-5 or 1-5-1, on the piano, and I would intone along: "One . . . FIVE . . . one . . . One . . . FIVE . . . one." At night, using my daughter's piano, I would repeat the exercise. In the shower, walking down the street, I would sound out the patterns, the way you repeat a number to yourself so as not to forget it. I needed to internalize those eight numbers, to make the "one-FIVE-one" instinctual and fluid.

Danielle needed to break me down and rebuild me, to strip away decades of behavior. The best way to fight old habits, as W. Timothy Gallwey suggests in *The Inner Game of Tennis*, is to "start new ones."

With "Time After Time," the best way to overcome my difficulties was to simply stop trying to sing it. Instead, anchored by my eight-note safe space, we began making childlike sounds. There were raspberry-like lip trills and trills that segued into long, sounded vowels. There were las, das, and mas (when infants make these sounds, it's called canonical babbling). There were bouncy little sing-song phrases like "me-may-MA-mo, me-may-MA-mo, *mooooooo* . . ." There were whoops and cries, hisses and sighs.

In one of my favorite exercises, the instruction was to let my tongue hang lazily over my front lip, release my jaw, and just say, "Blah blah blah." This Novocain-like mumbling felt weirdly good, and I imagined how satisfying it would be to let this rude utterance fly in everyday life.

The tongue, called "the worst enemy of the singer" for its tendency to get in the way of exiting sound, seemed on some days to consume the bulk of our time. Nowhere but the dentist did the inside of my mouth receive such careful scrutiny. But it was important: A raised tongue shifts air toward our nostrils and makes our voices sound nasal. No one likes to hear this, according to research.

Doing these exercises, I imagined myself regressing to my preliterate infancy, freed from the burden of words. Which was sort of the point. For even though the same apparatus enables both acts, a lifetime of speaking can be poor preparation for singing.

"We have seriously ingrained habits when it comes to speech that get in the way of making the sound the way we want it to be," Amedeo told me. My shoulders hunched when I talked, my chin jutted forward, my throat muscles constricted, my jaw clenched, my tongue was as tense as a spring.

This was all fine enough for everyday chatter. But trying to bring my speaking voice into singing was like overhauling an old leaded-gas car, accustomed to chugging along with stop-and-go traffic at low speeds, into a streamlined Formula 1 race machine.

I needed to move air, fast and free. So I produced mostly vowels: easy to make, flowing down my open vocal tract, stripped of the speed bumps of consonants.

"The vowel is the voice," writes one vocal pedagogue, "and the consonant is the interruption of the voice." In English-language speech, we spend five times as much time producing vowels as consonants. In singing, that ratio can hit *two hundred* to one.

Lyrics were to be avoided; they harbored bad habits.

So Danielle would have me go through songs singing only simple vowels; during one solo car trip I sang the whole *Chet Baker Sings* with "oohs" and "aahs," an exercise that had a pleasing purity to it.

When I thought less about singing, a funny thing began to happen. In one exercise, Danielle would have me sound out the words "no NOT now!" to the ever-ascending three-note scales she was playing on the piano. She wanted me not to sing it but to say it, as if I really meant it.

"No NOT now!"

"C'mon, I really want to."

"No NOT now!"

"Try to imagine you're telling your daughter."

"No NOT now!"

"Try to send it out the window!"

"No NNNNOOOTTT now!"

"Send it across the street!"

Focused as I was on getting my message across, we would comfortably reach places that were at or *above* the same notes I had been so struggling with in the song. It was not that my vocal range had magically expanded; it was that I had stopped thinking about it. I just wanted to make sure I was being heard.

THE TROUBLE WITH EVERYDAY HABITS

Few things are as habitual as our speaking voice. We drop some sixteen thousand words daily without a thought as to the way we're doing it. And yet speech can be hard on our voices. I seemed to have a chorus of people telling me my speaking voice needed help. How could I sing if my speaking was so afflicted?

Roger Love, a Los Angeles voice coach who's worked with performers from Gwen Stefani to John Mayer to Jeff Bridges, reassured me that speech often lay behind the voice problems of singers. My own case was instructive. I sometimes lapsed, Love said, into the low-energy growl known as vocal fry. My vocal cords were "getting slammed" as they tried to make sound without enough air coming through, "like a bad door hinge that doesn't have any WD-40." My "stomach was not coming in enough" when I spoke, producing an inconsistent airflow, adding to the strain.

"Have you ever noticed you speak in spurts?" That's what Mark Baxter, a Boston-based vocal coach who's worked with performers ranging from Aerosmith to Aimee Mann, asked me during a phone conversation. I was using my larynx to "clamp off" air as I squeeze out "quasi-phrases." This could lead to swelling, and thus friction. "It's no different than walking on pavement versus snow," he said. "Resistance makes you work harder."

I also seemed to "drill the same tone" when I talked. I had a repetitive *speech* injury. "Do you lose your voice a lot?" Baxter asked. I did, in fact. I was constantly getting hoarse at dinners with friends or after presentations. Giving a talk, he said, "you're feeling exposed, you're trying to impress an audience, it's going to be extra Tom! All those dysfunctional behaviors get flung up a flagpole and amplified."

But I began to wonder about that strain. Might there be something amiss not in the technique but in the instrument itself?

And so, one day, I found myself in the Manhattan offices of Michael Pitman, director of the Columbia University Irving Medical Center's Voice and Swallowing Institute. He bounded in, white-coated and smiling and full of energy and purpose, in that way of busy New York doctors. Carly Cantor, a speech pathologist and longtime musical performer, soon joined us.

I told Pitman about the dire assessments my voice had recently received. "Your speaking voice is not optimal, for sure," he said. I thought, "At forty-nine I learn this?" His own voice, I noticed, seemed crisp, absent of any diesel-engine-sound vocal fry.

My main problems were common ones: "People speaking from their throat, not carrying enough breath to the lips, not getting the sound to the front of the face." And I was asking more of my voice. "It's like being a runner. You can run five miles and be fine. If you try to run a marathon, if you have any inefficiencies, you're going to get hurt." Many of his clients were teachers. "They use their voice constantly, and they're not really taught how to."

Most likely, my habits were hurting me. Still, he suggested an examination by laryngoscope. "We can go through the nose or mouth," he said. "Through the nose is just as good, and you don't get that gagging issue." And so up my left nostril snaked the little clear tube.

Cantor asked me to read a paragraph of text, then had me sing out a number of vowels. The two talked over what they were seeing on the screen. "Hmmm, you do have a little gapping," she said. "Look how much stiffer that side is," she said to Pitman. The tube was retracted, and like a team of sports commentators we turned to the video replay.

The laryngoscopic view down your own throat, if you've never seen it, is not for the faint of heart. Imagine you are a naturalist who has fed a thin cable, armed with an illuminated camera at its head, into a dark, murky burrow in a rain forest. After snaking through darkness, you emerge into a yawning chamber, lined with bulbous, veiny, glistening walls, and you suddenly find yourself staring directly into the eyeless face of some horrible creature, with two large bone-white guillotine-bladed teeth opening and closing in an eerie shimmer, stretching thick ropes of mucus between them, nothing but the mottled skin of the trachea looming beyond. That this repulsive apparatus can produce some of the most beautiful sounds on earth should be a cause for almost boundless wonder.

As I stared at my own vocal folds thrumming in slow-motion glory, Cantor told me, "You do have a little bit of atrophy there. You're not closing as well as you could." It seemed I had a "vocal fold paresis," a not-uncommon condition, often the result of an illness. With one fold nearly paralyzed, the pair were vibrating out of whack, particularly at the higher frequencies.

This didn't mean I couldn't carry a tune—for no one's folds are perfectly symmetrical—but it did mean I'd have to work harder. "You're going to be more susceptible to inefficiencies in your technique," she said. "You're going to have to be more accurate than other people."

Getting through the *passaggio*, the vocal break, was going to be harder. People routinely compensate for vocal fold paresis by making on-the-fly muscular or respiratory adjustments, but that could cause even more strain. I could undergo surgery, but a more common response was voice therapy. As Cantor described some of the techniques involved, I realized they weren't so dissimilar to my singing lessons.

The diagnosis left me feeling as if some wind had been knocked out of my sails—or my vocal folds, as it were— just as I was getting going. Even before I opened my mouth, I faced a hurdle, lurking inside.

But there was hope. The thing that might help restore my voice to its full strength was learning to sing.

*

If singing had become a kind of physical therapy, I couldn't shake the feeling there were other forms of therapy going on.

I never actually talked about how I was feeling, but those hour-long sessions seemed to touch an emotional nerve. Singing, it's been shown, activates many more regions of the brain linked to emotion than speaking does.

And, almost inevitably, I'd leave feeling elated, humming some random harmony my entire walk home. A simple tongue exercise would send me into fits of near-hysterical laughter. As I sounded out nonsensical, childish phrases—"ooh wooh blah blah blah"—sometimes lying on the carpeted floor, like a helpless infant, I would feel weirdly vulnerable and exposed, as if I were showing Danielle some part of me no one had ever seen. Though no words were being said, it seemed confessional.

These simple exercises were vocal calisthenics, getting my voice in shape to do the later heavy lifting. But they were also an attempt to get me to lower my guard. As Amedeo told me, "Let's enjoy ourselves and let the sound come out and stop being so intellectual about it." Maybe in trying to open up my voice, I was opening all sorts of other things that had been held back.

This is the thing with the voice: *You* are the instrument. Which means the sound is not purely a matter of engineering and physics but everything that lurks in a whole, messy person.

One day, with Danielle off for maternity leave, I had a singing lesson with Mark Baxter, the vocal coach I'd spoken to on the phone. As he often does, he was teaching that weekend in New York. He had the flowing shoulder-length hair of a rock singer and an intense demeanor. If I sometimes felt almost mothered under Danielle's soothing tutelage, Baxter seemed more the stern dad.

"I call myself a vocal therapist," he said, perched behind a piano in a midtown rehearsal studio. Baxter, author of *The Rock-n-Roll Singer's Survival Manual,* has talked any number of noteworthy performers down off a ledge. "I've never met a singer who's happy with their voice," he told me. "Everybody feels like an impostor, and everybody's waiting for their cover to be blown." (U2's Bono, for instance, has said repeatedly that his voice "annoys" him.)

To assess the voice, you needed to assess the person. "I just wait for somebody to come through the door and see what condition they're in." A familiar client may be experiencing a novel life event, like a divorce. "There's all kinds of issues. Everything collects and becomes the voice."

What was lurking in mine? I wondered. After putting me through a series of exercises, during which I noted that my voice was "a little quavery," he nodded emphatically. "It's mostly because you're doing it softly. It's the same thing as riding a bike. If you do it slowly, your front tire is going to wobble."

As we worked through the exercises, he was growing increasingly exasperated. "You speak twice as loud as you sing!" He wondered about my childhood. Did I grow up in an environment where making sound was discouraged? Not particularly, I responded, but then again, I was a quiet, shy, bookish kid.

He asked me to exhale a steady hiss of air for as long as I could. I got to about fifteen seconds. "The goal is *sixty!*" he shouted. I was a cyclist, he reminded me, I *had* the lung volume. The problem was panic, not oxygen. I needed breath control. "It's ironic that we have to go back and teach breathing," he said. "It's innate!"

The hurdles were mental. I was holding back the "undisturbed stream." How could I sing when I could barely breathe? He opened the lid of the piano and played a few notes. "It's playing at the same volume, but there's more sound coming out," he said.* I was putting a lid on myself, dampening my own voice.

*

It wasn't always insecurity or inhibition that was getting in the way. Sometimes it was my body. I suffered, for instance, from jaw tension, widely regarded as one of the key problems in singing.

Our jaws are immensely powerful, but our closing muscles are nearly four times stronger than our opening muscles. No wonder we might have trouble letting the jaw freely dangle in a way that would aid singing.

Danielle would often ask me to lie on the floor and find something to concentrate on. This "constructive rest" was meant to reduce any tension that might have built up over an ordinary day. "Our voice is a part of our body," she said. Tense muscles get in the way of producing optimal sound, literally squeezing off the flow of air and shutting down the resonators.

Once I'd released the bulk of my muscles from any further obligation, she'd ask me to make a small sound, as effortlessly as possible. At first, my sounds—"mahs" and "ahs"—were almost imperceptibly quiet, "snow falling from a bamboo leaf." Then, gradually louder, with increasing "intention," but always with the thought "What *less* can I do to make this sound?"

Almost invariably, it became easier to make sounds and at the right pitch. There it was again, that key to getting better: doing *less*.

More than a century ago, an Australian actor named

* Something similar happens when we sing different vowels. Sing the word "food" and then "father," using a similar amount of energy. Because your mouth needs to be more open to sing an *a*, "father" will be louder.

F. M. Alexander noticed he was becoming increasingly hoarse after his Shakespearean recitations. Watching himself in a mirror as he spoke, he noticed he "tended to pull back the head, depress the larynx, and suck in breath through the mouth so as to produce a gasping sound."

When he tried to correct the behavior, Alexander found he quickly reverted to old habits. The trick, he eventually discovered, wasn't to try to do "what was right" but rather to *stop doing*. Rather than focusing on an end goal—like singing correctly—he focused on the process, or what he called "the means whereby."

Alexander's celebrated "technique," as it would come to be known, was as much about "unlearning" as learning. But undoing habits was much harder than doing them. "When you are asked not to do something, instead of making the decision not to do it, you try to prevent yourself from doing it," he wrote. "But this only means that you decide to do it, and then use muscle tension to prevent yourself from doing it."

Unlearning is hard because old behavior never fully goes away. It surfaces in what Rob Gray, who directs the Perception and Action Lab at Arizona State University, described to me as "action slips": You're driving to the grocery store on a Saturday, but you accidentally start driving to the office. Action slips happen especially in "high pressure" moments. Gray gives the example of the former NFL quarterback Tim Tebow, who was famously plagued by a tendency to revert to a low throwing hand in games. This had worked at the college level but was considered a liability in the faster-paced professional game.

In singing, I had plenty to unlearn, especially during those high-pressure moments. When I tried to sing a higher note, my whole body would tense as I attempted to scale the musical peak, craning my neck upward like a giraffe reaching for high leaves. This only raised my larynx, making it harder to produce that very note.

Rather than trying to suppress this habit, Amedeo had an elegantly simple solution, the one hinted at in *The Inner Game of Tennis:* Replace one habit with another.

When I hit a high note in a phrase, Amedeo would have me do something counterintuitive: Go *down.* The act of slightly bending my knees was a physical cue to keep my larynx down. Suddenly I was thinking more about bending than singing, and the notes came easier.

YOU'VE GOT TO SOUND UGLY
IF YOU WANT TO SOUND PRETTY

Have you ever wondered why it can feel so satisfying to sing in the shower?

You're alone. You're warm. The air is humid, moistening your throat. You're standing erect. You're at once relaxed and pleasantly invigorated by the water. There's little to distract you from the simple tasks at hand. You set the tempo and the pitch. And the tiles provide wonderful resonance.

Now imagine singing while driving. You're sitting, hemmed in by a compressing seat belt, a position that inhibits the free flow of air. Without any warm-up, you probably started right in with the first song you heard. The air is drier. To keep yourself alert, you may be drinking dehydrating coffee. The stress of traffic and the vigilance required for safety keep you perched on the edge of tension. Distracted by the surrounding environment, you follow along to the radio, your voice swallowed up by the sound of the song and the ambient car noise.

I'd slowly begun to realize how important it was, when

practicing, not only to give it my full "mindful" attention but to create the right conditions. Practicing suboptimal technique could lead to suboptimal results. This is the argument against baseball's tradition of pregame hitting practice: Hitters swing as hard as they can, at pitches good and bad, at pitches that are far slower than anything they'd ever see in a real game.

I began to think of my goal as to always be creating that singing-in-the-shower feeling, no matter where I was.

Warm. As in any other muscular activity, warm-ups were key for avoiding injury and boosting performance. A few lip trills, or scales sounded into a straw if I had one handy (straw phonation, as it's known), help give your vocal muscles a quick refresh.

Relaxed. Lying still for a moment, massaging the jaw, letting my tongue spill out with a few "blah blah blahs."

Energized. Danielle would ask me to "brighten" my face, one of those little neuromuscular adjustments that would help "energize" the sound.

Resonant. To create "space" in my mouth, I would do the little prescribed exercises, like starting a yawn (but not going all the way) or speaking like the cartoon character Yogi Bear to help lower my larynx. Another favorite was exhaling and then inhaling on a *k* sound, in an effort to lift my sagging soft palate and make my voice rounder and more resonant. Give this a try. Make the sound *kuh-kuh-kuh;* then do the same on an inhale. As you do, try to imagine the back of your mouth gently inflating, like a frog's.

Standing. Amedeo would constantly be calling me on my posture as I stood slouched, a hand in my pocket. Would an upright bass produce the right sound if it were all crinkled up? she wanted to know.

*

We'd since moved our sessions to CAP21, a rehearsal space in Manhattan populated largely by drama and musical theater students less than half my age.

The hallways were a constant buzz of flighty energy. Through the alarmingly thin studio walls, I marveled at the vocal acrobatics around me, worrying that my thin rasping was seeping through. These people were on a *career* track. What right did I have to be here?

In learning to sing, I'd been learning many things. I'd been learning the motor skills to move my body in the right way. I'd been learning how to warm up and practice efficiently. I'd been learning how to watch for—and correct—bad habits. I'd been learning about my voice itself, what it was, what its limits and potential were, and who *I* was, my limits and potential.

And I was learning about music itself. We were now working on songs, which introduced new layers of complexity. I soon realized that to consciously sing a song is to suddenly hear it, and understand it, in a way one never does when simply listening. Songs I thought I knew well seemed suddenly unfamiliar to me, like scrambled jigsaw puzzles.

In speech, we never worry about having enough air to make it to the end of a phrase, even though we partially hold our breath to talk. We instinctively know how to pace ourselves.

In song, I was constantly running out of steam, often because I was doubling down too early in a phrase. Familiar words began to trip me up. In R.E.M.'s "Nightswimming," I'd want to pronounce the word "clearer" as I did in speech—"clear-er." But singing that was a rather grating mouthful; much better to go "clee-ruh." "R, g, and k tend to be real hard for singers," Danielle said.

Singing was making my native language new to me again. As the *Music Educators Journal* put it, "The singer has two languages to master—music and text—while the instrumentalist has but one."

I still suffered from a pronounced vocal break, that moment where the set of muscles that produces "chest voice" reaches its limit, and so hands over the job to the "head voice" muscles. "It's like a sloppy gear change," Amedeo said. It sounded to me like a pubescent yodel.

We were trying to "connect" the two voices, through simple scale exercises like "ma-OOOO-ahhhh." I'd try to sing these without an audible shift, but there usually was. "It's going to sound ugly before it sounds pretty," she said, "but it *has* to sound ugly."

We were never quite sure what condition my voice was going to be in. Like an ancient violin that hadn't been well cared for, it could be thrown off by the littlest thing. I could relate to the singer Ian Bostridge's lament that his "life is governed by phlegm." At home, besieged by my "ugly" noises and gripes about mucus, my wife burst out, "Couldn't you have taken up model-ship building or something?"

Still, I was making progress. I was hitting notes more regularly. I was hitting *more* notes, stealing into tenor territory. I could suddenly pull off a G4 (when Art Garfunkel, toward the end of "Bridge Over Troubled Water," sings, "I will ease your *MIND*," he's G4).

There was a new confidence. I would slyly bring up some impossible-seeming challenge, like the E5 in A-ha's "Take On Me" ("in a day or *twooooooo*"). How does he *do* that? (There were long YouTube videos with tips.)

Danielle would assure me that someday I'd hit it— without hurting myself. More important, I was beginning to be able to diagnose, and correct, my own problems. I could hear I was nasal and try to "make room," or I could discern I was flat and try to wake up my face.

One day, she speculated that I might have hit a plateau. "You've made a ton of progress. I continue to hear you make progress. When we start to *own* our progress, that's when we stop being a beginner." Early on, I was just trying to follow along to exercises, or trying to recapture at home what we'd done in the studio, without knowing how. Now I had a better sense of the progress I wanted to make and what it would take to get there.

There was more to achieve, and I wasn't going to stop the lessons. But I felt it was time to move beyond what had become the cozy confines of the rehearsal studio and into the world.

CHAPTER FOUR

I DON'T KNOW WHAT I'M DOING, BUT I'M DOING IT ANYWAY

The Virtues of Learning on the Fly with a Group

THE CHORUS EFFECT

Every Monday evening, I travel from my Brooklyn home to the Lower East Side of Manhattan. There, on a block sheltered from the souk-like bustle and roaring traffic of Delancey Street, I make my way to a hulking nineteenth-century neo-Gothic building.

It was once Public School 160, but for the past few decades it's been home to the Clemente Soto Vélez Cultural and Educational Center. I climb the stairs, past the theater space, past the class doing "mindful capoeira"—is there a mindless variety?—and take a chair in room 203. The paint is faded, the windows struggle to keep the cold out, and the ancient wood floors are marked by regularly spaced depressions where restless schoolchildren once shuffled their feet beneath their desks.

This is the rehearsal space for the Britpop Choir, which mostly performs, as the name portends, a range of popular music from the recent past in England (Oasis,

Adele, David Bowie, Queen, even "boy bands" like Take That). The choir is some fifty strong, though on most nights three dozen or so people will be packed into the room. They will be arrayed, in a semicircle of chairs, around the director, Charlie Adams, a native New Yorker who grew up in London, lived for a spell in Liverpool, and then returned stateside a decade ago. She is always crisply turned out and filled with seemingly boundless reserves of enthusiasm and stamina, which she draws upon as she sings and shouts over her boisterous flock.

For the next ninety minutes, a kind of magic happens. People troop in from the dark streets, a bit subdued, shoulders sagging with the start of a new workweek. Adams asks everyone to rise for a warm-up. There are vigorous shakes of the body, a variety of stretches, a litany of contortions of the face. There are lip trills—a roomful of which sounds like a spiraling cacophony of mutant sparrows. There are scales and little harmonies. And then the work begins. In just ten sessions, each lasting an hour and a half, the choir, with its constantly fluctuating membership, must learn half a dozen or so new songs (burnished by an existing repertoire) in time for an end-of-cycle performance, typically at some Manhattan live music venue. Throats are cleared, lyrics sheets clutched, and, at a prompt from Adams, the first tentative notes sounded.

During that hour and a half, the energy of the room changes completely. What at the beginning had all the promise of a homeowners' association board meeting transforms into a rollicking party, as if some virus had been set loose in that warm, cloistered room and infected each of its inhabitants. There are moments, when everyone's voices have merged into a pulsating whole, in which a kind of transcendence—sonic, emotional, maybe even spiritual—seems to take place. As the composer Alice

Parker described it, "It's as if all of our inner ions have been scheduled to be moving in the same direction at the same time."

Sometimes, there's too many ions buzzing; Charlie will have to shush us like boisterous kindergartners to actually get anything done. By 9:00 p.m., when it's time to return the folding chairs to the corner, the room is positively charged. People filter out on a proverbial high note, excitedly chatting as they descend to the street below. Still coursing with energy hours later, the singers will not find it easy to fall asleep tonight.

The room, as we have left it, is silent. There is no evidence of what went on there, what sonic artifacts were created (except for when I remembered to record the sessions on my iPhone). But sometimes, as I struggle to hold some harmony or remember a lyric, I almost cannot believe the sounds we are making. It feels as if we have whipped up some majestic storm that the room struggles to contain, driven on by Adams, who stands in the eye of this ferocious noise.

We not only generate our own sounds; we help propagate those of others, simply by standing in their presence. The room becomes a crackling "diffuse field"; the sound pressure is the same, everywhere. As we sing, our own voices diminish in individual impact but grow in collective resonance. The phenomenon is called the chorus effect.*

"In a cognitive sense," writes the acoustic researcher Sten Ternström, "the chorus effect can magically dissociate the sound from its sources and endow it with an independent, almost ethereal existence of its own." There have been times that I felt less as though I were singing and more as if I were feeding my breath to some invisible

---

* Guitarists, for example, can use a chorus-effect pedal to boost their sound, as on Nirvana's "Come As You Are."

supraorganism—vaporous, thrumming, omnivorous—pervading the atmosphere.

While everyone is trying to hit their notes with precision, perfection, curiously, does not explain the power of the sound. Rather, the chorus effect comes thanks to the inevitable human tendency to stray, ever so slightly—sometimes more so—from perfect pitch.

In our choir, as in any, if everyone sang at exactly the same, note-perfect pitch, exactly in unison, the result would simply be *more*. It would be louder, bigger, and a bit monotonous.

But when everyone is just a little bit off from one another, thanks to the little pitch variations known as flutter and wow, an enchanting, "quasi-random" sound is created, fuller and richer than would ever be possible from a single source. When this "blend" is right (and this takes work, by the director and the choristers), and no one singer is distinguishable from the others, the listeners are pleasantly flummoxed by a sound that seems to come from everywhere and nowhere.

What I find more remarkable than all this is the very fact that I am here. Before joining, I did not really see myself as a "choir person"; nor, apparently, did many friends or family members, judging from raised eyebrows when I said I had choir practice.

I can honestly report, however, that Monday has become my favorite day of the week. It's not just my sense of the calendar that has been changed by the choir, but my whole life.

*

I had wanted to move beyond the experience of my voice lessons, where I was singing to one person. I wanted the stakes to be higher. I wanted to take this little lab-grown thing out into the world. Danielle had suggested some kind of solo recital, which immediately filled me with dread.

I am a person who writes sentences all day in isolation, someone who, despite sometimes giving talks to hundreds of people, can barely raise his voice around a crowded conference room table (in those rare moments when I actually find myself around a crowded conference room table). I routinely try to outsource to my more outgoing wife any number of real-world interactions that I find acutely painful. How could I sing onstage when I can barely handle the customer service booth at the grocery store?

A choir, I thought, could be the ideal compromise, even though, frankly, the idea still struck me with some terror. I'd be singing, but singing with others, and so sheltered a bit from the white-hot spotlight (not surprisingly, research has found that choir singers report experiencing less stress than soloists).

At the time, I really had no larger thoughts about group singing—what it would entail, what it might mean—beyond the fact that it was a *group*. The last choir I could even remember seeing was an ensemble doing Handel's *Messiah* at the Metropolitan Museum of Art. They were fantastic, but for a novice like me, with their flowing robes, their songbooks, their angelic sopranos and booming basses, they might as well have been from another planet.

By chance, my friend Katherine, a designer in Seattle, had also been looking for a way to sing. While she admired people's "gusto" for karaoke, she didn't think it was for her. "Karaoke doesn't seem to me to be about the love of singing," she said. "It seems like love of showmanship."

Many of the choirs she looked into, meanwhile, seemed too high caliber or vaguely "nerdy." Friends told her of a local amateur choir they enjoyed that performed popular songs, with orchestral backing. She felt, however, as I did, that she needed some training, so she began taking voice lessons.

And then, one day, she finally summoned the courage to attend the choir's rehearsal, which she called "super intimidating." Hoping to stand small in a crowd, she discovered there were only a handful of singers. She did not read music, which would make learning her parts difficult.

"It would have been so much easier," she said, "for my newbie middle-aged self to just turn and walk out and continue training indefinitely."

But she wanted a *goal*. She wanted her voice lessons aimed at something. Learning the songs (she used Notability, a program that will sound out the musical notes you input) focused her attention, while needing to adequately sing the parts provided motivation.

The choir provided something else, something I could wholly identify with. "Freelancing from a home studio has made my life so insulated," she said. Her friends all came from earlier versions of her life, people she worked with, created things with. "They are lovely friends, but I miss *doing stuff* with people, rather than simply dining with them."

Emboldened by her tales of how deeply she had fallen for choir, I went to the internet and typed in something like "amateur choir New York City." I soon realized the word "amateur" can have many different connotations, and it's certainly not synonymous with "beginner." In a city like New York, stocked to the rafters with musical talent, it can mean something like "as good as you can get without actually getting paid."

The choirs that surfaced in the search results seemed frighteningly above my station. There were, for example, auditions. For one, the singer was asked to perform a song not in English. I myself was sometimes singing *English* as if it were a second language, so that seemed out.

"PLEASE DO NOT BRING AN ARIA," warned the audition instructions for one choir. If only I could! Singers were not expected to be "ace sight-readers," it went on, in a gesture meant to be reassuring but that also, unsubtly, implied I'd have some grasp of the skill. I could barely read notes, much less *sing* them. And an audition? That was singing alone—just what I was looking to avoid.

I was about to start another search, for something like *"really really* amateur choir New York City," when a listing for the Britpop Choir caught my eye.

As a fan of bands like Oasis, Blur, and Pulp, I was immediately intrigued. One phrase stood out: "Whether you're a pro or just fancy you're Beyoncé in the shower—there's no audition to join." This could be it, I thought. But I began to analyze that sentence. Wait, did that mean pros might be there? And even in the shower, I don't fancy I'm anywhere near Beyoncé.

When I clicked through a few of the sample videos, I saw a roomful of people who looked as if they were having tremendous fun but who also looked, and sounded, supremely confident. I would watch each video a few times, trying to mentally Photoshop myself among the singers. I just couldn't make the conceptual leap.

Still, emboldened by the mantra of this book, I sent an inquiry, which led me to my first encounter with Charlie Adams, the founder of the Urban Choir Project.

Over the phone, I told her what I was looking for and confessed I had no experience. "One of the things we pride ourselves on," she said, "is that we're a place where quality meets the accessible."

This is a tricky place to inhabit. "'Amateur' is a weird word," she said. "We say 'community choir,' which has its own connotations as well." The Britpop Choir did not use sheet music—"we learn everything by ear," Adams said. For some, this was a relief. For others, it was a red flag. "In the beginning," she said, "we had a couple of people who came and felt it wasn't up to the standard they were looking for."

I was looking for something very specific. I wanted to be somewhere that would take in a rank novice like me, but I did not necessarily want to be surrounded entirely by rank novices. I wanted to be somewhere that was pretty good as I got better.

In the egalitarian world of community choirs, which I wholeheartedly support, even this last notion, which may seem rather harmless, can be a bit controversial. When I contacted the director of one of the so-called Can't Sing Choirs, which celebrate inclusivity over skill and have become popular in recent decades in England, explaining my project and looking into a possible visit, the response was cautious. "I'm not sure we are 'lifelong learning' though," she wrote. "We just want to give people the freedom to sing without feeling the pressure to improve." I had visions, unjust no doubt, of being doomed to the ragtag, disharmonic choir in the movie *Sister Act*, before Whoopi Goldberg arrives to give it some polish: a world of perpetual semi-competence.

The Britpop Choir seemed to strike a happy medium.

On the one hand, as Adams told me, "all of my work is not about developing people to be stars. It's more about using singing as a way to bring people together."

On the other, she said, "it's not really fun for anyone if it sounds *bad*." While vocal technique was not taught per se, given time and encouragement, she hinted, people sounded good. She recalled one woman who had joined a few years prior. "She was absolutely terrified," she said. "She could hardly hold her harmony." Now she was virtually leading her section.

While "bringing people together" was still the focus, she admitted that, lately, the Britpop Choir had been evolving. They'd sung for a commercial, they'd collaborated with a dance company, they'd filled in as spontaneous backup for a well-known recording artist. "They're pretty good," she said. "It's not a prerequisite, but we do find that most people who come have a bit of experience." There were people who had sung onstage, in studios. There might be a diva or two. With their busy slate of side gigs, it was turning into a semiprofessional operation.

I suddenly did not like the way this was going. It turned out there was a waiting list. Then Adams told me she actually ran another group, the Brooklynite Choir. It had a bit more of a "neighborhood feel," she said, which I took to mean "novice feel." It was closer to my home; it was closer to my level. I could join up straightaway. I felt as if she were trying to warn me away from Britpop—*get out while you can!*

I joined Britpop. It seemed that fate had driven me to it, and in a wayward journey like mine, even if I seemed to be heading into the rocks, I had no better captain.

*

On a warm spring evening, I entered the rehearsal room on Rivington Street, the one I had seen in the video, for the inaugural rehearsal in a new cycle. People were hugging, excitedly catching up. I slunk into a chair in this former schoolroom, taken back to the first day I joined a new school in eighth grade, not knowing a soul. As I suddenly recognized a few people from the website's video, I had a vaguely out-of-body feeling: Was I really here?

The room was overwhelmingly female. The men could be counted on one hand, as if all the others were off at war. This is a widespread phenomenon in the world of choirs, in America at least. It was not always so. Singing in colonial America, notes the historian J. Terry Gates, was dominated (as were most public activities) by men. By the 1930s, a survey of high schools found equal numbers of male and female singers. More recently, an analysis of high school choirs found the number had shifted to 70 percent female, 30 percent male, a cultural turn whose reasons are not entirely clear.

Adams, perennially on the lookout for male singers, told me, half jokingly, that she could start marketing the choir as a way for single men to meet women. There were rumors of an unnamed "guy from London," prior to my arrival, who had been something of a choral Casanova.

The room gradually fell silent as Adams, having just returned from maternity leave, moved to the center of the room. "To people who are just joining us today, welcome to the Britpop Choir!" she said, looking my way. "I'm Charlie. I conduct the choir"—and then, trailing off slightly, "I guess." But her modesty belied a striking efficiency. She gave a quick spiel about newcomers—there were several others besides me—not being nervous. "I'm not going to put you on the spot and make you sing solo—unless you want to." Charlie reminded me of a school-teacher, the kind you thought was cool, that you wanted to be. I was well older than she was, but in that curious way of the student-teacher relationship I somehow felt younger.

She quickly sorted people into sections (from our phone conversation, she had already pegged me as a bass, which is not really the bass of a classical choir, but here, anything below tenor—and, really, just most men).

"Tom's surrounded by ladies," she joked. "Hank, help him out!" Hank, I would soon learn, was a lieutenant of Charlie's: an actor, singer, teacher, and general multi-octave magpie who could cover up audio sore spots—mine included—like a liquid Band-Aid. Within moments, before any introductions had even been made, we were off and singing.

We spent that entire first session working on "Dreaming of You," a song by the English band the Coral. During pauses, I tried to briefly mingle, mostly with the two other men in my bass section (in a choir, I soon learned, your section tends to become much of your world).

One of them, Roger, a tall Asian American man with a deeply resonant voice—that would give way to a strangely endearing, much higher-pitched cackle when he laughed—would become my lodestar in the choir. He'd been with Britpop nearly since its inception, becoming de facto leader of the section. I could sense he knew what he was doing, and so for that session (and many afterward) I simply tried to shadow his every move.

I pasted a smile on my face for most of that first session, nodding along as Charlie tossed out an instruction like "Basses, you're going to sing the alto ones' part, down the octave." Because I'd been singing only by myself, and had only the barest grasp of musical theory—recently gleaned from my piano-playing daughter—I might as well have been instructed to field-strip an AK-47. I simply tried to do what felt intuitively right and what didn't sound too different from Roger.

*

Without realizing it at the time, I'd thrust myself into an intensely immersive learning environment. If we learn, in large measure, by *observation*, I now had dozens of people to observe. If learning is helped by feedback, I could tell, via the voices of those around me, if my singing (or theirs) was off. If learning is prompted by motivation, then I was spurred on by the feeling that I was part of something bigger than myself.

More than a century ago, pioneering psychologist Norman Triplett, analyzing the records from bike racing, made a seminal observation about the history of the psychology of performance: Cyclists who raced against competitors, or so-called pacemakers, rode faster than cyclists who rode alone.

"Social facilitation," as he called it, demonstrated something we now consider obvious: Humans seem to perform better in the presence of others. Surrounded by good singers, I was pushed to up my game. Social facilitation comes with a catch, however: It seems to work only with simple, or well-practiced, tasks. There would be those times, when I showed up not having learned or practiced some part, when the presence of others made me perform worse. I suppose this only upped the motivation to learn as quickly as possible.

What is most striking about that first rehearsal, when I listen to the recording now, is that I cannot actually hear myself. I was doing barely more than lip-synching, providing an inconsequential bit of sonic infill. "Social loafing," as it's called, is the flip side of social facilitation: when the presence of others encourages or allows you to work *less* hard.

It would take some time before I would find my voice.

SINGING: THE ORIGINAL SOCIAL NETWORK

The ritual that goes on in room 203 every Monday night is a familiar one throughout the world.

In the United States, according to a 2004 report, "more Americans engage in the public performance of choral singing than in any other art form. In fact, no other public for artistic expression even comes close." In England, the number of choruses—both of the "can" and of

the "can't" sing variety—is said to be at an "all-time high."
A national program, Sing Up, is aimed specifically at getting more schoolchildren singing. A rise in attendance at
British cathedrals from 2000 to 2012 was largely attrib-
uted to the fact that services are sung, as they have been
since the mid-seventeenth century. And let us not forget
the string of popular U.K. reality television programs in
which the unflappable choirmaster Gareth Malone turns
tuneless workplaces, groups of military wives—even entire towns—into well-lubricated vocal machines. Choirs
in Australia report long waiting lists, while in Sweden,
with its high levels of social capital, choir singing is a "national pastime."

There's good reason for all this. If singing alone makes
you feel good, as I discussed in the previous chapter, singing with others makes you feel even better.

Singing in choirs—which, I should preface, is just
fun—has been found to increase people's sense of happiness and well-being. Singing with someone else engages
a wider range of brain activity than singing alone. Choir
singing has also been found to boost people's oxytocin
levels and increase one's tolerance for pain. One study
found that group singing, but interestingly not group
conversation, lowered levels of the stress hormone corti-
sol. In another bit of research, people suffering from a
stress-related gastrointestinal disorder were asked to join
a choir; a year later, they reported less pain and had lower
levels of a hormone associated with the condition than a
group that did not sing.

Singing together is preventative health care by other
means. And not just physical health. Choirs have been
deployed, successfully, as a "therapeutic instrument" for
people in mental health programs. There have been choirs
for the homeless; choirs for people with loved ones who

have gone missing; "complaint choirs" (started, appropriately, by a pair of Finns during a Helsinki winter looking to channel people's griping into something positive); prison choirs; choirs to comfort the terminally ill; choirs for autistic children and adults; even a post-Katrina "Hurricane Choir," designed as a coping and recovery mechanism for people displaced in the wake of that disastrous storm.

Why do they seem to help? "Singing is joyful in and of itself," as one report noted. But, more important, what choirs seem to do is use the power of music to help satisfy an even more powerful human impulse. Singing, quite simply, is social glue; it helps join people together.

The Britpop Choir is capped at fifty, which, as it happens, is roughly the upper limit on favored group size of our hunter-gatherer ancestors—perhaps the sweet spot of social cohesion.

As anthropologists have suggested, other primates rely on one-on-one grooming for social bonding (and endorphin release). But human groups were too big for that level of attention, so we needed other measures—like those protolanguages of singing or making music together. In what they called the "ice-breaker effect," one group of researchers found that compared with other social leisure activities, newly formed singing groups "experienced much faster bonding."

One reason is synchrony. Doing things together, successfully, at the same time and at the same *rhythm*, has been found to be a powerfully pro-social agent. There are certainly other activities that can help promote social bonding; I've no doubt the mindful capoeira folks down the hall got a similar charge from their activity, as does anyone playing team sports. But singing in harmony, which requires people working together, breathing together, being *literally in harmony*—even the heartbeats of choral singers begin to synchronize—seems particularly effective.

When the sociologist Robert Putnam investigated, in a now famous study, why certain regional governments in Italy seemed to work much better than others, few of the reasons you might expect—party politics, levels of affluence—seemed to matter. What did seem important was "traditions of civic engagement." One of these was "membership in choral societies."*

As I spent more time with the Britpop Choir, I began to view the choir as a small-scale model of what a vitally functioning participatory democracy looks like. Everyone had to pitch in to make it work. You had to show up, memorize the lyrics, hone your parts. We were learning together, in what has been called a community of practice. You had to work with people, to anticipate their actions. If you were a bit weak on a part, someone might give you a lift; you might return the favor on the next song.

The presence of everyone's voice was vital to achieving the best sound, and no one voice—or group of voices— could be too strong. The variety of voices was not a hindrance but rather the very strength of the sound. People of different ages and races, from different backgrounds, with different levels of experience, were coming together to work on something that they were an integral part of and yet was greater than any of them. It was the rising tide of voices that lifted one big boat. It seemed like a little twelve-dollar-a-week utopia.

And the sound we made was fantastic.

---

* I do not want to posit choirs as a magic bullet for solving the world's ills. It has been pointed out, for example, that choirs were used to create "social capital" in the regime of Nazi Germany. See Shanker Satyanath, Nico Voigtländer, and Hans-Joachim Voth, "Bowling for Fascism: Social Capital and the Rise of the Nazi Party," *Journal of Political Economy* 125, no. 2 (2017).

*

It was around this time that I began singing into my phone with strangers.

I'd found that the positive charge that came from singing with other people in choir seemed almost addicting. I began to wonder if there were other ways, in between rehearsals, I might satisfy the need. One day, poking around online, I found a strangely named app called "Smule."

It was simple. You only had to plug some earbuds into your phone, search for a favorite song in the site's database, and then start singing. After recording a tune, you could tweak your performance with a variety of Auto-Tune-style filters and effects. You could film yourself or simply record an audio track. I recorded a few solo songs. It was easy, and the sound was decent. It was fun, if a bit sterile.

Then I discovered the "duet" option and felt as if I had unlocked the magic of the service. Now I would record my own "original content"—roughly half of a song—put it out into the world, and nervously wait for someone to join. Or I could join the duet someone else had already posted, hoping they were pleased.

And so, suddenly, I seemed to be singing with the entire world. I did John Lennon's "Imagine" with an Indonesian woman wearing a head scarf. I sang R.E.M. songs with a guy from Virginia whose profile picture showed him firing an assault rifle. I sang 1970s songs with middle-aged people and contemporary songs with teens and twenty-somethings. Some people had quasi-professional recording setups with big microphones; more than a few people were singing from their parked cars. Some were singing from their *moving* cars (I always avoided them). Some were belters; some were near whisperers.

I used Smule like a sandbox, a place where I could play

around and work different vocal muscles, tackling tongue-twisting freestyle raps or singing songs in my rusty Spanish. After my daughter tried it, she said, "Now I see why you disappear into your room for so long."

Like the choir, it had the whiff of utopia: people across time and distance and language and culture, all singing the same songs. As with other social apps, you could leave comments, give likes and "favorites," and gain followers. I was leery of trolls, but the people I sang with were always respectful. The praise they gave out was, to a fledgling singer, intoxicating. I had the habit of singing fairly constantly around the house, which could—understandably—annoy my wife and daughter. On Smule, people were not annoyed. They seemed happy I had shown up to sing with them. I thrived on comments like "Uh, you nailed it." It became like a secret support network.

Curious about the app's origins, I got in touch with Jeff Smith, the CEO of Smule. A longtime Silicon Valley entrepreneur and musician, he'd had the idea that a technology like the smartphone could help people make music, and make music together.

"Music is the original social network," he told me. At first, Smule created things like a smartphone piano. But no instrument is as expressive as the one all humans possess. "The voice is *you*," Smith said. It was the fundamental form of expression. "You look at a blues guitarist, they're moving their mouth. It's imitating the voice." As a frustrated singer himself, he wanted to make it less intimidating. The way to do that, he reasoned, was to sing with someone else. "You're likelier to sing with someone you don't know across the globe than someone you do know standing in front of you," he said.

The ancient connective power of music was brought into the gamified world of social media, and it seemed a powerful match. Singing mostly ended at singing, but sometimes it led to deeper connections. There were, he told me, more than one hundred reported "Smule babies," thanks to people who had met doing duets.

I was not looking for love, or even necessarily friends, but I began to feel a sense of connection with some of my regular singing partners. Here we were, separated by time and distance, opening ourselves up in this curious way, forging this shared experience. There was a woman from Texas, a longtime singer who had traveled to New York City as a teenager with her choir and used it as a way to reconnect with singing and relax after work. One of my most regular partners was a man from the U.K., a former performer with a sardonic wit who had once played on the legendary John Peel radio show. He told me the site had unexpectedly become a tool for managing his clinical depression; "sing your blues away," he told me.

I sang for a while with a woman whose voice I particularly liked and who, I later learned, had died from sudden cardiac arrest. A group of us—people I knew only from singing online—did a group song in her memory. Given that we'd never met face-to-face, it seemed strangely poignant.

Love, loss, life itself: Singing encompassed as much as music itself did. Whatever the sentiment, it just seemed more meaningful, and more fun, to do it with someone.

*

Meanwhile, I was getting to know some of my fellow singers in the Britpop Choir and discovering that they too had many reasons for being there, beyond, of course, the love of singing. One person told me offhandedly at a bar one night she'd joined on a bit of a lark and almost instantly realized "it was what I was looking for in my life."

Moments of transition—new beginnings—seemed to

be a theme. Roger, my compatriot in the bass section, told me he'd been in choirs since he was a kid. Before his voice changed, he did several solo turns in a Mandarin-language choir in suburban New York. He got back into singing on the heels of a breakup as he was undergoing a moment of "self-exploration and renewal."

He had logged a few years with another, more traditional—and all-male—choir before ending up at Britpop. "When you join a choir in which men are at a premium," he joked, "the bar is lowered on how good you have to be." While he had other outlets in his life, like tennis and painting, he told me the choir had become so important to him that if he were offered a job in another city, he'd have trouble taking it.

Sarah, a vibrant, outgoing alto who quickly became a friend, had played music her whole life, participated in several choirs, wowed the crowd at a variety of New York karaoke bars, and even given co-workers singing lessons in a "skill share" program. She was currently learning a "heavy metal scream" with her own voice teacher. For the past decade she'd been part of what she called an "all-girl accordion orchestra" (laughing, she remembered that the comedian Jon Stewart, introducing the group at a benefit concert, asked, "So what's your gimmick?"). But after the group's conductor, also a kind of personal mentor, died a few years ago, the group stopped playing together as regularly. "I didn't realize how much I missed having a regular rehearsal," she said. "It's really good for my brain."

As social an activity as our choir felt in the moment, it still took effort to meet people beyond our immediate section mates. Rehearsals were intensive, and once they were over, people tended to rush home. A drinks outing or two was organized, which could be tough on a Monday evening.

I became friendly with Laurence, a Frenchwoman

with an infectious laugh and the seemingly effortless style Frenchwomen often seem to possess. We started talking mostly because I kept running into her in my neighborhood, which happens to be filled with expats drawn by the local public school's well-regarded French-language immersion program. We were roughly the same age, we both had kids in the local school, we were both novices when we began. I sensed a choral soul mate.

One evening, over tea at a neighborhood café, she told me she'd first met Charlie when she'd signed her kids up for an after-school singing program. "Because they were little, I was attending every session," she said. "And I just had this kind of crush on Charlie in a way. Just seeing how much energy she had."

One day, Laurence asked her if she had any adult programs. "I'd never sung before, not even karaoke," she said. "I just showed up. I had no idea if I would enjoy or stick with it." Arriving at her first rehearsal, she was in a state of near panic. "I was pretty freaked-out," she said. "I felt that a lot of people had singing experience, that I didn't fit. I was so worried. They're going to think, 'This French girl, who has no voice, what is she doing here?'"

Monday nights became a momentary refuge from her home life. The marital tensions she was experiencing, which would soon give way to a separation, always seemed more pronounced on Monday, perhaps because of the stress of returning to the workweek. She slowly grew more comfortable in the choir and began to prize the feeling of weekly uplift it provided. There was also a regenerative feeling of novelty. "I kept thinking, 'It feels so good to feel like it's never too late to start something new.'"

Suddenly singing, to the casual surprise of her friends, became her *thing*, an island of identity. "It came at the perfect time," she said. With her marriage of twenty years seeming in irreversible decline, it provided not only an energy boost but the sense she could do things for herself. "When you have kids, you can't remember what you need, what you want," she said. "You're just kind of tagging along." Perhaps tellingly, her husband, as she recalled, while not discouraging her from joining the choir, did not attend any of her performances.

As we spoke, she suddenly remembered something. Toward the end of her marriage, her husband was "always complaining about my voice." Perhaps owing to stress, he had become "really noise intolerant" in general. But her voice became a focal point. "I tend to be a bit loud," she said. "There's nothing I can do. Usually when I speak or laugh loud, it's because I'm excited or happy." She even began looking into hiring a voice coach. "Maybe that's the solution, if I change my voice." The costs were prohibitive: A good voice coach in New York can cost upward of a hundred dollars per hour; the Britpop Choir was no more expensive, per session, than a movie. Meeting Charlie, she thought singing might help her "adjust" her voice.

The week she and her husband decided to separate, she remembers not being able to stop crying during the rehearsal.

"I wasn't crying in the street," she told me. "But singing moves you. Charlie came to me afterward and said, 'I've never seen you like this.'"

A few years on, Laurence now sings in both the choirs Charlie runs, and even recently did an informal audition that Adams was putting on for a group of core Britpop singers that she could call upon when last-minute singing opportunities came up. "Charlie was supersweet," she said. "She said she was so happy to hear my voice, by myself."

We had all come to the choir from different places, with different stories and different motivations. But we were all of us beginners, trying to start something new, trying to start over. Some people were looking for new directions; some were trying to rediscover old passions.

For some, the stakes were even higher. They were trying to get their lives back.

*

One night, early in the cycle, I was surprised to notice a new member in our vanishingly small bass section. With his shaved head, Adidas sneakers, and Fred Perry polo, he struck me as the kind of guy you might see in the terraces at an English Premier League soccer match. As it turned out, Adrian was a coach from north London who'd come to the United States to work with Red Bulls Academy. A week later, I started chatting him up, expecting to hear something about his love of the Britpop genre.

"I have a brain tumor," he said. "My speech therapist thought singing could be good for me."

Later, when we met over breakfast, he said he hadn't been expecting to tell anyone of his condition. He didn't know why he'd confided in me; maybe he sensed a professional listener. But it seemed to have lifted some sort of weight, and he proceeded to tell me the story.

On a hot August afternoon the previous year, returning from a swimming pool near his apartment in the Gramercy Park neighborhood of Manhattan, he was gripped by a seizure.

"I started pulsating," he told me. "I thought I was having a heart attack." A doctor, emerging from a nearby grocery store, summoned an ambulance. The emergency doctors immediately began testing his heart but found nothing amiss. He now felt fine, the two-minute seizure already a memory. He was sent to another hospital for an MRI scan on his brain. He waited, for hours and hours. A doctor finally came in and told him he would have to stay the night. "I was like, there's nothing wrong with me."

The next morning, he was told he had a mass in his brain. It was a tumor, and it would have to be removed immediately. Surgery was scheduled for later that week. On the phone with his parents, he suffered another mild seizure. His family began arriving in New York for the operation. When he awoke, he was told that 90 percent of the tumor had been removed (removing it all, he was told, would result in "significant damage"). He found he couldn't reply. "I couldn't speak. I could understand everything that was going on in the room; I just couldn't speak."

He was suffering from what's known as non-fluent aphasia. As Raymund Yong, the surgeon at Mount Sinai Hospital who performed the operation, explained to me, the lesion was in the left frontal lobe of his brain, near the region called Broca's area. This is one of the brain's primary "speech centers"; the other, Wernicke's area, is associated with *understanding* speech.

When the tumor was removed, a number of connections running to other parts of the brain—like fiber-optic cables with millions of wires inside—were, by necessity, damaged. Adrian did not lose the knowledge of *how* to speak, but he'd lost his ability to execute the motor commands necessary to actually speak. Other motor functions were similarly disrupted. He tried communicating with his parents by writing out answers, but because he couldn't move most of the fingers on his right hand, he struggled. He had trouble gauging distances. "Is this forever?" he wondered.

One day, a friend visiting him in the hospital played an album by his favorite band, Oasis. His larynx suddenly crackled to life. "I could sing along to it out loud," he said. "I remembered all the words." He could not have even a simple conversation. But he could sing.

Because singing generally happens in the *right* hemisphere of the brain, it's often "preserved" in the face of loss of speech. Singing Oasis, he was not producing speech but retrieving speech that had been encoded with melody. And, as Yong had told me, the right hemisphere has areas that are connected to and mirror the left and can be recruited as "backup."

Perhaps singing was a bridge. As Oliver Sacks suggests in *Musicophilia*, singing seems both to beneficially "damp down" the newly overactive right hemisphere and to help fire back up the "inhibited" left hemisphere, in a virtuous cycle. Adrian's brain was compensating by drawing upon resources in both hemispheres, which, curiously, is something that we typically all do as we get older.

"It was like a lifeline," Adrian said of his spontaneous vocalization. "Suddenly I thought, 'Okay, it might come back.'" But he was only beginning an intensive regimen of rehabilitation: cognitive therapy, speech therapy, group therapy, physical therapy. "It was unbelievable," he said.

Once-simple tasks had to be relearned. Not cognitively—for he knew "in his head" how to do things. But the neural pathways that would enable the necessary brain-body coordination had to be rewired. He could see things clearly, for example, but he had trouble getting his eyes to where his brain wanted them to go (a neuro-optometrist assigned him "eye push-ups"). Imagine that moment, looking into an open refrigerator, when you can't find something that's right in front of you. Adrian's day was filled with any number of refrigerator moments.

He was an experienced person trapped in the body of a beginner. A therapist brought him to a supermarket one day, armed with a shopping list. His task was simple: Do the shopping. Set loose among the aisles, he was overwhelmed by the sheer choice of items, the bustling shoppers clogging the narrow aisles, the lights and music.

"The first time, I couldn't do it; my coordination was off. I was a mess."

The sheer stimuli of New York City, with its roaring streets and thronged subways, were enervating. He had to navigate slowly, deliberately, sometimes to the impatience of passersby who saw no visible reason why this fit young man shouldn't be moving faster. He found himself in support groups mostly populated by stroke victims, where he was the youngest member by decades.

A few weeks in, his speech therapist suggested singing might help. Among other things, the rhythm and slower articulation of singing seem to help kick-start the flow of speech. And so, much as I had done, he went to the internet and found Britpop. He and his future wife, a shoe designer named Roz, joined up (Roz, who came to support Adrian, has since become a dedicated member, even if, as she jokingly insists, she cannot sing).

Amid a heavy schedule of chemotherapy, among all his other therapies, he was now singing Oasis, with people. His speech has largely recovered, though it can still seem a bit slow and mechanical, and there are moments when his face will go a bit blank and he'll suddenly pause. "That means I've lost it," he said. He enthusiastically told his fellow attendees at a brain cancer support group about the benefits of singing. "They all think I'm mad," he said, laughing.

But by the start of summer, he had recovered enough to establish We Can Kick It, an organization using soccer to help cancer-afflicted children. With the World Cup looming, he launched an online "ice bucket"–style challenge in which people were to juggle a soccer ball ten times with their feet.

This was something he once could have done in his sleep and now had to teach himself "from scratch." I signed up for the challenge, despite being a poor soccer

juggler. Wanting it to look decent for the camera, I practiced for weeks. We both got to our ten.

But the process of skill acquisition for each of us was
different. I was blazing trails in my brain to a destination—
the skill of soccer juggling—I'd never reached. He *knew*
the way to the land of proficient juggling, but impassable
obstacles had blocked the old paths in his brain, so he was
finding new neural routes to get to a place he had been
before.

ALMOST AN AMATEUR

As much as I was enjoying the choir, I often felt as if I
were getting away with something. Sooner or later, I'd be
caught out, my lack of talent revealed. Like an anthropologist embedded with some strange new culture, I
sometimes felt as if I were trying to politely mimic what
the people around me were doing without actually understanding what was going on.

During rehearsals, Charlie was typically at the center, scanning the room as we moved through our parts. I
was that kid in class who doesn't have the answer and so
tries to avoid scrutiny, which is a bit hard when you're the
tallest person in the room. Sometimes, though, her eyes,
masked by the reflection in her eyeglasses, would narrow
with concentration and settle on me, on my *mouth*, her
face betraying no reaction. I would secretly panic: Am I
doing something wrong? I had nightmares of her saying,
"Okay, Tom, we're all going to have to hear *just you* on
that part, to make sure you're not hopelessly sullying what
we've all worked so hard for."

Thankfully, that never happened. Her gentle critiques
were only ever leveled at sections, so we could take refuge in the diffusion of blame. Even this felt intimidating;

every minute the basses spent going over a part alone with Charlie felt like five (even if most other people were just looking at their phones).

During one session, Roger, who I was later told had a reputation for "scaring off" new members with his exacting standards, noted that I was a "bit flat" on a passage. A pro, of course, would take this in stride and simply adjust pitch. With my fragile beginner's self-esteem, I felt as if my entire reason for being had been called into question.

But I was grateful for the feedback. One thing that had become apparent in choir singing was that, depending on the whims of acoustics, you sometimes could barely hear yourself. You could simply sing louder, but then you ran the risk of being heard above everyone else. Also, due to the "Lombard effect"—we talk louder when the sound around us gets louder—raising your voice will probably just make everyone raise theirs as well. Because a choir in full voice can sweep up a lot of errors, you might be blissfully singing off-key and scarcely be aware of it.

I thought I might have had a leg up in all of this with my voice lessons, but the truth was more complicated. The voice coach is there to nurture the individual voice and develop its unique expressiveness. The choir director needs a warm, competent body to complete the blend. The needs and demands are different; as one article described it, "Choral directors are from Mars and voice teachers are from Venus."

With Danielle, I was trying to coax vibrato into my voice; with Charlie, vibrato would be a distracting nuisance. There's an old line of thinking that singing in a choir can even be *bad* for the "solo voice." The two activities were little alike. Singing lessons were filled with repetitive drills designed to hone discrete skills, like taking endless penalty shots at a goalkeeper. Singing in a choir was like suddenly being thrust into a live soccer match, having to read the game, knowing where you needed to be, anticipating other players' actions, all before a crowd.

Singing with a choir, I realized, much too late, was a very distinct skill from singing alone. As we worked on "Linger," by the Cranberries, I'd routinely slip from my assigned bass part and sing the melody—the song as I knew it from the radio. To be honest, I sometimes forgot I *had* a bass part. This transgression would then infiltrate the ears of Roger, who, as he told me, wasn't a strong enough singer to be able to entirely resist the influence. Being able to hold one's line, no matter what tempting morsels of multipart harmony were around you, was a hallmark of expert choral singers.

And I was no expert. With bass Roger in one ear and tenor Hank in the other, I sometimes felt as if I were in a game of sonic tug-of-war. Half the time I was probably splitting the difference.

I really felt off my game when Charlie would have us do the occasional "jam": We'd all get started singing some part in a song and then walk freely about the room, still singing, improvising if we liked. This was meant to be fun, a kind of social mixer with harmony, but I usually felt totally unmoored and exposed.

Novices like me, it turns out—and there is research— prefer to sing in the same position, next to the same people, and close to other people (expert singers pretty much prefer the opposite). Mixing singers in a choir, shuffling up the sections, is said to produce the best sound, but it also tends to make amateur singers unhappy.

Even when we step out of our comfort zone, we still need our comfort zone.

*

After ten weeks, it was time for our performance, at (Le) Poisson Rouge, a well-known music club in Greenwich Village. Like a final exam, this had loomed for weeks. I scrambled to remember lyrics; I struggled with high notes.

Even our wardrobe scheme for the night—band T-shirts—presented me with a challenge. I had plenty of band shirts in my college years, but decades later my closet was bereft. And so there I was, in the basement of Urban Outfitters, rummaging through Pink and Dr. Dre T-shirts. I brought my daughter to make it seem less conspicuous. I found an age-appropriate New Order shirt.

Then, suddenly, it was showtime. Because of the tightness of the stage, we were arranged in such a way that I was positioned a few singers down from Roger, in the back row, among singers I typically was far away from.

What's more, when we launched into our first song, "Road to Nowhere" by the Talking Heads, I found I had the *reverse* experience I sometimes felt in choir: Now I felt as if I were hearing only *me*, as if I were soloing to the whole place. Damned acoustics!

Even worse, we were set to perform Toto's "Africa" together with the Brooklynite Choir. Each choir knew the song but had never rehearsed it together. Suddenly there were strange faces and voices among us, as if our little hunter-gatherer group had been joined by a rival clan. Who *were* these people?

But here I was, in middle age, singing onstage for the first time since the third grade.

As it happened, my daughter, then seven, had joined Charlie's after-school program, called Broadway Show-stoppers. A few weeks earlier, my wife and I had gone, with other parents, to their small performance. Their show, like almost any children's performance, seemed a miracle. We were on the verge of tears simply seeing her take the stage. The copious errors were forgiven because they're children. How full of promise they seemed, their voices ringing with pure, unadulterated joy.

Now to my night, and the venue is crowded, with friends and family, who in general are showing great enthusiasm. My daughter is beaming at me and the choir, almost starstruck.

But there's also an inescapable touch of pathos. We are thirty-, forty-, fifty-, sixty-somethings. We're no longer so full of limitless progress. No one is planning, or even much dreaming of, a career in song. Our errors betray less the headlong enthusiasm of children than a glaring lack of competence. The parental smile of eternal indulgence gives way to a more complicated expression: respect for what we are doing, a bit of tolerance that we're not professionals, maybe even a bit of nostalgia—for these audience members too were probably once onstage, doing what we were doing.

But even by the forgiving standards of the audience, the show was considered a success, and I felt as though something in me had irrevocably changed. I kept singing. One show became two, three, four. I joined the little "professional" splinter choir that had side gigs. We provided backup for a concert in the Bronx that mixed Dutch and Puerto Rican musicians. We sang along with groups who had actual records and fans. We sang to a group of older people, many in wheelchairs, at a hospital on Roosevelt Island. I doubt if they knew any of the songs we sang, but they smiled and tapped their feet, and we did seem to briefly brighten the gray institutional air. We sang on a stage to passing commuters in the middle of New York's Port Authority Bus Terminal as part of an effort to spread holiday cheer; the only ones who stayed for the whole show were the khaki-clad, automatic-rifle-clutching marines standing guard near the Au Bon Pain. They didn't break cover and smile or tap their feet, but I hoped they wanted to.

In a world of endless, meaningless Muzak, it felt life affirming to be filling these spaces with our own breath. At a performance we shared with our sister group, the Brooklynite Choir, I beamed with pride when one of their singers told me she was "jealous" of the rich, deep sound our bass section was putting out.

I became a regular, going out for drinks with "the girls," where we dished over various characters in the group: the woman who did not seem to actually sing but never missed a rehearsal; the one who never came to a rehearsal but weirdly arrived at performances knowing exactly what to do; the sudden disappearance of a new choir member who, we suspected, had a voice that was not quite fitting in. It does happen, if not very often.

I was growing increasingly attached to this outfit. Much as Roger had described, when the discussion came up around the dinner table, as it sometimes did, of decamping New York for some other place, one of the first things that came to mind was this: Would I be close enough to come in for rehearsals?

Before I knew it, the Britpop Choir was fulfilling any number of needs in my life. There was the simple getting out of the house, being among people, working on something that wasn't work. There was the way I would leave rehearsals, every time and without fail, on an undeniable high. And there was the high-intensity vocal workout I was getting. While I was loving my voice lessons, they weren't cheap. But joining a choir is the next best thing. Your pitch-making skills will improve; your sense of timing will sharpen. And you'll be doing it all—well, at least at Britpop we were—in a festive atmosphere.

Over drinks one night, late into a cycle, with another

performance looming, Roger turned to me and grew serious. "There is a craft to choir singing," he said. "We're there to enjoy it, but a note's a note. You don't get an award for showing up. From the first cycle to now, you are way better. You've done your homework. I don't know what this means for your vocal career, but you're on it."

There'd been no audition, but I felt as if I'd finally passed. I felt as if I were almost an amateur.

CHAPTER FIVE

SURFING THE
U-SHAPED WAVE

The Agony and the Ecstasy of the Advanced Beginner

SURF SHOP CLERK: Hey, man, guys your age learning to surf, it's cool, there's nothing wrong with it.

JOHNNY UTAH: I'm twenty-five.

SURF SHOP CLERK: See, that's what I'm saying—it's never too late.

—*POINT BREAK*, 1991

HAVING FUN UNDER SUPERVISION:
THE ROCKAWAYS

Surfing has cost me two wedding rings, many thousands of dollars, and a few millimeters of intervertebral space in my spine. And I'm still not that good at it.

I was drawn in the way most middle-aged novices are: Surfing was an object of long and distant fascination that I wanted to try before it was too late. Something that might test me in new ways.

When I was growing up in the ocean-starved Midwest in the 1970s, surfing trickled into my consciousness, as many things did, via television: a clip or two on *Wide World of Sports*; the special "Hawaii trilogy" of *The Brady Bunch* in which Greg suffers a scary-looking wipeout into a reef (I can still hear the eerie music as the taboo tiki idol worked its evil magic).

I don't think I saw a surfer in person until I was in my late twenties, on a magazine assignment in Orange County to interview the noted surfer and shaper Donald Takayama—a task that was definitely over my head. After spending the morning with him in his shaping bay, I watched a crowd of kids on shortboards buzzing like agitated water striders around the encrusted pilings of the pier at Huntington Beach.

Over the next few decades, I maintained a kind of low-grade secret crush on surfing, the sort I once had on an older woman who worked at a hip coffee shop in my college town. Like her, surfing seemed wrapped in mystique, perhaps slightly dangerous, and ultimately unattainable.

The pursuit doesn't exactly hang out a big "Beginners Welcome" sign. At insider websites like Beach Grit, "vulnerable adult learners," particularly those mythopoetically rhapsodizing about the life-changing joy of waves they first rode the week before, are mercilessly mocked. Surfers, the Australian pro Barton Lynch once observed, are "more cocky and judgmental than any group of people in the world." Even if you barely paid attention to surfing, you'd no doubt heard about angry locals, always men, threatening "kooks" at coveted breaks. The bar to entry, on various levels, seemed high.

Even though I had moved to New York City, a place surrounded by water—and even, I heard, decent surf breaks—my infatuation remained theoretical, my relationship platonic. New York life can be provincial; the Rockaways might well have been another country. How would I get there? Where would I go? Who would show me the ropes? Nobody I knew surfed.

So instead, I just soaked up the mythology, devoured the books and watched the movies, learned the evocative names of surf breaks: Mavericks, Jaws, Trestles, Horseshoes, and Outer Log Cabins (the best waves, one surfer insisted to me, ended in *s*—an easily disproven theory but tantalizing nonetheless).

I tried to imagine myself as a philosophical, monk-like waterman, rising predawn to consult buoy readings. This straight-edge part of surfing—the all-consuming sense of purpose, the somber rituals, the hard-forged unity with the elements—attracted me more than the sun-streaked hedonistic side of things.

Someday, I would inhabit this role of "surfer" I had envisioned for myself. I hoarded it, in my imagination, some fantasy refuge against life's drudgery. In my mind I was always packing it in to go live in some small beach town, surfing in the morning, writing in the afternoon, reading in the evening. And yet "someday," as a unit of time, can be hopelessly expansive. Reality kept intruding on my surfing dreams. Or maybe because surfing was a dream, I had no need to make it reality.

*

And so several decades passed before I found myself, one late, cold November weekday afternoon, on a desolate, windswept piece of beach in the Rockaways, about to lie prone on a nine-foot slab of blue foam. In the slate-gray sea, two- to three-foot waves broke in the distance. Herring gulls, clamorous and territorial, were parked on the jumbled rock jetties. Overhead, a steady procession of large jets drifted down the flight path to JFK.

I was joined by Dillon O'Toole, an instructor with

Locals Surf School, a small Rockaway outfit. He'd arrived suddenly, as if out of the mist, carrying little more than a couple of boards and a small, desert-camo backpack with a "Bernie" button on it. A tall, tanned, bearded twenty-something with a deep, comforting voice, Dillon, like most Locals instructors, had grown up in the Rockaways and had been on a board since he was a kid. He could have been my son, but I felt childlike before his authority.

As I lowered myself to the board, I played out a scene familiar from any beginner break from Waikiki to Bondi. You might have seen this: a circle of black wet-suited souls air paddling on land-bound surfboards, necks uncomfortably arched, looking like stranded, flailing seals, being watched over by a bored-looking minder with a zinc-tinted nose. The idea is simple: Before you get in the water, where the board would become an unstable, *moving* proposition, it's best to experience the basic dynamics—where to position yourself, how to turn, the proper stance—on dry land. And, of course, the "pop-up," the act of swiftly transitioning from a prone, paddling position to an erect crouch, bent at the knees, arms outstretched for balance. "Pretend you're an archer drawing his bow," Dillon told me.

The pop-up is a funny thing. To the beginner, it's *the* crucial act in surfing. With the instructor cherry-picking waves, and pushing you into those waves, all you have to do is hoist yourself off the deck and survive that rocky transition, and your work is basically done. If you can manage to not fall off that big, wide, beginner-friendly wedge of foam that is the soft-top board, you are—at least according to the dictionary—surfing. You're tapping into a magic that had enthralled the writer Jack London, back in 1908, as he first spied a Hawaiian native upon the waves at Waikiki: "Straight on toward shore he flies on his winged heels and the white crest of the breaker."

Much later, when you're doing something that more

closely approximates actual surfing, you won't think much of the pop-up. It will just happen, instinctually. You'll be thinking of other things. But in the beginning, it's everything. I would visualize it; I would practice it on my living room rug.

Rockaway, in surfing parlance, is a left-handed beach break, or jetty break. In some ways, it's perfect for learning. The sandy bottom is free from reefs, rocks, or other hazards. It's blessedly non-sharky. You don't face a long paddle to get to the waves.

But it also has its challenges. The particular bathymetry of the seafloor here means waves tend to break steeply. "When it gets big and hollow, it's like a ninety-degree angle," Dillon said. You need a much faster pop-up than at a point break like Malibu. And because the sand that helps create the breaking wave is itself always shifting, the way it does in a desert, you never quite know what you're going to get.

Once I'd perfected my beach pop-up, we moved into the ocean. "This isn't so bad," I told Dillon, nestled in my thick, hooded winter neoprene. Then an unexpectedly large wave basically broke on me, and the wall of water felt as if a thousand tiny needles had been shot into my face.

Leading me through the waves by the nose of my board, up to his neck in the ocean, Dillon turned toward the horizon, shielding his brow with his hand. I saw an endless, swirling plain of greens and shadows. He saw something he liked. "Okay," he said, "get ready."

I arched my back, planted my toes perpendicular to the board, and looked ahead. "Slooowww paddle," he said, in his low, soothing voice. "Dig!" I paddled harder. I felt frothing at my heels and the slightest tilt of the board. "POP!" he shouted. Suddenly the ninja I had been on land was nowhere to be seen. I started to drunkenly clamber to my feet, my hand still clutching the board's rail. As I toppled over the side, the frigid water blasted up my nasal cavity like a satanic neti pot.

On the second try, I briefly got to my feet but made the mistake of looking at them as I did. In surfing, as in cornering on a bike or in a race car, the mantra is "Look where you want to go." This brings up a phenomenon familiar in skill learning: Beginners are always looking *at themselves*. New cyclists look at their hands on the handlebars; new drivers look at the hood of the car. The better you get, the farther away you start to look. By looking down, you're subconsciously orchestrating a series of downward muscle movements. In surfing, they say, "If you look down, you'll go down."

Which is precisely what happened. My weight shifted toward the nose, and my board, and me along with it, plunged forward. It's called pearling, or nose-diving. As it begins to happen, you fixate even more, and it just gets worse.

According to a theory from the sports psychologist Gabriele Wulf, we do worse at an activity when we focus on ourselves, instead of some "external" target. This idea shows up in almost every sport there is. Darts players do better if they focus on the board and not their own arms; golfers do better if they focus on the hole and not their elbows. Even musicians, it's been shown, seem to do better if they focus on overall sound rather than on their fingers strumming the instrument. Wulf, who says the findings have been replicated across 180 studies, thinks a focus on the self can prompt "micro-choking," getting in the way of automatic movement—which is what we're talking about when we're talking about skilled behavior.

And so, at Rockaway, Dillon wanted me to focus not on the front of my board but on an onshore building. Look at that, the theory goes, and the rest will take care of itself.

My pop-ups had many ways to fall apart, however. My

arms would be too far forward when I tried to pop up, putting too much weight at the front. I would pop up too late and feel the pulse of the passing wave. I would stand too tall or bend with my back rather than with my knees, both of which would wreck my balance. Sometimes, distracted by the turbulence of a larger wave, I wouldn't pop up at all, instead taking a long toboggan run to the shore. In any other context, this would be fun in and of itself. Here it just reeked of failure.

It felt as if I had a checklist in my head that I was frantically trying to run through, in real time, in the fraction of a second I had to pull it all together. Proper board position? Check. Eyes on the shore. Check. Archer's stance. Check. Then I'd focus so hard on my board position I'd forget to look at the shore. One rule was always being neglected at the expense of another.

This is classic beginner's behavior. A few decades ago, Stuart and Hubert Dreyfus, brothers and professors at the University of California, were studying, on behalf of the U.S. Air Force's Office of Scientific Research, how people went about learning complex skills. Looking at pilots, second-language learners, and chess players, they came up with their widely influential "five-stage model of adult skill acquisition." From a humble "novice," skill learners progressed to the "advanced beginner" stage, then on to a sort of midpoint of "competence," before climbing further to "proficiency," finally summiting at "expertise." Experts, noted the authors, tend to become one with their skill. Airplane pilots no longer think of flying a plane; they're just flying. As expert walkers, we no longer think, like the infants in chapter 2, about *how* to move our body down the sidewalk. We just do it.

In the "novice" stage, the learner rigidly adheres to "context-free" rules. Beginner drivers are told to stop at red lights; beginning chess players learn to "always" do this or that (for example, don't move your knight to the edge of the board). But what if a driver comes to an intersection where the red light has malfunctioned? (This was a classic problem in the "beginner" stages of self-driving cars.) What if your chess opponent responds to your textbook move with something unorthodox? Beginners judge their performance, the Dreyfuses suggested, by how well they follow rules.

On the surfboard, I was trying to follow a set of fundamental rules, without otherwise paying attention to what was going on in the real world. That's because simply trying to *observe* the rules was consuming all my mental bandwidth. I'd have relative success on one wave, then completely fail when Dillon pushed me into the next. He would say, "Yeah, on that one you needed more of an angled takeoff" or "That wave just kind of died."

To move to the next stage, that of the "advanced beginner," I'd need to start incorporating "situational aspects"—or context—into my surfing. I'd need to know when and how to apply rules depending on the situation. This was a hard enough transition in any activity. But what makes surfing so difficult is that the situation is *always changing.*

Surfing, you might think, is similar to snowboarding, and it is, in the simplest terms of maintaining balance on a plank that's going down a slope. But now imagine you have to jump to your feet and land in the proper position as that board begins descending. Imagine you're carving down not a mostly static mountain but a constantly quivering, shape-shifting mass of Jell-O. Imagine you have one moment to make the right move before the opportunity is lost forever. Imagine that if you fall, your board can become a deadly, boomeranging projectile. Imagine that instead of a cozy lift ride back, you have to power through an "impact zone" filled with pummeling waves and other surfers. Snowboarding during a mild avalanche is probably a fairer comparison to surfing. In his book *Kook*, Peter Heller is told by one sage surfer that it's not something you pick up in a year but a "life path."

My life path was just a few steps old. I knew it wouldn't be easy. Jack London spent four hours in the water on his first day and had this to report: "I was resolved that on the morrow I'd come in standing up."

When I finally did that, on my second lesson, I proudly reported to my wife and daughter, later that evening, "I surfed! It was amazing!"

I didn't fully appreciate at the time how little of the code I had actually cracked, how hard the gains would be, or how dispiriting it would be to go *down* in skill before, hopefully, I would begin to go back up.

*

I soon began to cherish my Rockaway outings. Once a week or so, I would drop my daughter off at school and drive to the beach, against the flow of incoming commuter traffic, trying to tell my protesting work ethic that this *was* work and never quite believing it. I'd queue up *Chet Baker Sings* and try to practice my vocals during the forty-five-minute trip.

As much as the exhilaration of riding waves, I looked forward to simply being in the water. I tried to cultivate surf buddies, as much for safety as companionship. There was Diana, a fellow parent at my daughter's school, but she moved to Hawaii. Henrik, a stoic, modern-day Viking from Denmark, was a good surfer, maybe too good—there were days I couldn't join him—but he moved to Copenhagen. If syncing ability was hard, syncing schedules was even harder. So I usually went alone, which is typically not advised. And yet I relished the idea of just me and the sea.

When I faced land, Rockaway, or more properly the Arverne section of Rockaway, presented a curious post-card view—a cluster of public housing blocks next to an upscale New Urbanist–style development that seemed more Florida than New York. There was a billboard, shilling new luxury condos, that showed a well-groomed man wearing a suit and holding a surfboard—"the wrong way," as some surfer had cackled to me.

Rockaway had its charms. It felt like a small town, for one. Once, Henrik and I finished a session and returned to the surf shop where we'd stored our gear. The door was locked. We stood on the sidewalk in dripping wet suits. Suddenly Dillon came rolling along on a beach cruiser. "They keep the key at that pharmacy across the street," he said, and pedaled off. We got our stuff, locked the shop up, and returned the key.

When you're on a board and turned toward the sea, however, looking for waves—the dying, wind-shaped traces of distant storms—you suddenly feel the city melt away. Bobbing rhythmically, set to the frequency of whatever the day's swell pattern was, freed from your smartphone, you look into the endless, skyline-free horizon, letting your mind spill into that empty space.

"Seahab," the writer and surfer Allan Weisbecker calls it. I don't know if you need science to convince you it will make you feel better, but let's just say no study has found a majority of people feeling *worse* after they emerged from a surf session. As with choirs, surfing's been used as a thera-peutic instrument for everyone from children with neu-rological disorders to veterans with post-traumatic stress disorder.

I would wonder, why hadn't I done this sooner? In under an hour I could go from the urban bustle of Brook-

lyn to a wild expanse where there were often more dol-
phins and seabirds than people. It was meditation by other
means. And there was plenty of time for contemplation.
As one analysis of a surf competition found, the process of
actively surfing waves makes up only 4 percent of a typical session. Half of the rest of the time is spent paddling,
the other half, waiting. Another lesson: Surfing, like life,
rewards patience.

I would sometimes, at the end of a lesson, meet someone else like me, the next incoming beginner, looking
excited and tentative at once, like a puppy walking on
snow for the first time. In the summer, the numbers would
swell, with competing surf schools jostling on the beach
and in the water. It wasn't uncommon to see four or five
beginners taking off on the same wave. Most places, this is
a no-no, but in this atmosphere it was not only tolerated
but encouraged, with a hearty shout of "party wave!"

This was all a fairly recent historical development, as
described to me by Mike Reinhardt, founder of Locals,
along with Mike Koloyan. When Reinhardt grew up in
the area in the 1990s, there were no surf schools teaching
droves of beginners "down for the day." Surfing hadn't yet
had one of its periodic, ever-growing upward swings in
popularity. Like most local kids, he'd just started going
down the block and trying to learn on his own, often the
hard way. When the two Mikes (with students they often
go by "Blond Mike" and "Dark Mike" to make it easier)
first opened the school, in 2012, Reinhardt told me, "We
got a lot of shit from salty locals who said, 'Oh, those surf
schools, they're just pumping out more kooks.' "

Most students, he insisted, were "surf tourists." They
wouldn't be crowding the water for long. "They may take
a five-lesson package with us, but surfing five times isn't
usually enough to do this on your own, and safely."

The upside for the short termers, Reinhardt said, is

that unlike with some other sports or activities, you didn't have to be good at surfing for it to feel incredibly fun right away. "If you're learning to kickbox, you're getting your ass kicked by the trainer for the first six months. You're going to have to be good at it to get some fulfillment."

Dillon had noted a number of "archetypal" surf students. There were, he said, the people like me, the winter people. "The person who's fully committed. Whatever happened in their life, they want to learn." Then there was the person who was there "to have a good time, make sure they're safe, and get some good waves." The "leisure lesson," he called it. And then there were people, usually in the summer and usually tourists, who come for "the roller-coaster ride," as he described it. "They're not really there to absorb anything. They just want to stand up a little bit, get wet, and that's it," he said. "A good chunk of the lessons," he noted, "are for Instagram bragging."

The surf writer Nick Carroll, citing some research he'd done with Australian surf schools, found that only 5 percent of clients ever came back for another lesson. "Most," he noted, "were happy to be able to say they'd had a go at it." The majority washed out after a few years.

*

I could understand why, for the path forward wasn't easy. This seemed particularly true later in life. Teaching kids to surf, Reinhardt told me, was often about helping them conquer irrational fears. "They'll be screaming at a tiny wave, and all of a sudden they're riding it and laughing."

Adults, however, have *rational* fears. "They know what they have to lose if they twist their arm and can't work or have to go to the hospital and pay the bill."

Kids are also in it just for fun; adults, Reinhardt said, tended to come charging in with strict goals. He cautioned against this. "Surfing can be frustrating," he said. "You can't put too much pressure on it, because, after all, what the hell are you doing it for if you're not trying to enjoy it?" Women, he theorized, were often better learners than men. "I think they're more patient with themselves," he said. "Men are just so macho, like, 'I gotta crush that wave.'"

This speaks to a classic problem faced by beginners: setting unrealistic expectations. It makes little sense to lay down strict goals ahead of time for advancing in some discipline when the novice barely understands what the discipline *is*, what will be required, or how they'll actually progress. Unmet goals can destroy motivation as much as they drive it.

The objective should be learning itself. "Focus on *process*, not *product*," suggests the learning authority Barbara Oakley. Much of our pain in learning, she argues, comes from getting hung up on results.

More than age or fitness, the prime determinant in learning to surf is the calendar. Reinhardt told me that people will book a package, show up for the first two or three lessons, begin to get a feel for it, then miss a week or two as some work-related thing comes up. Then it gets colder and the commitment level drops off. "They've missed a whole winter and have to start from scratch in the spring," he said. One's schedule must match up with the wave conditions, which were, more often than not, suboptimal or nonexistent. The Rockaway surf reports were often filled with uninspiring qualifiers like "some rideable surf if you're desperate to get wet." Usually, I was.

Surfing favors people with money or time. On top of that, learning to surf requires three things: motivation, practice, and feedback. Unless you lived right on the beach, just getting to the break took some work. Repetitive drills were impossible when weeks passed without waves.

And feedback, even with a coach, is often difficult in surfing. Dillon told me he often struggled to see what was happening as I disappeared behind the wave he had pushed me into. It had taken him years to develop a sense of what someone's feet might be doing from the way their shoulders were moving, and still, after some wipeouts, he was as clueless as I was as to why they happened.

Maybe this was a good thing. Too *much* feedback can hinder learning. Learners can become overwhelmed by it or too dependent on it. They fail to respond to their failure. You needed to get worked, as surfers say, in your own way, and *you* needed to figure out why.

Surfing humbles you. The degrees of freedom of the human body, combined with the ocean's unpredictable and unstoppable masses of kinetic energy, make for deeply unstable alchemy. Add to that my age and my high center of gravity, and let's just say I wasn't a natural for success.

Around this time, William Finnegan's totemic book *Barbarian Days* came out, and I, along with anyone I knew who surfed—and many who didn't—lapped it up. One line stopped me cold: "People who tried to start at an advanced age, meaning over fourteen, had, in my experience, almost no chance of becoming proficient, and usually suffered pain and sorrow before they quit." After *fourteen*? He offered a grudging concession in the next sentence: "It was possible to have fun, though, under supervision, in the right conditions."

Finnegan could come off like an aging hipster railing about how good it was in the old days, and I'm sure he had a point. I wasn't one to question his surfing bona fides, and, besides, having fun under supervision was exactly what I was doing. Did I need to be *proficient*? That's stage four in the Dreyfus model. I would happily settle for stage three: competent.

Soon, I was feeling confident enough to alternate lessons with time out on my own. I'd ride straight and all the way up onto the beach on my Styrofoam aircraft carrier, thinking I had it pretty dialed, only to be later told this was a kook's move. I'd spy one of the Mikes in the water with a student and give a solemn nod, as if I were some grizzled veteran of the lineup, and then get sideswiped off my board by an errant wave. I lost one of my wedding rings to the finger-shrinking Atlantic.

Poetically, I would lose the other in the Pacific.

*

Little did I know I was about to take a steep plunge down the U-shaped curve.

This is a fascinating, more or less inevitable part of the learning process. It occurs in various ways and for various reasons.

In the world of chess, for example, a player's rating often rises fairly swiftly as one learns and practices. Beginner chess is typically a battle of who can make the fewest blunders, and a bit of initial strategy and tactics goes a long way. But then you start meeting players who *know* that strategy and those tactics, and you start to lose. The expert beginner quickly becomes the intermediate novice.

A classic case of U-shaped development is with children learning grammar. In the beginning, because their speech is largely imitative, they will often get verb tenses right, without understanding why. As they slowly learn the rules of grammar, they confidently begin to apply rules across the board; they "overgeneralize." So where they once said "spoke," they suddenly say "speaked."

In one fascinating experiment—that I successfully replicated with my seven-year-old daughter—young children were shown to correctly understand the common-sense notion that when you add a cup of ten-degree water to another cup of ten-degree water, you get two cups of ten-degree water. But children between six and nine, it turned out, often got it wrong. Why did they seemingly go backward? Because they now knew how to add, and emboldened by this shiny new ability, they suddenly think the water is *twenty* degrees.

In the Dreyfus model, novices live in a world of rules to be learned and followed. Getting to the "advanced beginner" stage requires actually *applying* those rules. This also means knowing when *not* to apply rules, or how to act when no rule seems to apply.

This isn't as easy as it might seem. For me, the first sign of trouble came when, on a work trip to Portugal, I signed up for a day's lesson at my first non-Rockaway surf break, a spot south of Lisbon whose waters were warmed by a nearby power plant.

After first assuring the instructor of the time I'd logged in the water—*yeah, I got this*—I promptly dazzled him with a stunning inability to get up on my board. The break was unfamiliar, the board was new, the timing and shape of the waves seemed all wrong.

Here was a valuable lesson: At least until you are wildly proficient, every new surf spot turns you into a beginner again. What you learned to do well in one place may not work so well in another. Even a different *day* at the same spot can knock you back. With waves, change is the only constant.

The instructor, growing impatient with my attempts, told me my pop-up was all wrong. He showed me a method—clumsy, I thought—that involved going to one knee, then dragging the trailing leg up, then standing. As I later learned, this is called the two-step pop-up. It sort of worked.

Back at Rockaway, Dillon shook his head. "That's what they do to get people standing for a one-day lesson," he said, "but it's not what you want long term." *Remember that earlier lesson: Doing well is not the same as learning.*

More trouble came when I decided that I needed my own board. I felt that the soft top, that staple of surf schools, marked me as a hapless beginner. I probably should have just embraced it. Dillon swore by the foamie's inherent fun factor; even on big days I would sometimes see him out on one, joyfully stomping on the nose and making sweeping carves.

At a local shop, I picked out a seven-foot-eight-inch board. Known as a midlength, it falls somewhere between the agility of a shortboard and the grace and ease of a longboard. The next day, Blond Mike saw me walking to the beach, confidently toting my new sled. "I don't know," he said, surveying the board. "To my mind you lose the benefit of both the long- and shortboard."

I tried to shake off the comment. I entered the water and, for the next hour, rode precisely zero waves. The board wasn't only shorter; it had a lot less volume. It was like trying to tap-dance on ice. I had fallen for another classic novice syndrome: downsizing my board too quickly.

As a beginner surfer, I simply had to pass the barest threshold of performance to feel successful. Now I faced new thresholds, the upward slope of the U. I had to start spotting my own waves—a skill that really only comes with time and experience. You need to develop an eye for waves; beginners eagerly try to catch everything and quickly get tired. I had to paddle into my own wave, which required more strength than I really had. I had to time my pop-up and correctly angle my takeoff approach.

I'd not only plateaued; I felt I'd gotten worse.

What had actually happened was my metacognitive window had been thrown open. Before, I didn't know what I didn't know. Now I was getting a sense of what surfing really *was*. My pop-up was the same, but now it was up to me to know when to deploy it. Which wasn't easy. Surfers take quick over-the-shoulder glances up to the moment they catch the wave, because that wave always has the capacity to change. To paraphrase Heraclitus, no one surfs the same wave twice. The rules I'd learned might work, but only at the right time and on the right wave.

*

It eventually dawned on me that I needed a bigger picture. I needed to escape my confines and push past the limits of what I knew. Like the learners in the Infant Action Lab who bravely attempted steep cliffs at the very edge of their ability—and even beyond—I needed to head to the "zone of proximal development."

I'd heard from a friend about a surf camp in Costa Rica that had really helped her surfing: a week's worth of intensive surfing, video analysis, a small student-to-teacher ratio. And February in the tropics meant no thick wet suits, no shivering curbside undressing in the company of inquisitive pigeons. I gleefully imagined myself ripping down the line, bare-chested, later lounging beachside with a fruity cocktail.

One cold but sunny December afternoon, I was winding up a session at Rockaway. The waves were substantial; the tide was dropping. There were a handful of other surfers, and I had caught some decent waves.

Suddenly another was coming. I began paddling, noticing a bit too late that it was rearing up higher than I expected. I reflexively tried to jump to my feet, and the next thing I had any awareness of was my face hitting the sandy bottom. There was a dull thunk, and I could fleetingly feel—almost smell—the cold, grainy, punching-bag firmness of the ocean floor. I felt a ripple of nausea and dizziness pass through me, and I rolled along the bottom for a moment before stumbling to my feet. If anyone else had noticed anything, they weren't saying.

Later, after sliding into an MRI tube, I was told my tumble had resulted in "2–3 mm anterolisthesis of C2 on C3 and of C3 on C4. There are mild degenerative end-plate changes, mild disk space narrowing, and small to moderate marginal vertebral body osteophytes at C5–C6 and C6–C7."

Or, as my doctor cheerfully put it, "there's some bumps and scrapes." My nerves were constantly pinched; I could barely move my neck. "Finnegan was right," I thought. "Pain and sorrow." Weeks of physical therapy loomed.

Here was the downside of adult learning: having the body of an adult.

Surfing is not without its risks. In an analysis in *The American Journal of Emergency Medicine*, a majority of the more than twelve hundred surfers surveyed had suffered at least one acute injury—most often to the head, most often from their own board. Most of those injured were self-professed expert surfers.

Still, I counted myself lucky. What if the angle of impact had been a few millimeters different? What if I had been knocked unconscious and no other surfers noticed or, as on some days, there *were* no other surfers?

Costa Rica was mere months away. After a follow-up visit, my doctor gave me the go-ahead. But on the eve of heading into my biggest waves yet, I felt that my confidence was at an all-time ebb.

CLIMBING THE TREE OF KNOWLEDGE:

NOSARA, COSTA RICA

Nosara is a collection of small oceanfront villages on Costa Rica's Nicoya Peninsula. One of these, Playa Guiones, is a dusty little expat-friendly enclave brimming with tanned and impossibly fit Americans and Europeans who buzz the mostly unpaved roads on ATVs or beater bikes. It's a *pura vida* playground of beachy boutiques, pressed-juice stands, and scores of stylish rental houses set amid the tropical foliage. There's a strong teak-and-thatched-roof-*palapa* vibe, with people doing aerial yoga to the sort of gently propulsive, forgettable ambient music that seems to play on a constant loop from Tulum to Kuta.

It also has the beach, a bucolic arc of sand unmarred by direct beachfront development. Guiones, thanks to geography and oceanography, serves like a big satellite dish for waves, picking up a constant transmission of pulses from the Pacific Ocean. This means it has pretty good surf, day in and day out, for most of the year. Not surprisingly, this has made this otherwise remote town—reached via a bumpy traverse of dirt roads—a mecca for all sorts of surfers.

Nosara is also the home of Surf Simply, the "Surf Coaching Resort" I'd booked in the hopes of elevating my skills. It has a waiting list for spots stretching nearly two years, but thanks to a cancellation I landed a week in February.

When I arrived, on a Sunday afternoon, the place—a set of bungalows on a leafy hillside—was quiet. After storing my bags in the room, I was pouring some water from a freshly hacked coconut when I met Danny, a fellow guest for the week and, I'd later learn, a climate scientist at an Ivy League school.

Danny said he was headed for a quick surf. Did I want to come?

The camp didn't technically begin until the following morning. I was weary from travel and still feeling incredibly gun-shy about surfing itself. I wanted to say no but found myself nodding yes. We grabbed some boards, lashed them to the side racks of beach-cruiser bikes, and pedaled the half a mile down to the beach. As we rode, Danny told me he was a returning guest hoping to refine some of the techniques he'd picked up the year before.

He had suffered a kind of surfing-related injury himself: Stepping on a skateboard in his driveway for the first time—skateboarding being commonly recommended as a way to practice surfing on land—he promptly fell and broke his collarbone.

The beach was sparsely populated, on land and in the water. As we began paddling, I was struck by how far out the waves were breaking, compared with Rockaway. It also occurred to me it was my first time surfing without a thick wet suit. By the time we'd made it past the huge wash of whitewater and out to a stretch of calm sea, I was already half-exhausted.

Danny waved at a surfer who was paddling over, an Asian American guy named Eddie whom he'd met on his last trip. A former New Yorker who had worked in finance and had moved to Nosara to surf and "figure out his next move," Eddie, I'd soon learn, was a staple in these waters. He was easy to pick out, with a relaxed style and a shag haircut that reminded me of the legendary big-wave surfer Mark Foo.

I made a few attempts at waves, but they felt half-hearted; I was still convinced I was a misstep away from permanent spine injury. It still hurt to swivel my neck around to look at waves. I was reassured that Danny, a bit out of practice himself, didn't seem to be doing much better.

Simply being in the water seemed important. I needed to shake the feeling I was playing with my own mortality.

*

That evening, at the resort, the week's guests gathered poolside with drinks on a set of low-slung couches for an introductory chat with Harry Knight, a tall, amiable Englishman who is one of Surf Simply's founders.

Low lights shimmered in the humid night air, and soft music percolated in the background. People were casually but stylishly dressed, their faces warm with that glow of the tropics. The whole scene felt like a reality television show—maybe *The Bachelor*, given the roughly four-to-one female-to-male guest ratio.

We went around the circle. There was Danny, whom I had already met. He had a nervous energy—he always seemed to be scrounging for food—and a dry, unfiltered wit: the Jeff Goldblum character in our little *Jurassic Park*.

He joked that he was the poster boy for adult improvement, given that he was the very surfer depicted on the part of Surf Simply's website that asks, "What Level Surfer Are You?" He is shown, wearing a hat for sun protection, riding "down the line" of a modest wave, competently if a bit stiffly. Behind him, meanwhile, a Surf Simply instructor, having executed a powerful "cutback," is propelling up the face of the wave, his board already beginning to launch into the air.

It's a dramatic illustration of how differently one wave can be surfed by two persons of varying skill level. "I could go down the line constantly and I'd be perfectly happy in life," he said. "But people always tell me I should do something else." He was there with his wife, Ellen, who had surfed years before, then given it up when she had kids. She wanted back in.

There was another couple, Michael and Shari, from Montana. Each of them picked a trip every year—hers tended toward surfing, his, mountain biking. Shari had been to Nosara twice; it was Michael's first time. Tall and easygoing, Michael had surfed for seven or eight years while living in California. "I've always found it extremely challenging to progress," he said, "more so than a lot of other sports I've done."

Shari, easy to spot in the water with her ever-present trucker hat, was quick to note that she lived in Montana and "didn't look anything like a surfer"—that is, not lithe and blond. Like me, she was, in part, trying to get over the fear factor. "There aren't many situations where you quite deliberately put yourself in the way of a big moving chunk of water that's coming after you at twenty miles per hour. It's intimidating."

Ulrike, my bungalow mate, was a pediatrician from Germany who lived in the Midwest. She'd long dreamed of surfing, and her first time had been at the camp the previous year. She joked that she didn't even know then which foot to place forward on the board. (Knight had an easy trick for this: "If you close your eyes, and have someone push you from behind, which foot goes forward?") "I learned a lot in my head," she said, "but just couldn't translate it into action."

The remainder of that week's surfers was a group of six women from New York City, their mostly non-surfing husbands left behind. I would end up particularly bonding with them; maybe it was a New York thing. They inhabited a different New York than I did, an Upper East Side sanctum of private schools and charity events and long summers in the Hamptons. Their husbands worked in finance. They had family compounds in Palm Beach and boutique vineyards.

Among them was Ashley, whom her friends jokingly referred to as Barbie (she was lithe and blond). "I'm the beginner's beginner," she said. "I'm nervous because everyone's better than me." There was Abby, a droll, self-described "Jersey Girl," a bit younger than the others, who had a fledgling fashion company. "It's been a while since I consistently surfed," she said. "I'm hoping my muscle memory will come back on day two." She, in fact, was my partner, because we were roughly matched in skill.

There was Vanessa, who off and on the waves looked as if she could have been a model for a surfwear company. She seemed particularly driven, making up for lost time. "I started surfing after I had kids and decided it was the best thing I had ever done," she said. "I was extremely frustrated that because I started so late in life, I'm never going to get really good."

"She rips! She's being modest, and she's got a paddle that is insane." This came from Kathy, who, I was to learn, was basically the reason the others were there. She seemed the troop leader, a vivacious raconteur who always seemed up for adventure, whether it was one more wave or one more game of Cards Against Humanity (one of the late-night diversions we would fall into).

"I'm working on my whitewater climb," she said. "I may have pulled one or two off, but I didn't move my feet enough." I nodded without actually understanding what she was talking about, for my definition of surfing had mostly dwindled to "Ride the board to the beach without getting killed."

We were about to undergo that curious experience of a group of mostly strangers facing a physical and mental challenge together. I imagined myself a Hercule Poirot type, in the thick of some seaside drama, observing the dynamics and getting to know everyone while also being a bit aloof. I sensed that we all had our reasons for being here. Some of these were the simple surf goals expressed that night, but others were more profound.

*

In one of the Surf Simply rooms, where we would go for stretching exercises or lessons on how to read a surf forecast, my eye was immediately caught by an impressively sprawling, flowchart-style mural, titled "The Tree of Knowledge," which occupied almost the entire wall.

"The Tree of Knowledge" was the intellectual heart of Surf Simply, a master blueprint of the whole DNA of the sport. It seemed a bit grandiose, but I respected the sincerity and thought that went into it. I would peer into its vastness, feeling like an explorer at the edge of the known world.

There were five main headings, for each of the Surf Simply skill levels—echoes of the Dreyfus model—with dozens of surfing skills branching off from each. I'd optimistically identified myself to Surf Simply as level two. ("Level 2 surfers can comfortably stand on the board and are focusing on catching unbroken waves.")

The numbers are a rough guide, for skill learning can be wildly erratic. Some days, I was virtually level three; other times I was flirting with level one. But I was struck by how vast the range of skills contained in the simple word "surfing" was and how few I'd even attempted ("whitewater floaters," "faded take off," "drop knee turns").

When I met Rupert Hill, Surf Simply's other cofounder and also an Englishman, I mentioned that I was surprised by how much surfing experience the other guests seemed to have. What I was really asking was, how long is this going to take me? "On average, level one will take you, surfing every day, a week or ten days. Level two, a month. Level three, a year. And level four"—he paused to reflect on the answer—"like a decade."

Ten *years* of regular surfing. I didn't even want to ask about level five. These numbers, he stressed, needed to be taken literally. He'll meet someone who says they've been surfing two years, only to find out they meant *one* week last year and *one* week this year. "They've been surfing for two weeks, not two years."

Ru, as he's known, confessed that he found surfing "the most difficult sport I've ever tried to learn." He paused. "Maybe except for boxing, where you're trying to remember all this stuff but someone punches you in the face."

He identified in surfing something I'd seen in my other attempts at skill acquisition: that the idea of what you thought of as being competent at something didn't really match what actually being competent at that thing was, by the time you got there.

"The more you learn, the more you realize you don't know," he said. "The further away the finish line gets with every piece of new knowledge."

Hill and Knight met years ago, in Cornwall, where they both learned the sport in the heart of England's surf scene. When Hill first came to Nosara, in 2007, he was the prototypical surf instructor, a guy with a car and some boards strapped to the roof. Knight followed soon after, and they opened a surf shop in town, where they'd do walk-in lessons.

But they were thinking of something more than the usual one-and-done model of vacation surf lessons. They started to think about more of a proper pedagogy. They'd taught plenty of beginners, and had coached competition surfers, but the middle—"where 99 percent of surfing was"—seemed curiously bereft of coaching. In the secretive, guild-like, historically male-dominated world of surfing, skills were often treated as just something you had magically imbibed in the water as a young grom (that's surfer talk for a kid) from some mystical elder with flecks of seaweed in his stubble.

Hill and Knight wanted to demystify surfing. "There is a mystique that is earned, but too promoted," Hill said. He was never one of the "cool kids" of surfing. "I really wanted to take this thing that was for the cool kids and say, 'It's just as much yours.'"

Rather than build up the mythos of surfing, they wanted to break it down. "The industry norm," Hill said, "is that people really don't approach surfing as a sport." Rather, it's presented as a *lifestyle*. Hill thinks all *that* stuff—"sitting in the ocean and being overwhelmed by nature"—just happens on its own.

To get better quicker, he suggested, you needed to treat surfing as a sport, with all the tools that entails: a rigorous, thoughtful skills development plan; video feedback and analysis; and drills.

Which is why, the following morning, when Abby and I first met our coach, Jessie Carnes, we were told we were going to spend the entire day "in the whitewater." Meaning we would be catching only the waves that had already long broken. The place where kids and tourists frolicked.

Knight advised us to not feel slighted. "We use the whitewater not as 'this is where you go as a beginner, and then you can go out the back'"—the term for riding out past where the waves were breaking. "We're using it to get high repetition, to learn motor skills." The sheer number of hurdles in catching unbroken waves meant, for us, that there'd be only a few chances in a few hours. The whitewater was like a tennis serving machine, endlessly sending waves like balls.

Our dismay was also tempered by the fact that everyone else was in the whitewater as well. More experienced surfers often blanched at this. Knight recalled that Eddie, for instance, a Surf Simply alum, asked him, "I have to do *what*?"

The whitewater was not only helpful, Knight said, but *harder*. "The faster the board goes, the more stable it becomes," he said. "It's like riding a bicycle very slowly;

it's incredibly difficult." He found it amusing that people thought of the whitewater as the "safe zone." "If you can get somebody surfing well in the whitewater, they're going to rip the wave to shreds when they get out the back."

And so, after some introductory stretching, Jessie led us into the water. A former top-ranked competitive surfer from Florida, she was irrepressibly sunny. Jessie would smile so much that at the end of the day there would be creases where her smile had broken through the heavy-duty sunblock, so it looked as if she were smiling even when she wasn't. She had us start the morning lying prone on our surfboards, working on simple turns in the frothing surf. She was trying to instill in us the idea that a surfboard was like a control panel, with various buttons to press to make it do what you wanted.

In the whitewater, I did feel a bit like the chastened "advanced beginner" being sent back to square one—as if I'd really come so far from my first days. But Hill had told me most of what you did in surfing could actually be done on your knees. "The only reason we stand is that allows you to press those buttons with more power and speed." And besides, the whitewater was *fun*, like boogie boarding as a kid. I could grab a wave at will and still have a longer ride than I'd ever had at Rockaway. We moved to our feet and started making big carves. We leaned back on the board to slow, or moved forward to accelerate. We grabbed the rail and practiced little moves like cross stepping up and down the length of the board.

I resolved to embrace it, to become the Kelly Slater of the whitewater. And I tried to remember the idea that had arisen in all my skills: You had to crawl before you could walk. In singing, I needed to do pitch-matching exercises before I could sing songs. In chess, it was best to study tactics and strategy before simply letting yourself loose upon the sixty-four squares. If I were to simply go and start messing around in the big waves, I'd be in over my head, figuratively and literally.

There would be time for that, and as it happened, a larger swell was predicted for later in the week.

*

We soon fell into an intoxicating routine. Mornings, we'd gather for breakfast around a large table, a bounty of brightly glistening tropical fruits arrayed before us. On a television nearby, an endless spool of surf videos played—a world of expansive blue horizons and sweeping aerial photography, as surfers, all streaked hair and zinc-nosed, gave moody, soulful glances into the camera when not hucking "airs" off some Indonesian crest. The videos were always on mute because Hill didn't like the music they featured. Instead, we bathed in a soothing stream of Astrud Gilberto and Miles Davis.

We'd surf, break for lunch, then surf again. Afternoons would feature a class or two on a subject like surfing etiquette or how to read a surf forecast. All this was detailed on a surfboard-shaped chalkboard in the communal space. Given the playful, slightly raunchy spirit of the group, I wasn't entirely surprised to come down one morning and find that the itinerary had been tampered with. Whatever had been planned for 10:00 a.m., we were now, apparently, going to "EAT ASS." I still recall the particularly English look of prim, silent disapproval that flickered across Knight's face as he eyed the board for the first time that morning.

Nights we would return for a dinner, at the resort or at a restaurant in town, then a few mescal-fueled rounds of Cards Against Humanity with "the girls." One notable game was interrupted by a scorpion, which I was commanded to dispatch. Disconcertingly, it scurried into an electrical outlet.

Or Kathy, also an aspiring singer, and I would grab the guitar and try to start sing-alongs, mostly to 1980s alternative rock staples. With our little dorms, our classes, and our sophomoric humor and gossip about the instructors, it all felt like college. I probably hadn't had as much fun *since* college.

In the water, it was dawning on me that I'd jumped off the deep end. We'd finally gone "out the back," past the whitewater. Just getting there proved a whole new experience. The required paddling length was three times what I was used to. And where at Rockaway I could often power through oncoming waves by lifting my body a bit off the board, letting the whitewater rush through, here the waves were too big; they would knock me back nearly to shore.

So I had to learn an entirely new maneuver known as turtling, which we'd practiced one afternoon with Jessie in the resort's pool. This involved sliding off the board as the wave was approaching, then quickly ducking under the board, "dropping like an anchor," and grasping the rails. As the wave rushed by, the idea was to thrust the board in the opposite direction. If all went well, the wave thundered past you with little impact. If it didn't, you'd get the board ripped out of your hands.

My quiet winter Rockaway surfing also hadn't prepared me for the maelstrom that is a crowded surf break. Just paddling out, you had to look not only for incoming waves but for the constant cross traffic of surfers going down the line.

Sometimes I'd reemerge from a turtle dive, wipe the water from my eyes, and instantly see a surfer bearing down on me. In those moments where I had foolishly put myself in someone's path, there were two probable outcomes. One, I was in the way of someone really good.

They'd angrily shake their head but could easily avoid me. The second scenario was that I was in front of someone who barely knew what they were doing. This meant they wouldn't angrily call me a kook—something I was strangely sensitive to—but it also meant they didn't have the skill to avoid me. I would simply plunge below the water and hope for the best.

Before going for a wave—one of the several hundred that rolls across your average break in an hour—you had to make sure one of the seemingly dozens of other nearby surfers wasn't also intending to go for it. Sometimes you went for it anyway—because you were never entirely sure if someone was going to make their wave—only pulling out at the last moment if they did.

It often seemed like high-stakes game theory, the "surfer's dilemma" of how a growing pool of surfers could share a finite supply of waves. Surfing, to a strategist, is what's known as a "mixed-motive game"; it's best if at least *someone* catches a wave so it's not wasted, but each person would prefer it was them. This leads to a fragile peace, and it was almost inevitable that you got in someone's way. As Danny had told me, his least favorite part of learning to surf was the idea that "others in the water would typically prefer me not to be there."

On the second day, with Abby and Jessie and me finally "out the back," I realized with a start that the waves looked massive, at least twice as high as what I was used to at Rockaway. Thankfully, they seemed to break at a more forgiving pitch.

We spent some time learning how to read those waves, to tell which way they were breaking or to gauge the steepness and speed of the wave by how dark it was. As we floated, Jessie mentioned offhand that she occasionally saw venomous sea snakes in the water. They weren't harmful to humans unless, she added, you got stung between your fingers, which I thought about every time I thrust my slightly splayed hands into the water for a paddle. Sometimes, bobbing placidly past the impact zone, everyone would suddenly drop to their boards, like a spooked herd of gazelles, and start rapidly paddling out to the open ocean to avoid an unexpectedly large wave rumbling through.

Jessie gave me specific instructions. When a wave was approaching, I would begin paddling—roughly five paddles—toward an imagined "six o'clock" position on the beach. Then with the wave upon me, she wanted me to shift my focus toward seven (or five) o'clock and "turbo paddle" three times. Just before the pop-up, I was to push down on the right (or left, depending on the wave direction) rail of the surfboard, hooking the board to the molecular tension of the wave face. Then I'd pop up, keeping my vision focused down the line of the curling wave, aimed toward three (or nine) o'clock.

This attentional focus was key. In wave-pool experiments where surfers were equipped with waterproof eye-tracking devices, expert surfers' glances immediately shot to that part of the wave where they were headed. Novices, meanwhile, looked at themselves. They weren't thinking of where they were going; they were thinking about how to stay balanced, which only made it harder to actually stay balanced.

*

The instructions I was being given all seemed a bit surfing-by-numbers.

Which was precisely the point. Coaches, Hill said, will advise something like "drive through the turn with more power," without explaining the fundamental steps that make that happen. "That's like teaching someone to be a comedian by saying you should really be funnier." Rather than tell someone they need to be "in better rhythm with the wave," Hill will go through a video with a student and have them try to properly time the maneuvers. Surf Simply will sometimes put students in the water with just fins and a mask and let some "waves pound over them," as Knight put it, to help them get a feel for it all.

On my first few attempts, I didn't catch the wave at all. I soon realized I was obsessed with the idea of my board's nose plunging beneath the surface and me being pile driven into the ocean floor. But that very fear of pearling *was making it more likely I would.*

There is often, in moments of anxiety, a disconnect in skills learning between instinct and proper technique. In singing, when you approached a high note and your only thought was stretching upward, it actually helped to bend your knees and dip *down.* In skiing, beginners lean back to avoid falling, when they should be leaning forward. In surfing, when your brain was screaming to apply the brake, you needed to punch the accelerator.

"People worried about nose-diving are slowing their paddling and weighting the board back to lift up the nose," Hill said. "Which is the opposite of what you want to do." On a steep wave, you needed to commit even *harder,* to speed your paddling and get your weight forward to get down that steep slope even faster.

Soon, Abby and I were both managing to ride the waves—thanks to a push from Jessie. Getting pushed is a hallmark of learning to surf; to paddle well, you need a particular muscular strength that's really only developed through paddling. I felt sheepish about this, but Knight had told me about a group of Australian commandos who had come one week—"the most ripped guys I'd ever seen." They all needed pushing.

My first proper Costa Rican wave, a six- or seven-foot

right-hander, was just sheer, stupid bliss. It was ten sec-onds that felt like ten minutes. To anyone looking from the shore, I was just another tourist on just another aver-age wave, but I felt like Neptune, on some sea chariot, ready to "touch the elemental magma of our souls," a line from journalist Matt George quoted in *The History of Surfing*.

It was also all a bit hectic. On one ride, I suddenly found myself barreling toward Ulrike, who was in the water and holding on to her board. As we locked eyes, I felt my board pointing straight toward her. Knight shouted, "Left!" and I was just able to carve away, wiping out in the process. Jessie pushed Abby into one wave just as a guy on a shortboard was popping up. The breach of etiquette forced him off the wave. Jessie apologized pro-fusely and said, "She's just had the ride of her life!" He shook his head, smiled, and gave a thumbs-up.

Later, we reported to a little hut with a television monitor for our video coaching session. The land-side view of the day's events was often not a pretty sight; video feedback was a sobering reality check. In the water, I felt as if I were careening down the face of monster tubes. On the video, I looked like the "fun dad" in a kiddie pool. And where a proficient longboarder would stand tall and non-chalant as they flowed down the line, my face was knotted into a grimace, and I was hunched over, all thin and bent; for my troubles I earned the nickname Gumby.

However valuable the feedback, it was inexact. "The feedback the ocean gives you is not consistent with your personal skill level," Hill said. "The ocean is this big uncontrollable variable." People might go out and do everything right and still have a mediocre surf, or they might have the ride of their lives through the fortunate intervention of a coach and a bit of luck.

"I would urge you to have this in your head," Hill said.

"Don't beat yourself up in the sessions that went badly, and don't pat yourself on the back too hard when you have a really good one."

It seemed like a good mantra. You just did the best you could. It might work out, it might not, but the rest was out of your hands.

Later, lying in bed, I could still feel myself skidding down a wave, the press of breaking water at my back. When I closed my eyes, I would see dark bands moving toward me on an undulating and endless horizon. I could feel myself twisting in position, craning my aching neck, trying to position myself into the center of that life force, to see where it would take me.

ON THE VIRTUES OF STARTING LATE

The legendary pro surfer Phil Edwards once said, "The best surfer is the one who's having the most fun." Like many novices, I heard this early and took it to heart, even though I largely suspected it wasn't true. It seemed like something a pro surfer might say to make hapless schmucks like me feel better. To my eyes, the best surfer was the one who wasn't flapping violently at waves that rushed beneath him, or getting tossed into the washing machine on the ones he managed to catch.

Harry suggested I reverse the equation: "The better you get, the more fun you can have in a much wider range of conditions."

Our group was certainly having fun. Through the course of the week, I was struck, more than once, by the image of forty-somethings brimming with glee as they picked up or refined elemental skills.

The lower down they were on the learning curve, the more profound the effect. They became better surfers, but you could see them developing in other ways before your eyes. These were people who'd temporarily abandoned the safe harbors of adulthood—their bankable competency at work, the familiar rationalizations of what was age appropriate, that fallback move of relinquishing the idea of growth to their children—to take part in a challenging, risky, and maybe even futile endeavor.

"So many people get to midlife and they don't want to do things they're not good at," Hill told me. "Constantly doing things that you suck at is a great life lesson in itself." Whether it was moving from whitewater drills to unbroken waves, or going from competent riding down the line to powerful cutbacks, you could read the change in people's faces. The self-doubt and even fear at the beginning of the week had faded. They had a new idea of what surfing was and who they were.

I was beginning to get a sense of what surfing meant to some of them. Ulrike, my bungalow companion, spoke of a close friend who had developed brain cancer and died five months later. Her long-delayed goal of getting to the water had acquired a new urgency.

Dorritt, one of the women from New York, had told me that for her surfing was a way to try to recover from a wrenching divorce. She equated gaining confidence in the waves with regaining strength emotionally. If you could handle what the ocean dished out, you could get through almost anything.

And you never knew what life, like the ocean, would throw at you. Danny, after our week in Costa Rica, received a diagnosis of lymphoma. He was still surfing, but also "more cautious about the situations I put my body in."

Kathy, whom I'd secretly dubbed the Queen Bee of the group—for she just seemed to draw people into her orbit, through charisma and sheer life energy—had regaled me the whole week with riotous stories of her surf adventures.

Like notches on her surfboard, she had logged time with a ragtag bunch of instructors all over the world. There was "Hawaii Joe," actually from New Jersey; or another, a pilot-surfer who told her, as they flew in a small plane over the Indonesian archipelago, that he could "bring any woman to orgasm in fifteen seconds." It took longer just to get your wet suit off.

Along with Vanessa, she was also easily the best surfer of the group. I wanted to know how this mother of three had become so committed, and gotten so good, in midlife.

"I used to watch the surfers from the beach by my house," she said. This went on for years. I imagined her as a character in a Jane Austen novel, cloistered by insecurity and societal expectation. One day, with her friend Ashley and a group of other moms, she finally braved the waters. "I half stood up, once," she said. "My ribs felt bruised. We emailed each other about our various surf ailments and never spoke of it again."

Like an itch that you can never fully scratch, it kept coming up. Around five years ago, she said, her family was on holiday in Waikiki. Her kids—those catalysts for adult learning—wanted to try surfing, and one of the local surf "uncles" told her she should try too. Her husband, eyeing the genial old instructors, encouraged her. Just then an instructor named Trevor, whom she described as a "younger, cuter, less buff version of Laird Hamilton," showed up to give her the lesson. "My husband just laughed," she said.

She spent the whole morning catching waves on what felt like Jaws—the famous break in Maui—but that the grim truth of photography later revealed to be a "lake-like surface." She thumbed through the photos, looking for "hot-mom shots," finding instead one of her "on my lake-like non-wave, with my bottom unflatteringly at half-mast, full crack showing, in the face of this poor kid."

"Horrified," she told me. "But hooked." So began the long hours, the endless repetition, the stutter steps of progress. She made the beginner mistakes. She looked at her board so much on pop-ups that an instructor suggested writing the words "Look up" on the nose. She did.

She took a heavy soft-top board to her own nose, breaking it and requiring twenty stitches. "I had a complete cast on my face," she said, "and was ordered out of the water for six weeks." She got back in after five.

She would change, shivering, in winter parking lots so as not to get the car sandy. Looking back, she said, "I thought I was such a badass surfer back then. I look at the pictures now and laugh. I feel like the better you get, the worse you realize you are."

Metacognition—your knowledge of what you know—is a harsh mistress. As a beginner in any discipline, you not only lack skill; you lack a larger sense of what you don't yet know. Suddenly you're in bigger waves, and like those infants in chapter 2 the old rules about what worked no longer apply. Kathy told me she'd always had her foot on the brakes a bit, terrified of getting held down by waves, thrashing and squandering breath when she did. "A wise instructor told me, 'There's no point in fighting, because the ocean always wins.'"

It took her several years to become calmer when the conditions were out of her comfort zone, and she still gets butterflies "even on the smaller days." She had a near encounter with a shark in Hawaii and was still shaking the next day in the water. The instructor kept saying, "What shark?" and winking.

Now she feels a prevailing sense of calm in the water. "There are no computers, phones, complaining kids. You must be totally in tune with what you are doing." It is her husband who now feels uneasy if she goes out alone. A friend had joked, "He didn't mind that you were going to Tortola for three days with a hot surf instructor, but he doesn't want you going out alone?" Her husband jokes that surfing itself, not any instructor, has "become her affair."

She has earned the nickname Just One More for her propensity for staying in the water. She's sported reef rash and black eyes. Once, after heading straight from a surf session to a black-tie charity dinner on Long Island, and to the general amusement of her neighbors at the dinner table, she reached for a fallen napkin and a stream of ocean water gushed from her nostrils.

When she first started, she had the idea of surfing a monumental wave like Pipeline. "I had no idea how insanely far that was from my reality," she told me.

Now her goals, honed by experience, are more reasonable. Having started later, she knows that she needs to get "years' worth of waves to catch up with what I missed" but also that "my body will give way to the strains of surfing faster than, say, golf." She always laments to Vanessa, who is eight years younger, that she has so much more time to learn.

Starting older does yield one huge benefit. "It makes me appreciate every second I have out there so much more," she said.

*

If you were to visit Rockaway Beach in the early summer, somewhere in the vicinity of Sixty-ninth Street, you would see the ocean populated by a frolicking mass of children riding colorful soft-top boards close to shore. Look a bit harder and you might spot someone standing up tall among the Lilliputians, a stupid grin on his face. That would be me.

The first summer after I'd started taking lessons, I

enrolled my then seven-year-old daughter in Locals' surf camp, my thinking being I didn't want her to have to wait until she was getting junk mail from AARP to decide if surfing was something she wanted to try. As with chess, I felt as if I were reflexively trying not to let gender get in the way. Fathers are more likely to engage in rough play with sons than with daughters and seem more willing to let sons take risks than daughters. Fathers, it's been argued, are actually the main "gender socializing agents" when it comes to children. By getting her on a board early, I wanted to instill in her the feeling *Here's another thing I can do.*

Summer, which brings much smaller waves and much larger crowds, is basically off-season for serious Rockaway surfers. But having come all that way, I thought it seemed wrong to simply sit on the beach and spectate, as other parents mostly seemed to do. I would cadge a spare soft-top from one of the Mikes and paddle out. Luckily, my daughter was still of the age where seeing her father ride up alongside her in the water was a source of pride, not embarrassment. She (and I) would puff up if one of the tanned and toned young instructors complimented me.

I had an ulterior motive in enrolling her in camp. If I could interest her in surfing, I'd have a future sidekick, one I could enlist to tilt the democratic voting process over our family holidays in favor of places that just happened to be near surf spots (my wife had tried it once and still wasn't sold).

And so we surfed. We surfed a spot near Bordeaux that happened to be, to my daughter's glee, right next to a nudist resort (they didn't surf). We surfed with a former pro and her kids in Lisbon on a crowded swimming beach and enjoyed ice cream afterward. We surfed rocky Makaha Beach in Lima, where a tough Brazilian instructor pretended not to hear her protestations that she was getting tired. If she'd been alone with me, she would have folded sooner, and I would have humored her. Not wanting to look soft in the eyes of the teacher, she persisted, riding her biggest waves to date. We surfed off Costa Rica's Papagayo Peninsula in uncharacteristically small seas, but this allowed her, for the first time, to catch her own wave.

As I marked her progress, I realized I'd more or less reached level three—"competence"—in the Dreyfus model.

In this stage, learners begin to become *emotionally involved* in their learning. In the beginner or advanced beginner stages, learners, they write, cling to rules: "If the rules do not work, the performer, rather than feeling remorse for his or her mistakes, can rationalize that he or she had not been given adequate rules."

At Rockaway, I could explain away a wipeout by saying I hadn't yet been taught the particular response to a particular kind of wave. But with competence comes a personal stake in failure or success. You have to *own* your mistakes, and if you do well, you're happy not simply because you did well but because of the choices you made that led to your success. Early on, I got a thrill from riding a wave, but later satisfaction would come from paddling to the best spot to *catch* the wave.

I had the sense I would be happy staying at this level. I know it seems anathema, in this goal-minded, performance-driven age, to be content with something less than mastery.

A character in David Foster Wallace's novel *Infinite Jest* scornfully describes the "Complacent type" in tennis, "who improves radically until he hits a plateau, and is content with the radical improvement he's made to get to the plateau." Eventually, he starts losing, because "his whole game is based on this plateau." He professes the "love of the game" but has a "tight and hangdog . . . smile."

But surfing wasn't competitive for me. There wasn't any marathon finishing time or cycling PR I was trying to beat. I didn't have any quantified performance metrics. I didn't know what "losing" meant in surfing, other than perhaps losing the joy of doing the thing. If the day came when I felt bored riding down the line, I could start experimenting with other things. I could travel to new places; I could buy a new board.

I was far from jaded. The smallest waves at Rockaway gave me a little charge when I saw them on the surfcam. Where a friend might complain that the waves were not up to a certain standard, the fact that they were *waves* was usually enough for me. There was nothing I was bored about in surfing.

Did I hope to get better? Of course. But surfing was not my job, not my side hustle, not even my life's passion. It was just another of my "capricious and tenacious enthusiasms," in the words of the writer James Dickey. I wanted to be as good as it took to keep it being fun for me.

If I'm doomed to be a mediocre surfer, I'm okay with that. The word "mediocre," after all, comes from Old Latin, meaning "halfway to the top." That seemed a fair climb from my starting point of nothing. A plateau in surfing seems like something I could happily ride for a long time.

CHAPTER SIX

HOW WE LEARN
TO DO THINGS

THE ART OF KEEPING THINGS IN THE AIR

After I had struggled for months with my various skills, it seemed time to take a step back and think more about how we actually learn skills. But I didn't want a mere textbook exercise. I wanted to learn *something* as I learned about learning.

Juggling seemed perfect. It's almost a pure motor skill; unlike, say, walking, there's little functional reason to keep multiple objects aloft in the air, other than to prove it can be done.

It's long been used as a convenient way to study human performance. Juggling showed up early in the psychology literature. The study that helped popularize the idea of the "learning curve"? Its subjects juggled. The cover of one widely used textbook, Richard A. Magill's *Motor Learning: Concepts and Applications*, depicts—you got it—a juggler!

As Peter Beek, a researcher in human movement sci-

ences at Amsterdam's Vrije Universiteit, explained as we
sat in his office one afternoon, there are many reasons why
juggling is an exceedingly useful way to study learning.

You need a task you can easily do in a lab. You need a
task that no one can do right away, that has to be *learned*.
Yet you want a task that isn't too difficult so people don't
immediately give up. Most people can begin to learn
three-ball juggling in a few days.* Juggling success is easy
to measure: You juggle balls, or you drop balls. Last, learning is aided by motivation, and unlike the typical range
of weird, monotonous experimental tasks used in motor-
skills research—moving cursors with joysticks, tapping
out sequences on buttons—juggling is actually *fun*.

Unlike some of the other skills I'd set out to acquire,
juggling wasn't a lifelong dream. I wanted to learn to juggle to learn about learning. Still, I couldn't help thinking
it would be a clever party trick. Months later, at gatherings
my daughter was invited to, I'd find juggling to be a virtual
dad superpower.

For here's the thing about skills: Once you acquire
even the most rudimentary basics of something like juggling, you've already set yourself apart from the greater
part of humanity. Take an informal poll of your friends
or co-workers. Chances are very few of them can capably
juggle three balls. Four? Even fewer. Five? Now you're
spending time in juggling chat rooms.

This is one of the secret payoffs of skill learning: It
may take you years to become a master, but with just a
little time and effort you've learned something that others
can't do—that you yourself, a short while ago, couldn't

* Three balls is generally considered the entry point of actual juggling, which
is broadly defined as the ability to manipulate more objects than one has the
hands for.

do. As minor a pursuit as three-ball juggling may seem, for me it once had the air of impossibility, until suddenly, magically, it did not.

*

The first step was finding a teacher. In New York City, where the local bulletin boards bristle with ads for lessons of all stripes—improv theater, sausage making, tarot-card reading—this wasn't a problem. I quickly found Heather Wolf, who ran something called JuggleFit ("Learn to Juggle for a Healthy Body & Brain"). She lived one neighborhood away.

Over coffee in a leafy nearby park, she told me her story. Graduating from UCLA with a degree in sociology, she returned to her real love—playing the electric bass— and enrolled in L.A.'s Musicians Institute. One day, she noticed a job posted on the bulletin board: The Ringling Bros. Circus needed a bassist.

"I didn't even know the circus had a band," she told me. "I just always wanted to tour." For the next six years, she lived on the circus train. One season, a new show was announced in which the whole cast—but not the musicians—had to be able to juggle. She figured as long as everyone else was learning it, she would too. She kept at it, eventually learning to juggle five balls, the entry point for expert juggling.

"I'm not the best juggler in town," she said, though with a touch of New York City chutzpah she added, "I do believe I'm the best juggling *teacher* in town." People who are experts, she explained, "may have forgotten what it's like to be at that early stage." This was something I'd heard from various motor-skill researchers: As cool as it might sound, you don't want Michael Jordan or Lionel Messi teaching your kid's basketball or soccer camp. He would struggle to explain what *he* does, much less break it down for a nine-year-old.

Like many New York enterprises, Wolf's juggling was a side hustle. An avid birder, she spent most of her time working on the website for Cornell University's Lab of Ornithology. Her roommate used to clown for now-defunct Ringling. "He's not with the circus anymore, but he tours all over, with people like Britney Spears. Clowns in New York get a lot of gigs, actually."

A week later, we were in my living room. She produced three colored scarves. Sensing my vague disappointment—where are the balls?—she said that "juggling in slow motion" would not only help me trace out the pattern in the air but boost my confidence. One way to improve learning, research has suggested, is to make skills seem easier in the beginning.

As I held two scarves in my right hand and one in my (dominant) left, she asked me to simply throw the scarves, one after the other, to the top corners of an imaginary box positioned over my head. I did, and the scarves fluttered to the floor. Easy enough. Next, she wanted me to throw and then catch the scarves, once. Not so bad. Then she wanted me to keep repeating the process. This quickly became overwhelming, and my flurry of scarves looked as if I were frenetically ransacking a bargain bin at Macy's.

"I can do a bit of mind reading when I teach people to juggle," Wolf said, "and I can tell you're thinking of this as a pattern."

Just throw to the corners, she reiterated. Don't *think* of the overall pattern you're throwing; just throw. Wolf didn't want me to think of the catches, either; if I just kept throwing to the corners, my hands would move to where they needed to be for the catch.

"The key to learning juggling," she said, "is not thinking."

HOW THINKING GETS IN THE WAY OF LEARNING

"Almost everyone can ride a bicycle," observed the physicist David Jones, "but almost no one knows how they do it."

Ask the average rider how to turn a bicycle, and they'll probably answer, "Turn the handlebars in the direction you want to go." But this isn't technically true. As bike geeks from Wilbur Wright onward have noted, to go left, *you first have to steer to the right.**

Hardly anyone knows this because hardly anyone is aware of it. And we're not aware of it, because to actually know this fact, or at least to think of it while riding, wouldn't help us ride.

What makes skills so *skillful* is that we don't really know how we do them. This is why written instructions are so often of little use in skill learning. "Knowledge helps," wrote Jerome Bruner, "only when it descends into habits."

The problem with beginners is that they're always thinking about *themselves doing the skill.* When we do try to think about an "overlearned" skill like walking, we're likely to perform worse, under the theory of "reinvestment," as proposed by the motor-learning expert Rich Masters.

People who have had a stroke, for instance, often suffer from an "asymmetrical gait," or a limp. They must relearn how to walk, but because they're self-conscious of how

---

* The physicist Joel Fajans has a nifty method for experiencing this "counter-steering" for yourself. While riding downhill (so you don't have to pedal), take your left hand off the handlebar. As you do that, put your right hand, palm open, on the right handlebar, and slightly apply pressure. Because your palm is open, the bike can turn only to the left. But you will go right. See Joel Fajans, "Steering in Bicycles and Motorcycles," *American Journal of Physics* 68, no. 7 (July 2000): 654–59.

they now walk, they think about the mechanics of walking, which only makes it look more *mechanical*. To learn to walk well, they're going to have to learn implicitly. "The trick," as Masters has described it, "is getting people to learn to move without knowing that they're learning."

When we become skilled at something, it becomes automatic. We don't have to think much about it, because our brain, running on virtual autopilot, is constantly making predictions—and most of its predictions are true.

As Pablo Celnik, the genial, Argentine-born director at Johns Hopkins University's Human Brain Physiology and Stimulation Lab, told me during a visit one afternoon, the brain does this for efficiency's sake, but also because of an inherent time lag.

"Your brain receives feedback about what you're doing, and that takes time—about eighty to a hundred milliseconds," he told me. "We live in the past. Whatever we see now is actually about a hundred milliseconds ago for the motor domain."

These predictions help us get through daily life. When they fail, we look for explanations. We trip on the sidewalk, our brain gets this news one hundred milliseconds later, and we accusingly stare at the offending crack. The surprise violated our model. But when we try to tickle ourselves, nothing happens, because we already know what it's going to feel like. Our cerebellum has "canceled" the sensory input, suppressed neurons. There's no surprise; the model is intact.

When you first get on an escalator that has stopped working, you gingerly take a few steps. You may even "feel" motion. That's because your brain has trained itself, through many repetitions. It's ready for the escalator; it's *predicted* it. We know, in our heads, that it's broken, but we can't help thinking, in our bodies, that it's not.

BEING THE ROBOT, SLOWING TIME, AND
REPETITION WITHOUT REPETITION:
HOW WE GET BETTER AT SKILLS

Juggling, I soon learned, wasn't really the skill I thought it was.

Like many beginners', my mind's eye of juggling was what's known as a shower pattern—three objects being passed in a clockwise semicircle. But the shower pattern is much harder than the "cascade," the most common form of multi-object juggling. In the cascade, objects cross each other and land in the opposite hand. Traced out, it looks like a figure eight tipped on its side.

I'd also envisioned that jugglers were tracking each object in flight, which is precisely what beginners try to do. When my daughter gave it a go, her head was wildly snapping as she tried to monitor each scarf.

But, as Heather Wolf had shown me, juggling is less about throwing individual objects than throwing to a pattern, like tossing to a little algorithm in the sky.* It's little wonder so many noteworthy mathematicians, from Claude Shannon to Ronald Graham, were drawn to juggling.

In juggling, unlike most sports, you don't actually want to keep your eyes on the balls. Jugglers look to the *apex* of where things are thrown—that external focus again—and only ever have a peripheral sense of all those objects in flight. This has been confirmed by studies in which most of a juggler's vision was blocked, except for a thin slice up

---

* Claude Shannon, the renowned mathematician (and juggling enthusiast), even expressed juggling as a formula: $(F + D)H = (V + D)N$. F stands for the time a ball spends in flight; D is the "dwell time," or how much time it spends in the hand; N is number of balls; H is number of hands; and V, for "vacant," is how much time a hand spends empty.

near the parabola of the throwing arc, and they juggled just fine. Good jugglers can do it blindfolded.

Back in my living room, I was having better luck with the scarves. I could now keep the three scarves aloft for a number of repetitions, or what jugglers call runs. We moved on to balls. First, Wolf asked me to just throw a ball, with a relatively high arc, from one hand to the other. Easy enough. Then she wanted me to reel off three of those throws, but let the balls simply fall.

This would help me diagnose my throws. In juggling, the throw is *everything*. With a good throw comes a nearly automatic catch (*prediction*, again).

I was struck by how fast it all seemed. I got the first three balls in flight relatively well, but then I experienced a common beginner's malady: I rushed the fourth throw, which messed up the timing of the pattern. "You have more time than you think," Wolf said.

Over time, she said, juggling would come to seem slower. And it did. As you sometimes hear a professional athlete describe it, I felt as though I had more time with the balls. The pattern was as clear as skywriting; the balls seemed to *hang* in the air.

The neuroscientist David Eagleman, who has researched people's perception of time, offered me a compelling explanation of this slowing. When we start out with a skill like juggling, he suggested, novices pay attention to everything.

My early juggling went something like this: *Okay, I'm throwing one ball. And then another! Wait, I still have to throw another? What happened to that first one? Here it comes! I can't believe I'm throwing again—oops, here's that second ball! Did I just mess up my third throw? Should this throw be with my left or right? Wait, how did I get two balls in one hand? Why am I doing this again?*

The more things you have to pay attention to, the

faster time seems to move. But as you get better, you learn what to pay attention to. You have a better sense of what to expect. Suddenly you're not thinking about the balls at all. You're just tracing a pattern in the air. You have all sorts of spare attention. You can carry on a conversation while you juggle. Time seems more unoccupied, and thus slower.

Then you start to learn a new trick, and everything speeds up again.

*

Another classic novice problem I faced was that my throws, apart from being mistimed, were going everywhere. In juggling, little errors had big consequences: A throw that was just a few degrees off could end up being way off target by the time it came down.

"Be the robot!" Wolf would say. She wanted me to imagine I'd been programmed so my feet would stay still, my arms would be close to my sides when I threw, and I would move slowly and deliberately. My only job was to make clean throws, robot-like. She recommended juggling while facing a wall; with a natural barrier, I'd have little choice but to rein in my throws.

One key problem in skill learning is that our bodies have so many "degrees of freedom," as the renowned movement scientist Nikolai Bernstein put it. The human arm alone has, from the shoulder joint to the wrist joint, some twenty-six different degrees of freedom, or directions it can be moved. To do this, we need to effectively coordinate any number of the body's thousand-odd muscles and hundred billion neurons. The simplest act of throwing a ball starts to look like a busy airport control tower working in sync with an army of crack puppeteers.

Imagine trying to teach your child how to swing a baseball bat. There are all sorts of ways to swing it, but when it comes to baseball, only a small number of these will be useful. Novices, overwhelmed by the idea of orchestrating all these movements, tend to "freeze" their muscles, as Bernstein put it. They fight against their own bodies.

When I tried to teach batting to my daughter, her initial swing was like a gate: her feet planted, her knees rigid, her shoulders tightened, her forearms locked. She simply twisted her torso with the bat held in front of her and tried not to lose her balance. She wasn't unlocking those degrees of freedom.

Eventually, we learn to "unfreeze" the body and take advantage of muscles working in concert. We call it coordination. "One of the things that people learn as they get more skillful," as Richard Magill, a motor-skills expert, told me, "is to take advantage of what nature provides for free."

Learning a skill means doing the most with the least. Expert performers, we often say, "make it look easy." This is for good reason. When I visited New York University's Sports Performance Center, ahead of running the New York City Marathon, I was surprised to discover how riddled with inefficiency my running form was; for example, I unnecessarily clenched my shoulders. It seems a small thing, but over 26.1 miles it adds up, costing extra energy and interfering with breathing.

Pick any skill—from cello playing to cycling—and the findings are the same: As we get better, our movements become more efficient. This means "inhibiting" muscles that aren't needed and "exciting" the ones that are. If I ask you to clench your fist and raise only your pinkie, as you lift that one digit, you will be simultaneously instructing your other fingers *not* to move.

When Wolf advised me to "be the robot," she didn't mean to literally move like a robot, all herky-jerky (I was already doing that on my own). What she really intended was for me to *get out of the way* of my juggling.

Sometimes, she said, people will suddenly cry out, "I can't do this!" And she will have to point out, "You *are* doing it." The *robot* is doing it. The physical part of juggling is not really that demanding—simply throwing a ball from one place to another. What's hard is executing the "mental model" for each pattern. Poorly aimed throws are often just timing errors that disrupt the pattern.

When talking about skills, people often use the phrase "muscle memory." It's tempting to think that we're literally encoding some motion onto our muscles, that they harbor the memory of some act. But it's not really true. When you sign your name, your muscles seem to reflexively "know" how to apply pen to paper. But you could also draw a huge version of your signature on a chalkboard. You could spray-paint it on a wall. You could trace it out in the sand using your toe. You could pee it into a bank of snow (I did this as a kid, in the name of science). You could pull off a fairly decent version of your John Hancock with a pencil clenched in your mouth.

None of those things involve moving the same muscles in the same way. Rather, you're executing a "motor pattern" that resides in your brain. The muscles are simply doing what the brain tells them (even as they tell the brain what *it* should be doing).

Muscle memory also implies that when you perform a skill, you perform it the same way every time, the way you "remember" it. But even the most repetitive motor skills are always subtly changing. We need to constantly adapt and optimize. For this reason, Bernstein argued that when we practice some skill, we shouldn't simply repeat

"the *means of solution* of a motor problem time after time."
In other words, we shouldn't try to endlessly perfect that
one technique that seems to work, under the same set of
conditions. That's too rigid; if one little variable changes,
the technique might not work so well.

Instead, we should try to *solve* the problem every time,
which means we might even use a different technique. He
called it "repetition without repetition." And so good juggling practice is not simply about trying to do longer and
longer runs of the same old three-ball cascade. I knew the
solution to that problem; I just had to get there faster and
more consistently.

What would help make me better was to give myself
new problems to solve: starting a pattern with my weaker
hand (which has already "learned" some of the skill from
the dominant hand), or changing the height at which I was
juggling. I would switch rooms, switch objects. I would try
to walk and juggle. I tried to juggle while sitting. I listened
to music; I had conversations.

With every subtle change, *I* had to subtly change. I
would act like Karen Adolph's learning-to-walk infants,
for whom what looks like willy-nilly randomness is actually the powerful learning strategy of variable practice.

It's not that good jugglers never make mistakes. But
their constant problem solving has given them many more
solutions. Expertise, the chess grandmaster Jonathan
Rowson notes, means running out of unfamiliar mistakes.
Expert jugglers not only know the moment a ball leaves
their hand that they have made a mistake; they know how
to correct for it, mid-flight.

"Once you have a bad throw," Wolf told me, "rein it
in. *Be the robot.*" The key, she said, is "that you control the
balls; they don't control you."

WATCH AND LEARN:

CAN ONLINE VIDEOS TEACH YOU EVERYTHING?

Did I need a *teacher* to learn juggling? Couldn't I just go on YouTube?

In short, yes: YouTube is filled with a huge number of juggling videos, and some aren't bad. Watching others, moreover, and imitating them is perhaps *the* fundamental way humans learn.

"We're built to observe," as Luc Proteau, a professor in the Department of Kinesiology at the University of Montreal, told me. Our brain has a host of regions, termed the "action-observation network," that's sparked when we watch others do something in our "motor repertoire" (watching a dog bark, for instance, not *typically* being a human trait, doesn't activate the region).

We're simulating doing the task ourselves, warming up the same neurons that will be used when we actually give it a go. The action observation network isn't a substitute for action—only doing something will fully engage one's motor cortex—but rather a dress rehearsal.

But you need to *want* to learn. When we watch people trying to learn to dance or tie knots, as Emily Cross, a professor of psychology at Bangor University, told me, the action observation network is "more strongly engaged when you're watching to learn, as opposed to just passively spectating." Learning, she suggested, "primes the brain for picking up new information."

The more we want to learn, the more we prime the brain. The more curious you are to know the answer to a question, the better chance you'll remember it. People who believe they will need to *teach* something that they learn seem to learn motor skills better than those simply learning them. Curiously, we seem to learn better when we watch the error-filled efforts of novices. When we watch the flawless performance of experts, after all, we're watching someone who isn't learning. Seeing learning happening actually helps *us* learn.

You can't always learn by watching, of course. But learning *without* watching is truly challenging. In a study that looked at three-ball cascade juggling, one group watched a video of a professional juggler. Another group was given simple verbal instructions and asked to "try to work out or discover the best way to juggle the three balls."

By the end of the third practice session, the group that had watched the video were juggling an average of seven cycles. The other group couldn't manage one.

*

With juggling, or any other skill, watching someone else might not be enough. You need someone watching *you*. What coaching gives you, and YouTube lacks, is feedback. Back in Brooklyn, Heather Wolf was constantly monitoring the position of my arms, the height of my throws, where I was looking.

She'd point out when I got things wrong, but more important, she'd point out when I got things right. While we tend to think of feedback as a diagnostic tool for fixing mistakes, a growing body of research shows that people not only prefer to be given feedback on their *successful* attempts at a skill; they seem to learn better this way.

There are more ways, after all, to get something like juggling or surfing wrong than right, so why not focus on the good results? And because positive feedback boosts learners' confidence and motivation, this might be more helpful than repeatedly pointing out what they did wrong, which might just make them more anxious and self-conscious.

You can have too much feedback, of course. As learners, we need to make our own mistakes, then figure out a way past them. We need to remember that poor *performance* does not mean poor *learning*. Every time I juggled, I was juggling a little bit differently; scientists call this trial-to-trial variability "noise."

My performance was all over the place. I'd juggle twenty to thirty runs of three balls one day, then barely manage a few runs the following day. But then I'd suddenly rebound. This was normal: An MIT juggling study noted that almost all of its subjects had a series of "breakthroughs" in which their success rate had suddenly and dramatically improved. Errors, or "bugs," the study observed, "come in bunches." I'd throw one ball too late, rush the next, then not throw the last one at all. If I somehow managed to correct that first bug, I'd be rewarded with a string of successful tosses. Early on, it's often just luck—beginner's luck, we call it—that divides a good and a bad performance.

I was like those infants learning to walk in Adolph's lab: stellar walkers one day, stumbling apprentices the next. But in all this variation I was gradually building up robust solutions.

Sometimes, these solutions don't come from watching how-to videos or from the input of coaches. Consider the case of Dick Fosbury, the renowned Olympic high jumper. As a young athlete in Oregon, Fosbury was struggling to stay on the high school track team as a high jumper. His personal best, five feet four inches, was typically the *starting* height at meets.

As failure loomed, he began mulling a return to an older style of high jump called the scissors, in which the legs are lifted one at a time over the bar, while the torso remains upright. It had been eclipsed in favor of the "straddle," a belly-down roll over the bar. Fosbury just couldn't make the straddle click.

With little to lose, he reverted to the scissors, barely clearing the bar at five feet six inches. It was a new personal best, but he realized he wouldn't be able to go higher without doing something different. In the midst of his next jump, he thought, "Lean back."

This little added motion wasn't pretty—one writer called it an "airborne seizure"—but it gave him the needed leverage. "I didn't change my style," Fosbury said. "It changed inside me."

Fosbury's improvisational adaptation of the scissors spawned a new style, called the Fosbury flop, that would revolutionize the world of high jumping. It wasn't the result of imitation, because no one else was doing it. It wasn't the result of coaching, because no one was coaching it. It was said to defy physics; people wondered if it was illegal. Fosbury, fighting to stay on the team, had discovered it through necessary exploration; he had learned it, literally, on the fly.

HOW SKILL LEARNING IS LIKE HIGH-INTENSITY INTERVAL TRAINING FOR YOUR BRAIN

After a week's juggling, I was a changed person.

I don't just mean I suddenly brimmed with confidence or that my outlook on life was a bit sunnier. I mean that I'd actually been changed.

This innocuous little act of throwing balls in the air has been found, in a number of studies, to alter the brain. This "activation-dependent structural brain plasticity," as it's been called, pops up in as little as a week. Juggling changes not only gray matter, the brain's "processing centers," but also white matter, the networked connections that bind it all together.

The changes often happen more in the visual cortex, not the motor cortex, which reinforces the idea that juggling is less about skillfully moving your arms and hands than about being able to track and predict where balls are going.

When we learn to do something, the brain responds in a particularly charged way—more so than when we merely do something we've already learned.

This does not mean, as is often reported, that our brains are "expanding." There isn't a change in the brain's size or weight. Rather, there's an internal reshuffling.

"Learning a new skill requires the neural tissue to function in a new way," as Tobias Schmidt-Wilcke, a neuroscientist—and juggler!—at Germany's Ruhr-Universität Bochum, told me. "It's not the case that the more we learn, the more we locally gather gray matter. It's all about reshaping and getting the job done within a very confined ground."

In other words, we don't just keep piling on the gray matter as we learn something (for we're *always* learning something). Just as our muscles get more efficient as we learn a skill, so does our brain. After an initial burst that comes with learning something new, gray matter density declines. We use only what we need, leaving behind just enough to get the job done; skill performance stays stable as density declines.

Here's one advantage of being a perpetual beginner: Rather than grinding out a marathon, you are putting your brain through a variety of high-intensity interval workouts. Each time you begin to learn that new skill, you're reshaping. You're training your brain again to be more efficient.

I had the sense I could *feel* these processes at work as

I tried to learn three-ball. It seemed to actually make my head hurt as I tried to puzzle out what to do. Eventually, I could do it without thinking. Then I'd try to learn some variation on three-ball, like a "Mills mess." And my head would pulse again—or so it seemed to me—with torrents of shifting gray and white matter.

When that pulse became more a throb, it seemed a good time to stop trying to learn that move. Indeed, a whole body of research has shown that sleep, or even just a short rest, is one of our best learning tools. The resting brain "consolidates" the memories of what you were just trying to do; a big part of any skill, after all, is *remembering* how to do it. Like in a sports broadcast, taking a break gives your brain a chance to do a slo-mo analysis of your last frantic burst of activity.

Curiously, the plasticity shown in learning to juggle didn't seem to depend upon how *well* one learned it. "The brain wants to be puzzled and learn something new," one researcher suggested. It likes learning for learning's sake.

It also doesn't seem to matter how old you are. A study that looked at a group of older subjects (a mean age of sixty years) learning to juggle found a similar brain plasticity seen in an earlier study in which the mean age was twenty years.

"Even if there's little chance you'll become an expert," as Schmidt-Wilcke had told me, "you should try to learn something new."

*

I had this advice in mind one day when I traveled to Manhattan's Upper West Side with Heather Wolf to meet a student she'd been telling me about.

In a light-filled corner apartment on a high floor, we met Steve Schrader. Gray-haired and compact, with a nimble gait, Schrader, after serving me coffee, asked where I'd come from. "Brooklyn," I said. He lit up and exclaimed, "I was there on Wednesday for my birthday!" He'd just turned eighty-one. A colorful forest of opened birthday cards lay atop a grand piano.

Schrader struck me as a wonderful old-world New York character. He was a lifetime denizen of the Upper West Side. "I don't go below Ninety-sixth Street," he joked. His father, Abe, an immigrant from Poland, had been a well-known garment manufacturer (nicknamed the Ultrasuede King) who once had a day named after him during the Ed Koch administration. Abe eventually sold the company and became, at age ninety, a day trader on Wall Street.

Steve had an even more varied path, and he seemed to me like a role model for lifelong learning. "In my life I've been something of a dilettante," he said. He haunted Greenwich Village in the days of Dylan. He played guitar, recorded a few CDs. He has painted. He sold dresses, taught high school, and ran a small publishing house. His true love—"there's only so many things I can screw around with"—is writing, and he gave me a few of his books: funny, elegiac essays about his life and the city.

A year before, Schrader added juggling to his repertoire. He'd had some physical problems—a gallbladder taken out, a pacemaker put in—and was feeling "very down." His doctor advised against his beloved tennis, which he'd picked up at forty.

At a local "aging in place" center, he noticed a class on juggling. "I found it very hard, though in truth the guy wasn't a very good teacher." He tried juggling on his own for a bit, but it wasn't taking. Then he found Heather Wolf. At first, he attended her group classes. "I felt I didn't fit in," he said. "I was about forty to fifty years older than anyone else." He had the sensation, as he often does at his age, that people were "looking past him." But he liked Wolf, so he hired her for weekly lessons. His goal, he half joked, was to get into *Guinness World Records* as the oldest person to learn five-ball juggling.

It wasn't easy. By now, I'd more or less mastered the three-ball cascade and moved on to "asynchronous" four-ball juggling. This is an impressive-looking thing, and as Wolf noted, most people at that point can't even tell how many balls you're actually juggling.

Like Schrader, my goal was five balls—the mark of the competent juggler. Wolf told me it might take one year, even with consistent practice. It might even take two. Schrader and I could take comfort in that Claude Shannon, the genius at MIT, had been equally flummoxed in moving from four to five balls. "It was something he could not master," writes Jon Gertner, "making it all the more tantalizing."

Learning to juggle, Schrader had encountered many of the same issues as I had. Without a coach, he'd practiced improper technique—like throwing with his arms too high—and locked in bad habits.

After struggling initially, he had encountered the virtuous cycle of skill improvement: The more you learn, the more you enjoy it; the more you enjoy it, the more you practice; the more you practice, the better you get.

He was also keenly aware of another truth in skill learning. "The older you get," he said, "the harder you have to work." In the juggling study that found that older jugglers had just as much gray-matter change as younger jugglers, another fact stood out. Over three months of training, 100 percent of the younger group (mean age twenty) achieved the target of sixty seconds of uninterrupted juggling. In the older group (mean age sixty), only 23 percent did. The study concluded with a recommendation that Schrader, like his father, had taken to heart:

"As people age, they should not do less, but do more to keep and maintain their abilities."

But here's another twist: The more learning older adults take on, the faster they seem to learn—the *more they become like younger adults*. Learning to learn, it seems, is a lifetime sport.

CHAPTER SEVEN

MEDITATION WITH BENEFITS

How Drawing Changed the Way I Saw the World, and Myself

Everybody ought to be taught to draw, just as much as everybody ought to be taught to read and write.

—WILLIAM MORRIS

WHY CAN'T WE DRAW WHAT WE SEE?

In 2017, Google released a list of its most searched how-to questions, a category that had grown more than 140 percent since 2004. It was a candid peek into human needs and wishes, big and small.

At number one: "how to tie a tie." You can almost feel the sweaty fingers of the job applicant (who presumably had already clicked through another favorite, "how to write a cover letter") before a looming interview. At number two, tenderly and heartbreakingly, "how to kiss." Farther down, "how to make pancakes" jostled with "how to make french toast," as parents, with floured fingers, grappled in the kitchen on Saturday morning.

At number five, nestled between "how to lose weight"

and "how to make money"—two prime concerns of contemporary life—there sat, almost quaintly, "how to draw."

It seems odd, on a list dominated by some of life's big pursuits, and a handful of lesser, more immediate ones, to find a skill that arguably stopped being hugely relevant—even in the art world—since the advent of photography.

Drawing, like singing, seems like a phantom limb of a skill, one we effectively left behind as children yet that continues to occasionally haunt us. I find it telling that of the very few things I remember from my early days in elementary school, one was singing in a school assembly, and the other was having my winter-scene artwork singled out by the teacher and hung above the chalkboard.

Like all kids, I just drew, without particular encouragement or instruction. Not that it was needed. I spent hours drawing epic, intricate scenes of unfolding action, blue Bic renderings of enemy forces attacking mountaintop fortresses or deep-sea divers being menaced by great whites. They weren't particularly good as drawings—there was no attempt at capturing depth or dimensionality—but that wouldn't have entered my mind. I drew, as most kids do, because it was fun and because there seemed to be some story or impulse I wanted to express visually.

"All children are born artists," Pablo Picasso famously said. "The problem is to remain an artist as we grow up." It's the sort of thing you see on the break-room coffee mug of an earnest art teacher, but there's something to the idea.

In one study, a range of subjects, from young children to adolescents to older adults, were asked to create drawings intended to express things like the concept of "angry." Expert judges, using criteria like "expression" and "balance" and "composition," were called in to rank the drawings. Unsurprisingly, the group that did the best were the adults who identified as artists.

But the group that did about as well as the artists? The

five-year-olds. Everyone else, from adult nonartists to older children, did worse. The study's author, Jessica Davis, suggested the presence of a U-shaped curve (similar to the one I'd found in surfing), marked by artists and five-year-olds at the high points, with everyone else in the trough.

What happens, the theory goes, is that children begin to draw less what they *feel* than what they think something should look like. They enter what the psychologist Howard Gardner called "the doldrums of *literalism,*" or a "pedantic preoccupation with the photographic aspect of drawings." They try to get technically better at rendering reality but find they don't possess the skill set.

As Angela Anning, a professor of early childhood education, notes, children are expected to learn—but aren't taught—the "technical challenges of representing space, scale and perspective." They sacrifice raw intensity for an attempt at realism and generally come up with something that, as Gardner notes, "is at once more carefully wrought yet also more wooden and lifeless." In the "angry" study, the adults and older children tried to draw anger itself, while the kids just drew *themselves,* angry.

And so most kids, myself included, come to assume they're "not artistic." We're taught writing and math without expecting to become writers or mathematicians, but somehow drawing becomes viewed as a strictly vocational exercise for artists in training.

I vaguely tried to keep it alive. On a postcollege extended trip through Europe, before the era of laptops and smartphones, I carried a notebook in which I wrote and occasionally drew simple sketches of buildings and street scenes. I did this because I had the romantic idea that this is what one did, preferably in a Viennese café.

Without fully being aware, I was aspiring to the Renaissance ideals expressed by Count Baldassare Castiglione in his famed 1528 work, *The Book of the Courtier,* a much-translated tome described as the "ultimate 'how to' guide" for advancing in court life. In it, he deemed drawing and painting "highly important" skills. For a long time, the "polite and useful" art of drawing was considered as basic a communication skill as writing, notes the historian Ann Bermingham. It was a "social practice" more than an aesthetic one.

Whatever sort of practice it was, I fell out of it, for decades. The arrival of my daughter, and the way she eventually turned nearly every surface in our kitchen into a gallery wall with her boundless doodles and sketches, reawakened the vestigial itch. I decided I would join her in drawing.

My motivations weren't entirely clear. I didn't consider myself artistic, nor did I assume drawing would open magical avenues of expression or creativity. Drawing is said to be a good way to actually acquire knowledge, because the act of drawing adds another layer of memory encoding in your brain, but I wasn't necessarily looking for that. I simply thought it might be good, for someone who sat looking at words on a computer screen all day, to work a few different muscles.

As Winston Churchill, a devoted amateur painter, once noted, something like reading—even reading for pleasure—after the "ordinary daily round of the brain-worker," simply worked the same tired faculties. "To restore psychic equilibrium," he argued, "we should call into use those parts of the mind which direct both eye and hand."

No matter what the goal, one thing I'd been finding in my efforts at learning is that it could be hard to predict what trying to learn something might do for you, how it might change you. Not knowing exactly what you might "get" from some learning experience was just another reason not to begin it.

But where to learn, and how?

An old acquaintance who'd become an energetic sketcher—even publishing a book of his depictions of restaurants—suggested I look at *Drawing on the Right Side of the Brain*, the classic book by Betty Edwards. More than any one person, Edwards, over the past several decades, has convinced many thousands of people, even many who didn't consider themselves artistically minded, that they could draw.

I bought the book and had a go at a few of the exercises. I found them interesting but sensed I was going to need more—more discipline, more feedback. By chance, searching for information about the book online, I saw that Edwards's son was going to be hosting a workshop in New York City. It would be five full days—more drawing than I had done since I was probably five. I signed up.

*

There is something about attending a class, even as a mid-career professional, that sends you straight back to elementary school. That whole first-day thing of walking into a strange room, trying to figure out where to sit, taking sly glances at your classmates, worrying if you've brought all the correct materials. That fear of doing or saying the wrong thing. The anxiety that everyone else in the room might be better than you. But also that strange, liberating feeling where your only job is to learn something.

And so there was that slightly nervous jostling as nine of us gathered one early December morning in a sleekly decorated residential loft in Tribeca. At the front of the class was Brian Bomeisler, the son of Betty Edwards. She had recently turned ninety, he told me, and "had slowed down a bit."

He welcomed us and told us we were about to pack a semester's worth of learning—forty hours—into one week. Like his mother, he was a painter—"a noble but not terribly lucrative profession." He'd been leading the workshop for several decades. With wavy white hair and thick black glasses, he had a languid, bemused air and would occasionally drift into nostalgic remembrances that were by turns wistful and whimsical.

Bomeisler had lived a bohemian New York City life that seemed hardly possible these days. He was trained at the Pratt Institute by Rudolf Baranik, a Lithuanian émigré—whose Jewish parents were killed by fascists in World War II—known for his abstract expressionist paintings and political activism. "He painted only in black and white," Bomeisler said, "and he wore only black."

He recalled another instructor of his who lived in tony Greenwich, Connecticut. "She would come down to Bed-Stuy, which was a bit seedy at the time, in these flowing chiffon gowns," he said. She had a knack, he said, for saying memorable things, in her "erudite mid-Atlantic accent." One day, he was telling her about an autumn train trip he had taken from Washington, D.C., to New York City. He was enthusing, in painterly fashion, about the many colors of the changing leaves. "She looked at me with this twinkle in her eye and said, 'Ah, yes, but did you see the colors *between* the leaves?'"

Early on, he lived across from CBGB in the days of Richard Hell and Debbie Harry, before it was a themed restaurant at Newark's Liberty International Airport. He moved to a loft in SoHo (the loft we were in belonged to a jewelry-designer friend of his), at the corner of Bond and Bowery, where he remained for the next several decades. "I watched the World Trade Center going up, and I watched it come down." He was now a divorced dad with alimony payments and two teenage daughters—"yikes!" he said, laughing.

His past was reflected in the city almost everywhere he went. Just across the street from where we were sitting, visible through the windows, was an apartment where the actor Robert De Niro was living back in the 1970s. "I helped build his roof garden," he said. Bomeisler was working as a carpenter, not an easy thing when you lived in New York. "We didn't have a truck. We traveled around on the subways with all our tools in canvas bags."

He'd end these reveries with a slight chuckle, then assume a serious demeanor.

"Drawing," Bomeisler told us, "is not a motor-skill problem. If you can sign your name, you can draw." He once had a quadriplegic in his class who drew with a pencil clutched between his teeth.

What drawing really was, he said, was a *thinking* problem. He was going to teach us not how to be artists—"I wouldn't even begin to know how to do that"—but how to "draw what we see in the world around us." And, importantly, how to ignore everything telling us we couldn't draw. "A lot of the skills I'm teaching," he told us, "are about the way you talk to yourself, about inserting more positive voices in your head rather than the ghosts we all have."

This was all in the spirit of his mother, whose PhD at UCLA, he told me, was on "anxiety and drawing"—not how drawing may help soothe anxiety, which I'm sure it can, but how many of us might feel trepidation at the prospect of putting pencil to paper. What made *Drawing on the Right Side of the Brain* such a revelation—the book has sold millions—was that rather than teaching people how to simply copy pictures, or pushing some particular drawing technique, "my mother's work," as Bomeisler said, "was the first to teach not so much about drawing, but about thinking."

Edwards saw drawing as a skill as "equally vital" as reading; just as reading gave one access to the insights of any number of other disciplines, drawing could help train our perceptual abilities to "guide and promote insight into the *meaning* of visual and verbal information."

The title was inspired by Roger W. Sperry's ground-breaking, Nobel Prize–winning research on "split-brain"* subjects in the 1960s. Sperry found the left hemisphere of the brain was focused more on language, analytic thought, and arithmetic. The right hemisphere, meanwhile, seemed more inclined toward processing spatial relations, recognizing faces, and conjuring mental imagery of two- and three-dimensional figures—exactly what would come into play while drawing.

Historically, Edwards noted, the right hemisphere had been viewed as the "minor" half, inferior to the left, where the bulk of our verbal processing occurred. In a language-dominated world, Edwards campaigned for the importance of this underdog hemisphere and visual literacy more broadly.

When beginners try to draw, Edwards suggested, they try to draw the world that they know, and are able to name, rather than what they're really looking at. We draw in categorical prototypes. Asked to draw a face, we draw what we think a face looks like, and the drawing we produce, while looking *face-like*, doesn't look much like an actual face.

In one of the book's exercises, readers are asked to reproduce Pablo Picasso's portrait sketch of Igor Stravin-

---

* In a now-obsolete process known as commissurotomy, the hemispheres in patients' brains had been divided in two, as a treatment against epilepsy.

sky. Normally, Edwards noted, the drawing, with its various spatial illusions, is difficult for novices.

But Edwards gave a simple instruction: Turn the drawing upside down. Suddenly they were much better at copying it. The secret to their improvement, she notes, was that they did not know what they were drawing. The parts of the drawing that were still recognizable, like the hands, were the most challenging. Faced with something it can no longer analyze—like an upside-down drawing—"L-mode" retreats, Edwards suggested, letting "R-mode" bloom.

Did they actually improve because of some temporary reorganization of brain activity? Critics have suggested Edwards's book stretched the neuroscience. Chris McManus, a professor in the Faculty of Brain Sciences at University College London, writes that "hemisphericity"—or "the idea that many people use only one side of the brain for solving a problem, and that, with proper training, we can voluntarily will the other side to solve problems"—is "deeply flawed."

Despite being widely disseminated in pop culture, the notion that people are "left-brained" or "right-brained" isn't backed by strong scientific evidence. Nor is the idea that the right hemisphere is more "creative." Sperry himself cautioned that the "left-right dichotomy" is an idea with which it's very easy to "run wild."

Bomeisler suggested the left-right concept was more metaphorical in nature. But he worked the metaphor pretty hard. "The left brain is powerful," he told me. "It really doesn't like to be set aside. When you have these little setbacks, in terms of right-hemisphere perception, the left brain says, 'See, I told you you weren't going to be able to do that, stupid.'" Even as a metaphor, as one critic suggested, the right-left formulation "perpetuates outmoded dichotomies of brain functions."

None of this means that Edwards's techniques won't help people draw things more accurately or that her book isn't filled with insight.

Artists, after all, have long suggested that looking at things in new ways was essential to depicting them honestly.

The critic John Ruskin, writing in the nineteenth century, argued that "the innocent eye"—or a "childish perception" of things "without conscious awareness of what they signified"—was essential to art. "When you go out and paint," Claude Monet counseled, "try to forget what objects you have before you, a tree, a house, a field, or whatever. Merely think, here is a little square of blue, here an oblong of pink, here a streak of yellow, and paint it just as it looks to you."

And leaving brain studies aside, there's all sorts of intriguing evidence that the way we label and think about things affects our ability to draw them.

In a well-known study from the 1930s (whose general findings have since been replicated elsewhere), people were shown a graphic symbol—say, two circles connected by a line. They were then asked to replicate it from memory. When they were told the object was a pair of eyeglasses, they drew it differently from the people who were told it was a set of dumbbells. In both cases, people departed from the original symbol.

The result was clear: What people drew was more influenced by the symbols in their minds than what was on the page.

*

One of the strongest sets of symbols we possess is the human head. "These symbols actually seem to override seeing, and therefore few people can draw a realistic human head," Edwards wrote. "Even fewer can draw recognizable portraits."

And so on to our first order of business in Tribeca. "We have reached the worst moment of the five-day class," Bomeisler said. "I'm going to ask you to do a self-portrait." These would not be analyzed, but rather stored away until the end of the class, then compared with a later effort as a way of gauging how much progress we'd made in a week.

First, though, we were asked to introduce ourselves. Among the students was Eric, a software engineer and aspiring yoga teacher from California. He'd read *Drawing*, done a few exercises, and was intrigued to try more. He'd turned the week into a learning vacation. Saki, a Greek finance professional, was taking a nine-month sabbatical to "explore the parts of my psyche that have remained unexplored over the years." Ursula, from Montreal, spoke five languages and had undergone "regurgitative experiences" in the Peruvian Amazon. Barbara, who worked as a server in a retirement community in Idaho, had been through "many a community college art class" and wanted the rigor of an intensive week to piece it all together. Nancy was a former math teacher ("I've lived my life on the left side of my brain") in Marin County who in retirement had taken a crafty turn, "spending my life with dirty, gluey, inky hands."

Once we'd concluded our biographical sketches, it was on to actual sketching. We were asked to take out the "self-portrait mirror" (a mirror with a set of crosshatched lines) included with the pre-packed portfolio that is part of the class. And then: Draw. The room went pin-drop quiet and stayed that way for nearly an hour.

My own effort looked like a mug shot sketch, if the suspect in question didn't actually dwell on this planet. My wife, when she saw the drawing, asked, "Is that Beavis or Butt-Head?"

There are, as any beginning drawer will soon discover, a number of rules of thumb about the typical proportions of the human head; for example, the face is about as wide as five eyes.

My drawing violated almost every one of these. My face was at once too wide and too long. The space between my nose and my lips was as wide as Park Avenue. My lips hung perilously low on my chin, like a Mr. Potato Head clumsily arranged by a well-meaning toddler. My eyes were crude hieroglyphs. Like most beginners, I'd drawn my hair as a collection of individual strands, which is never how it actually appears, unless you have the world's worst comb-over. There are scores of muscles on the human face, any number of wrinkles, and an archipelago of shadows—none of which I managed to capture.

This sketch was not from memory, where it would be easy to imagine people relying on concepts rather than reality. I had stared at myself intently in the mirror for an hour and still screwed it up.

I was reminded of something Edwards had written. My "pre-instruction drawing" represented *the age when I last drew*. Or, basically, stopped drawing. This was truly a portrait of the artist as a young man. I was a nine-year-old trying to draw a forty-nine-year-old. This seemed a strange thing. There are few areas in adult life in which our skills are so stuck in childhood amber. I'd been a beginner in drawing for five decades.

The following day, we were asked to draw a folding chair. Bomeisler stressed that we not think of it as a chair. "By not drawing the chair," he said, "you get a more complex picture."

I tried to look at individual parts of the not-chair, zooming in until it was abstracted bits of tone. I told myself, thinking of that famous painting by Magritte,* "This is not a chair." In my mind I suddenly started seeing it as just a collection of shapes and "negative spaces," the stuff between and around the not-chair.

When Bomeisler came by to look at my work, he noticed that the seat back I'd drawn seemed to be the wrong size. "It should be as long as the distance from the seat back to the cushion," he said.

"That can't be right," I thought.

Then I measured it, using the standard artist's sizing method—which you've probably seen in Bugs Bunny cartoons and the like—of a pencil held at arm's length and one closed eye. It *was* right. I just kept staring, but no matter how long I looked, I couldn't accept the actual size. How could I have rendered what was right in front of me so wrong?

*

Why can't we draw what we see?

A study that looked into this question found, as Bomeisler had suggested, that motor skills had little to do with it. Instead, the authors suggested, we suffer from delusions, or "false beliefs that are held in spite of invalidating evidence."

I was, in other words, still trying to draw "the chair," rather than a series of angles, lines, and shadows. Studies have been done in which children are asked to copy a series of angled lines. They do this well. When they're asked to copy the oblique, outline image of a table—which is where the original lines came from—they suddenly make errors.

I spent days battling these sorts of delusions. It wasn't easy. "I'm not sprinkling fairy dust and you're Michelan-

---

* Titled, appropriately, *The Treachery of Images.*

gelo," Bomeisler growled one morning. One of the few people to ever leave the class early huffed, "This was supposed to be my vacation. I didn't think I was going to have to work this hard."

In one exercise, I retreated to the corner of a bedroom to draw a view looking back out to the hallway. To accurately render something like an open door requires battling the perceptual phenomenon called shape constancy; for example, we think a door swung inward is still rectangular, the way doors are.

But when we view an open door, we're looking at a trapezoid. I had to measure to get the angles of my open door right; I couldn't rely on my eye. Artists actually seem to fall for these perceptual biases as much as anyone, but they've learned how to fix them on the page.

Drawing, it is often said, "teaches you how to see." It does, in a sense, but the truth is more complicated and more interesting.

Edwards gives the example that when we look around in a crowded room, people's heads, whether they're near or far, appear to be the same size (the effect is called size constancy). If you tried to draw it that way, you would sense something wrong on the page. But draw them at their correct, varying sizes, and the heads will *still* look the same when we actually see them on the page.

More than "how to see," drawing teaches "how *we* see"—the various shortcuts and hacks by which the brain renders the external world. We don't see the world that's reflected on our retinas. The brain, like an artist, sketches its own interpretation of what's around us.

Drawing also teaches you how *much* there is to see. The longer I looked, the more I saw. The shadow in the corner of the ceiling was actually several shadows lurking within each other. A single floorboard held a world of subtlety. While I wanted to try to capture every last detail,

Bomeisler advised that it was often more judicious—and better for one's sanity—to leave things out.

I found the sheets on the bed particularly hard to render. When I complained about this to Bomeisler, he said, "Let me get my special sheet pencil." It was a joke, of course, playing on the idea that there's nothing different about drawing a set of wrinkled sheets from drawing a wrinkled human face. It's all just contour and shadow. I had to dispense with the idea of fabric and geometric folds and just think of it as an abstracted landscape, a shaded topographical map someone had been sleeping in.

Drawing was the most absorbing thing I'd ever done, far more so than writing. With my phone shut off and put in another room, it was just me, a pencil and paper, and the space around me. Hours passed without my knowledge. It struck me as *meditation with benefits*. I entered a deep state of focus in which time and my worldly cares floated away, and at the end I had a souvenir to take home.

The artist Frederick Franck quotes the ninth-century Zen master Daie: "Meditation in a state of activity is a thousand times more profound than in a state of quietude." Nowadays we call it flow. I wasn't alone in feeling this. I heard someone in the class say, "It's the hardest I've concentrated in a long time." Ursula, from Montreal, said she'd gone so deep she "felt like childhood memories were going to come out."

Our final project was to revisit the self-portrait, armed with the techniques and experience of the week. This time, we mounted our self-portrait mirrors. A group of us set up in the hallway. Saki was next to me, and I tried not to be distracted by his drawing. I put in earbuds and fired up a Glenn Gould playlist, and suddenly it was lunch.

I came back half an hour later and resumed the portrait. I noticed after a while Saki hadn't returned from lunch, and his drawing, which he'd been furiously erasing, wasn't very far along. I started getting vicariously stressed but had hours to go before my own drawing would be complete—if there was such a thing. I would have kept going for days. A drawing is finished, Bomeisler told me, when anything you do to it will make it worse.

I took my drawing from the wall and mounted it to a wall in the loft, where an impromptu gallery of our work had formed. My portrait seemed dark, almost graphic, and moody. I had an intense gaze, which, more than any personal trait, simply reflected the idea I was working so hard on the drawing. Bomeisler compared it (favorably, I like to think) to the work of Max Beckmann, that chronicler of Weimar street life. But the eyes! They were huge. When I brought the drawing home, proudly displaying it in the living room, my wife, chuckling, said, "You look like a Beanie Baby."

"Most drawings are failures," writes Peter Steinhart. "Almost all drawing is merely practice." I took this as my mantra—as if I had any other choice.

The class had been a revelation. Once you started learning to draw, Edwards suggested, your brain was changed forever (and my brain, as described in the last chapter, had been undergoing lots of change recently).

Drawing wasn't such hard work, but *seeing* was. Once you started to put in the effort, it felt like a superpower that unlocked new layers of the world around you. I found myself stopping on the street to inspect the subtle dynamics of a cityscape reflected in a car's hood, or the textural pattern on the peel of an orange. I could zone out for half an hour in a doctor's office looking at things (a jar of cotton balls, the acoustic tiles in the ceiling) and wondering, "How would I draw that?"

In drawing myself, I had become intimately acquainted with my face as a thing. This was the same face that I looked at every morning in the mirror, but in trying to draw it, I felt like a mapmaker charting an unfamiliar territory. I could have taken a thousand selfies and not come to as intimate a relation with my physiognomy as I did in drawing a self-portrait. In an age inundated with the raw information of photographs—sheer data there for the taking—drawing seemed like wisdom that needed to be earned.

Some people who took the *Drawing* class, Bomeisler told me, "were like, 'I've learned how to draw, check,' and then they went back to their normal lives."

I knew I was only in my Paleolithic stage, a few primitive scratchings on the wall. "Never graduate from drawing," the artist John Sloan advised. Drawing had unlocked something in me. While I enjoyed creating something tangible, the drawings were almost beside the point. I was in love with the process, and so I went looking for more.

THE DRAWING THAT DRAWS ITSELF:
MY ADVENTURES IN ART SCHOOL

Stepping from the busy sidewalks of Tribeca, with its upmarket boutiques and spin-class studios, into the New York Academy of Art, you felt as if you'd accidentally wandered into an ancient Greek agora. There were plaster columns, replicas of busts by classical sculptors, statues of muscular nudes. You half expected to stumble across a Socratic dialogue in the lobby.

Housed in a five-story nineteenth-century warehouse once home to bookbinders and parasol makers, the academy was founded in 1982 by a group of people who were concerned that as art had become increasingly minimalist and conceptual, art schools were sending graduates into the world lacking many of the traditional skills of drawing and painting. One of the school's early patrons, ironically, was Andy Warhol, often considered a conceptual artist. There were art students, the feeling was, who would have trouble drawing a circle. "They could talk about conceptualism until they were blue in the face," as Angharad Coates, the academy's communications director, told me. "But they didn't know easels or brushwork."

Early on, the academy's approach was seen as a bit eccentric. The painter Eric Fischl described "lots of students painting people in togas, and they weren't ironic about it."

Accurately depicting the human form had long stopped being one of the central concerns of art, but here all students were still expected to learn *écorché*, the art of drawing or painting the human body as it would appear without skin. Despite its focus on classic techniques, Coates insisted the academy was not a retreat into classicism. "The idea was you'd have all this hard-core training," she said, "but then were expected to become a contemporary artist."

The academy had some initial financial and organizational woes, but had since settled into a respected, if quirky, part of New York's art scene. There was a lavish fund-raising ball every year. Iggy Pop, the "Godfather of Punk," dropped by to offer his famously lithe and muscular self as the nude model for a live-drawing class. "For some reason it felt important to me that I could just stand naked for a group of human beings and have an exchange," he said. Sculpture students helped cold-case investigators by rendering faces for the skulls of anonymous crime victims. The academy's director was a high-functioning former executive whose first encounter with the school was as a painting student.

I felt a bit intimidated about launching right into one of the academy's continuing education classes—even the ones termed appropriate for beginners—so I began with a few private lessons with Michael Grimaldi, head of the academy's drawing department.

We met one night in a cavernous room marked by scattered easels, splotches of paint and tape marks on the floor, and a clanging radiator. Grimaldi was tall and soft-spoken and moved gracefully, like the former Division I college fencer he was. He'd recently gotten back into the sport, after some fifteen years away, when his eight-year-old daughter began fencing. He realized, like me, that amid the "sound and smells of bouts" he couldn't stay on the sidelines.

Growing up in Manhattan, he had been surrounded by contemporary artists; Robert Rauschenberg and Julian Schnabel had lived in his building. "They were never discouraging about the urge to draw what you're looking at," he said.

When I told him I'd recently taken the Edwards course, he nodded knowingly, and some of what he had to say echoed what I'd been hearing. "Over the next few weeks we'll try to figure out ways of abstracting visual experience," he said. "We'll be deprogramming a lot of our biases with things."

When we try to draw a face, for example, we tend to overemphasize the things that are important to us. We make eyes too big and foreheads too small, because we look more often at, and invest more emotion in, people's eyes than their foreheads. We put eyes higher than they really are, which is roughly halfway down the head (studies have found that as many as 95 percent of nonartist subjects make this mistake). We intend to draw someone at a three-fourths portrait angle and still want to "frontalize" their eyes, because that's how we typically see people. The more things are invested with meaning or emotion, he suggested, the harder it is to draw them, at least initially. His daughter was a particularly tough subject. "It's somehow easier," Grimaldi said, "when you can look at things in a cold, detached way."

Our first subject was an overstuffed antique couch, placed on a riser and lit from above. The focus of the first lesson was "value," how light or dark something is. Unlike painting, with its variety of colors, pencil drawing was limited. "You're working in only one channel," Grimaldi said. "Value is notoriously difficult for us to achieve." It's also difficult to perceive. "When we look at a white object against a white wall, we're thinking they're both white," he said. But the fact that you can *see* the object, that it does not seamlessly blend into the wall, means there are differences in value. In drawing, it wasn't safe to assume anything.

With one pencil and a piece of paper, you needed to cover everything from deepest shadow to brightest sunlight. Before drawing, Grimaldi said, you needed to figure out the "lightest light" and the "darkest dark." By bracketing the extreme values, he said, you could more easily determine where the other values lay. For once you made a mark on a white sheet of paper, he warned me, you'll think it's darker than it really is.

The sheer range of values contained in any given scene could be overwhelming. He recommended squinting. "You're inhibiting your eyes' color receptors so that you're relying more on your rods, which are value receptors," he said. "If you walk into a dark room, you don't see color, you just see value."

The following week, we moved on to a cast statue, a fragment of a Roman copy of a Hellenistic Venus. In my imagination, the way this would be drawn was for me to simply start drawing, my hand faithfully following the contours I saw in front of me.

You could certainly do this. We were going for a precision rendering, however, and in the same way one doesn't build a house without blueprints, you don't draw something without first laying down a schematic. This sort of drawing looked vaguely architectural. "My teacher told me," Grimaldi said, "it isn't really a drawing; it's an armature of a drawing."

The first step was to sketch the basic "envelope," the geometric shape that connected the furthermost points of the figure and would establish the proportions. It looked vaguely trapezoidal. From there I would look for various "landmarks," things like the highest or lowest part of the drawing, and start to sketch quick lines between them. He compared it to hiking: If we got lost, we could figure out our position by triangulating our position vis-à-vis the landmarks.

He didn't want me to draw any details, just broad gestures. "We can always find mass and form later on," he said. If I found myself spending too much time in one area—usually it was the head—I should move on.

Everything was to be abstracted. Curves were to be drawn not as curves but as a series of small, straight lines. "It's a much faster way of approaching a drawing," he said. "It takes a long time for our eye and hand to draw a curve."

I noticed that he held his pencil not the way one does when writing but by its end. It twitched in his finger like the recording needle on a seismograph machine. Even this was meant as a way to avoid drawing particular contours or forms. Instead, the pencil fluttered back and forth, almost in time with his saccadic eye movements, like a real-time recording.

Artists tend to look at their subjects much more often than nonartists. By doing this, one argument goes, they reduce the need to keep the image in their working memory, where it very quickly becomes prone to biases and misperceptions.

When I suddenly realized I'd placed the flurry of

strokes that roughly represented one of the figure's arms too low, Grimaldi brightened. "The good news is when we find an error in the drawing," he said. "The bad news is when we don't." The longer you went without making a correction, the bigger the correction would ultimately have to be.

Gradually, from this trapezoidal box filled with slashing, crossing marks, the figure of Venus began to emerge. I had the sense that rather than my doing the drawing, the *drawing was drawing itself*. Long before I thought about the "eye" or the "foot," it was already shimmering into view as a simple by-product of calculating angles and gestures.

"You're actually doing really well with this," Grimaldi said. He seemed to mean it, but I was wary of rote encouragement, the way all sincere learners are. "Don't just tell me that they're good," my daughter once said, after baking chocolate chip cookies. "Tell me how they *really* are."

*

My amateur drawing career was under way as I waded into the continuing education classes the academy offered. Like an enthused schoolboy, I rushed to purchase the recommended list of supplies; a whole new range of *gear* is undoubtedly one of the greatest pleasures of being a beginner. As someone who pushes electrons for a living, I loved the sheer tactility of drawing: sharpening pencils with a razor blade, working the puttylike kneaded eraser, blending graphite with a paper "stump."

As I left my house carrying my portfolio, I noticed a surprised look or two from a neighbor and felt a secret satisfaction: Oh, sure, it's me, just off to *art school*. This bouncy confidence diminished when I entered the academy, filled as it was with actual artists, with paint-splattered pants, interesting hair, and accomplished work.

Still, it felt like being let into some secret world, and surrounded by these young artists in training as they washed brushes or kibitzed in the lunch area, I'd think back to my own precollege self: "What if I had taken this path?"

Even the continuing education courses, often labeled for beginners, were filled with talented people. In one course, I met Pat, a high school teacher from Brooklyn. He had been painting and drawing for decades. He told me he had a painting in his house that he had last worked on twenty years earlier and someday planned on returning to (talk about continuing education). But he'd reached a point of mental exhaustion with it, "where you're spending an hour in a half-inch square and still it's not coming out the way you want."

After a while, I could relate. In a class on the Bargue method, a famous nineteenth-century French drawing course that had influenced artists like Picasso, I spent many weeks trying to forge a convincing likeness from a plaster cast of an ear, which hung from an easel in front of me. Illuminated by an overhead floodlight, it was an intoxicating, infuriating mass of swirling shape and shadow.

Like confronting a bewitching whirlpool, I felt sucked into its unknowable vortices. "We are rendering three-dimensional form with a pencil," Ard Berge, the teacher, told me. "We are illustrating what it would be like to touch it." In a sense, we had to sculpt it, with a pencil rather than our hands. We had to dive down into the curling depths, follow the flow of the reflected light from above as it bounced back into the upper folds of the ear. "Rolling form," he called it. "Remember the song from *Rawhide*? Keep that form a-rollin'!"

I'd sometimes glance at the drawing of Andrew, a fellow student, seated to my left, and be struck by how different our works looked. Mine was loose and impressionistic, while his was exactingly precise, almost like an anatomical drawing. You could learn a technique, but your style just seemed to emerge on its own. At semester's end, when we all gathered our drawings, there were twelve ears, each as unique as a signature. "It feels sonic," Berge said, studying mine approvingly. "Like there's a pulsing quality to it." I felt transported back to grade school, my artwork singled out by the teacher. I don't know why, but praise for something you're new at can seem more satisfying than praise for something you've long done.

As I gradually grew in confidence, I would shrink less in embarrassment when someone glanced over my shoulder at what I was doing. I led impromptu drawing seminars at home, where I would place an object—like an orange—on the kitchen table and have my wife and daughter try to draw it. In the holiday card we gave to our building superintendent, I included a quick sketch of his Siberian husky, Logan. "You could totally sell these!" he enthused. I was heartened by his reaction, but it also reminded me of the way grandparents think their grandchildren are bound for Carnegie Hall when they squeak through their first song on the piano.

Then I took my first live-drawing class. It was one thing to have hours upon hours to stare at an inanimate object, and quite another to have a living, breathing person seated before you in short increments. The model would return from a break, sit just a bit differently, and suddenly the fold on a dress, or the light on her cheek, was different from what I'd drawn.

And as I tried to draw, I couldn't help but revert to my journalistic instincts. Who were they? Did they like the work? Could *I* be a live model? We couldn't address them in class, of course; it was seen as a violation of privacy, as well as a disruption to accurate drawing.

One afternoon, I ran into the class's current model, a lean, muscled man with streaky blond hair, in the elevator, back in street clothes. I asked him what he thought about while he sat there, placid and immobile. "Today I was thinking about stocks to buy," he said. I don't know if I expected him to say "the meaning of life," but his answer surprised me. Iggy Pop said he thought about his own songs; this guy was mentally tracking the market.

Meanwhile, my own thoughts were intruding on my drawing. "You're seeing what isn't there," the live-drawing instructor, Robert Armetta, said, fairly scolding me. I was putting in a literal eyelash where a smudge of darker value would suffice. "You're emphasizing that which shouldn't be emphasized, and you're deemphasizing that which shouldn't be deemphasized." I nodded. But there was more. I was committing that cardinal sin of drawing lines. "It starts to become too conceptualized, so formulaic." My pencil, he asserted, was too heavy. I looked down at it, in my hand, as if it were made of iron. "Everything should be light," he said of my hard-to-erase pencil traces, "because we're operating under the assumption that it's wrong." And indeed, I was. Somewhere along the line, my measurements had gone askew. "You were checking a to b to c, and c to d to e, but you weren't checking a to f. Does that make sense?" Not really, I thought, but I just nodded, a bit dazed.

As much as I still felt in over my head, one of the almost inevitable by-products of learning new things is the spillover effect of wanting to learn *more* new things.

And so it wasn't long before I'd signed up for a class that covered drawing *and* painting. The instructor, Adam Cross, told me that the class switched halfway through from drawing to painting. "Seventy-five percent of students just want to keep drawing," he said. "They're so excited by this thing they've unlocked."

In painting, with its new tools, its new technical challenges, I was a beginner all over again. Robert Armetta, in evaluating one of my sketches, had told me that those first glances, early in the drawing, had a special potency. "Your eye is fresher now than it will be the rest of the day," he said. With a drawing, over time, "we're lulled into this sense that things aren't so bad." Familiarity breeds contentment.

The beginning stages of a drawing were like being a beginner: the wide-awake clarity of the new experience, those tentative movements, the gradual winnowing out of errors, that freedom from past experience or habits, an empty horizon vast and white with possibility.

I had no idea where drawing would take me. I hadn't planned on painting, and yet there it was; I was even eyeing the sculpture classes. I thought again of Norman Rush's description of love as a series of rooms in which you keep moving from one to the next, each getting larger and better. "You never intend to go from one room onward to the next—it just happens. You notice a door, you go through, and you're delighted again."

This is how learning felt, once you opened that first door, the one marked "Beginners Welcome."

CHAPTER EIGHT

THE APPRENTICE

or, What I Learned

A man ceases to be a beginner in any given science and
becomes a master in that science when he has learned
that . . . he is going to be a beginner all his life.*

—ROBIN COLLINGWOOD

YOU'RE NEVER TOO OLD;
YOU'RE NEVER TOO YOUNG:
LEARNING AS A LIFETIME SPORT

There were many occasions in my series of novice under-
takings where I was embarrassed, unsure, outperformed,
and on the verge of giving up.

One of the most indelible moments was when I found
myself on a three-kilometer swim in the open ocean, off
the coast of the Abaco Islands in the Bahamas. There, I
found myself struggling to keep up with my nine-year-
old daughter and a seventy-year-old Frenchwoman who'd
given up a pack-a-day smoking habit and had recently
taught herself to swim watching YouTube videos.

---

* I know, another "man." But I didn't want to lose the spirit of the quotation.

How had it come to this?

A year before, I'd been sitting on a bench staring at my phone as my daughter did her weekly swim lesson for what felt like the thousandth time (one of the few times I wasn't looking at my phone was when I actually dropped it *into* the pool).* On this particular afternoon, I began to have that nagging thought, the one haunting this book: How many hours had I sat on the sidelines killing time? When was the last time *I* swam?

I managed a few hotel pool swims a year, a dip in the lake at my in-laws. The truth was, swimming in New York City was not easy; pools were expensive or crowded. I'd been in the water a lot surfing, but getting back to the board never required more than a few strokes.

But I'd been reading Roger Deakin's book *Waterlog*, a classic celebration of "wild swimming"—the simple act of taking a plunge in a river, lake, or the open seas. It seemed immensely appealing. In an increasingly "signposted" world, Deakin suggested, wild swimming promised freedom, as well as the profound metamorphosis of leaving behind one world for another. He sold it as a foolproof tonic. "I can dive in with a long face and what feels like a terminal case of depression," he wrote, "and come out a whistling idiot." With each page I felt myself pulled toward the water.

Watching my daughter backstroke back and forth, I had the sudden idea that we could all take a "wild swimming holiday." These had become increasingly popular, particularly in England, where bookshops were stocked with entire shelves of swimming-changed-my-life memoirs.

Unlike my annual bike trips, which were dominated by long days of suffering, carbs, and testosterone, here was

---

* Packed in a bag of rice, it lasted a week, then died.

something we might all enjoy. My wife, like me, was no aquatic fanatic but seemed to enjoy a dip whenever we could actually do it. My daughter would have the chance to apply what she was learning to the real world. We would be in nature—like, *really* in nature—we would work our bodies and calm our minds, we would bond as a family (as mentioned earlier in the book, learning new things together is a relationship tonic).

Low-impact swimming, moreover, was a lifetime sport. I heard this many times; it was often the first thing a swimmer told me. As a somewhat older parent who would be roughly of retirement age as my daughter hit full adulthood, I thought this sounded appealing. Swimmers, as one long-term study found, lived longer than people with a sedentary lifestyle. This you'd expect. But they also seemed to live longer than walkers or runners, for reasons that aren't clear.

Any swimmer will tell you, as Roger Deakin did, that swimming makes you feel good. For actual clinical proof of its antidepressant qualities, we can turn to a deeply suggestive study involving mice (which, by the way, innately know how to swim). The mice were subjected to a number of mild forms of stress over a period of weeks: Their cages were tilted, their tails nipped, their beds wetted. In New York such treatment would look like this: The landlord won't turn up your heat, the car alarm outside won't stop, your neighbor smokes constantly.

Not surprisingly, the mice began to seem down. They were soon dropped into water for a bout of swimming. Analyzing the subsequent changes to the mice's brains (specifically proteins in the hippocampus), the researchers concluded that it looked as if the mice had swum their depression away.

Try as I might, I simply couldn't find a *downside* to swimming. And so, after consulting with SwimQuest, one of a handful of swim holiday outfits, I decided on its trip to Mathraki, a small, rocky Greek island. The Ionian Sea tended to be warm, clear, and largely absent of things that might hurt you—sharks or, more likely, speedboats. I looked at Mathraki on the map, surrounded by expanses of blue, and read how Odysseus was said to have been held captive by Calypso on a nearby island.

Swept up in mythology and the romance of the open sea, I only later recalled that although I was relatively fit in general, swimming always quickly exhausted me. After a few laps, I found myself having to rest. If the pool was a struggle, why had I just blithely signed on for the deep, ungovernable ocean?

*

Deciding I needed to cram in some lessons, I contacted Marty Munson, a local triathlon coach. She wanted us to start in the pool. This itself was a revelation. Unlike that of my daughter, who was progressing by leaps and bounds, my own swimming was stuck in the 1970s, when I'd learned to swim at the YMCA.

Or *thought* I'd learned to swim. What I'd been taught, more than one person would tell me, was how not to drown. There's a difference.

As she watched me swim a few laps, Munson quickly diagnosed why I found swimming so taxing. Like many novices—or people stuck in the novice stage—I'd been trying to inhale *and* exhale as my head came out of the water on a front-crawl stroke. Exhaling, I learned, should be reserved for underwater, via what's called bubble breathing. In my frantic gulps of inspiration and expiration, I was inviting hyperventilation.

This breathing instruction may be blindingly obvious to you, but no one had ever pointed it out to me. There were other issues with my form, but tackling breathing seemed most vital. As the noted swim coach Terry Laughlin observed, "One of the major differences between swimming and land-based sports is that breathing in the water is a skill, and a fairly advanced one at that."

To get ocean experience, we headed for Coney Island, which, in the warmer months, has a vibrant open-water swimming scene. The morning we went, it was still cool, and we were alone. We donned wet suits and plunged into the water, the famous Cyclone roller coaster looming in the distance.

Swimming between jetties, I got briefly dizzy as the waves rolled me. It had somehow never occurred to me that you could get seasick *in* the sea, not just on it. I would come up for air and take a wave in the face, gulping mouthfuls of seawater. The wind slowed my progress, and the currents changed my course. "Open-water swimming," Munson told me, "is about practicing acceptance. You have to take whatever the ocean decides to throw at you."

It seemed another good mantra for life. If you could handle long swims in the roiling ocean, a crowded commute or busy slate of meetings would seem tame.

And yet I had plenty of trepidation as we arrived in Mathraki. Sure, we had crawled out of the sea, evolutionarily speaking, but humans have had a conflicted relationship with it ever since. Why was I subjecting myself and my family to the perils of this vast unknown? At least in surfing you were generally on *top* of the water.

Mathraki, one of the small Diapontia Islands that lie off Corfu, was a rugged, pine-scented outcropping that seemed to be largely inhabited by old Greek guys wearing New York Yankees caps who had lived in Queens before returning home to kibitz over Mythos lagers, tend their small Mediterranean gardens, and otherwise live out their dotage. We stayed at a small family-run inn where there seemed to be more chickens than fellow guests.

The innkeepers' son, George, who doled out the strong Greek coffees in the morning, also drove the SwimQuest safety boat. On the first day, after he'd taken us well out to sea and the other swimmers were already immersed, we hesitated, swaying, on the lip of the boat.

We were far from any shore, the water's surface an impenetrable, swirling mirror. None of us had ever swum in the ocean without land a Frisbee toss away. What might be patrolling these Stygian depths? The fear of deep water is called *thalassophobia;* there is no fear of shallow water.

One by one, beginning with my daughter, we dropped in. The water was warm, almost silken. In the distance lay the craggy walls of the coast of Albania. We began to swim, instinctively strung together for protection. I had the sudden feeling that the world had dropped from below me, that there was no limit to the abyss.

The paperback cover of *Jaws,* which had peeped out from every supermarket counter when I was an impressionable seven-year-old, flooded my mind. The foreboding was real. And yet the safety boat was always churning away nearby, and our guide, Mia Russell, a strong and experienced South African competitive swimmer, surfer, free diver, and self-described "mermaid," watched from above, often joining us in the water.

Our hesitation gradually yielded to bliss. Plunging into the water felt like entering another world, a series of blue rooms lit from below by diaphanous, reflected beams of light. The ocean became everything—the surging obstacle in your way but also a salty, buoyantly supportive caress. With the boat never far away, I was free to let my mind wander, as boundaryless as this underwater realm. We were like a little pod of whales, weaving in and out of coves, frolicking in the bath-like waters.

As the days progressed, we slowly began to conquer whatever apprehensions were holding us to the shore. Without even thinking about it, we were swimming longer than we'd ever swum before: Yards turned into miles; impossibly distant islands now seemed within reach. On our last night, my daughter won the coveted Golden Swim Cap for her pluck and determination in completing nearly all of the week's scheduled swims.

We emerged feeling we'd been *through* something. We are born in water, so why can't we be reborn? "Water is a form of therapy," Russell told me one afternoon. "It's this peace that overcomes you in the water, because it's quiet. You're floating. It's comforting. It's womb-like. It all comes out in the water." She has seen endless numbers of people "going through" things in the ocean, conquering fears, sorting out their lives, or overcoming personal hardships. Their goggles sometimes filled with tears.

*

We were hooked. My wife and daughter brimmed with the same fiery beginner's zeal I had.

Less than a year later, we signed up for another Swim-Quest trip, this time in the Bahamas. Russell was waiting for us on the dock at Great Guana Cay, a small barrier island in the Abacos. In Mathraki, she had christened my daughter her apprentice "mermaid," and in a solemn ceremony she now presented her with a mermaid pen.

There were ten persons there for the week, sharing an oceanfront villa. The group consisted entirely of women, save for myself and Guy Metcalf, an English swim coach and Russell's co-guide. John Coningham-Rolls, Swim-Quest's tall, gregarious founder, noted that this gender skew was not uncommon. "Most of the distance records in swimming," he'd told me, "are held by women."

There was a mother-daughter pair from the U.K. who had come straight to the Bahamas from another wild swimming expedition, a cold-water plunge in Sweden. There was a middle-aged English pediatrician who had lost her husband several years prior. She told me one evening that he'd always been expedition leader in the family, and in trying to find her own path, she'd come to the water.

The one who particularly captured my interest was Patricia, just turned seventy. She lived in Chamonix, where she skied, played tennis, and tended vegetables in her garden. She had retired a few years earlier after a varied career that included working on a film for the noted French director Claude Chabrol. She possessed an easy glamour—the woman could throw on a sundress and make it suddenly seem as if we were in St.-Tropez—and an unfiltered, rather dour charm.

One night at dinner, my wife received a compliment on the shirt she was wearing. She nonchalantly declared, "It's from H&M." Patricia suddenly slammed her hand on the table, startling everyone. "I am boycotting them!" she shouted. It had something to do with their global supply chains. But it was only one of a series of boycotts she seemed to be undertaking, and for sport we tried guessing which companies had or hadn't escaped her withering attention. When we pulled up to the dock at one oceanfront seafood spot for lunch, she noticed a cluster of bleached shells conspicuously close to the restaurant. "I feel as if I am in a conch graveyard," she said, with a weary Gallic scorn (she ordered vegetarian).

On an easyJet flight a few years before, she had stumbled across an article in the in-flight magazine on travel that combined trips with sports. "I saw people swimming in the most beautiful and amazing places in the world," she told me, "and I decided right then and there that I wanted to do that."

She wasn't much of a swimmer, however. She could do a slow hundred-meter breaststroke at the pool, pausing to take a breath. The swim trips she was exploring were on the order of a nonstop, three-kilometer front crawl. She went to her local pool but was told there wasn't a qualified coach for adults. There it was again, that subtle implication: *Learning was for children.*

Then she discovered YouTube and its cornucopia of instructional videos. She was particularly drawn to something called the Shaw method. She watched obsessively. She walked around her apartment with her arms bent in the proper style. Each time she hit the pool, she focused on some small detail, like the way her hand entered the water. Lacking a coach, she had her sister film her so she could compare her performance with the videos. Slowly, swimming two times a week, she got better. After six months, she could swim a kilometer without stopping.

After a year, she went on her first open-water trip. "I wonder," she told me, "why the hell I did not swim all my life." But the important thing was the doing, rather than the not-having-done. I thought of the philosopher Seneca, writing about "feeble old men" terrified by mortality when an illness appears. "They exclaim that they were fools because they have not really lived, and that if only they can recover from this illness they will live in leisure." Patricia wasn't waiting for that day.

*

Early in the week, I had tried to size up the group around me. SwimQuest had special weeks for people training for English Channel crossings and the like. But our week was billed as a "holiday." You could push as much as you wanted, but the distance or pace wasn't intended—or so they said—to be punishing. The safety boat, manned by Troy, who ran a local dive shop and had a joke-riddled banter as smoothly worn as sea glass, was always an option. Still, as someone who prides himself on a certain fitness level, I like to know what I'm up against. I decided, using rough parameters of age and appearance to assess the group, that I had nothing to worry about.

I soon realized my mistake. Once they entered the water, these polite older women transformed into powerful engines of hydrodynamic efficiency.

Patricia, especially, had an intensely fluid stroke. With what seemed like a minimum of effort, she was gliding through the azure waters. I found myself falling behind the group—and not for lack of effort. To my surprise, my daughter, who I'd worried would be unable to keep up, was actually passing me. "Technique, technique, technique," Coningham-Rolls had told me. Fitness gets you only so far in the water.

Later, at the house, as we gathered around a laptop like a campfire to look at video footage of our swims, my problems were on clear display. My arms weren't bad, the coaches told me. I had nice, high elbows; my reach was long. The main problem was my legs. I had thought I could overcome other deficiencies by simply pounding the water with legs conditioned from a lifetime of soccer. But I was kicking from my knees, not my hips. This was something Russell had cautioned me against in Greece, but the habit was sticking. As my knees bent, my legs dropped in the water, creating serious drag. And I was kicking furiously; for a moment, Russell thought the video had been sped up.

All that frenetic kicking was, as Metcalf noted, "pretty useless." Disconcertingly, I saw my daughter, she of the Golden Swim Cap, nodding in agreement. My "up-and-down kick," Russell said, was not "pushing the water backwards"; it was pushing it *down*. "If you did the bend kick really fast," she said, "you could actually go backwards."

Which is how I often felt I was going.

The days assumed a pattern: My daughter, whom I'd heard praised by the coaches for her "powerful kick" and "flexible ankles," was typically up front with the faster swimmers. I would keep up for a while but find myself flagging. With my incompetence masquerading as chivalry, I would swim near my wife, with her slower, steady breaststroke.

Trying to regain my dignity, when the day's swims were over and the others flopped into chairs to read, I would go on runs in the punishing, humid heat. On the fourth day, this backfired. After a seaside lunch in Hope Town, I started feeling light-headed. What I thought might be food poisoning was actually sunstroke. Chastened, I lay in the boat, drinking Cokes as Troy played me a selection of Bahamian "rake and scrape" songs, and watched everyone else swim. Patricia soon joined me, but only because she had another full week of swimming on deck and wanted to pace herself.

It was all a bit embarrassing, but it also felt, strangely, exhilarating. My travails in the water were actually one of the things I loved about open-water swimming. I appreciated that the ocean was, for me, one big blank slate. On a bike, I had a precisely calibrated sense of my performance metrics and an obsessive sense of obligation to meet or exceed them; I spent hours on the "sports social network" site Strava studying my rides, seeing what imaginary trophies I could amass or how I stacked up against people I knew. With swimming, I not only had no sense of what good swimming times were; I found I didn't care—and, well, good thing!

Didn't I want to get better? Sure. But I sensed that

this wasn't going to come immediately. As Terry Laughlin argues, "A good, efficient swimming stroke is one of life's more complicated skills, far more difficult to perfect than the ideal golf swing or the picture-perfect tennis serve."

More pressingly, I wanted to get from one point to another, on my own steam, in a little series of quests that my wife and daughter and I could do together and later commiserate about. I wanted us to see the beauty of the ocean—like the battery of slim, shiny barracuda that trailed us one afternoon as we swam—while it was still there to be seen. My daughter not only had a powerful role model in Mia but got to hang out with an intergenerational, international group of women, united by a common passion, who were putting her father to shame.

As for Patricia—who ended up winning the Golden Swim Cap—when she wasn't swimming, she was reexploring an old fascination with astronomy. She was trying to understand quantum theory. And she'd started playing pickleball, which is like up-sized Ping-Pong played on a badminton court. It's one of those "fastest-growing" sports you've never heard of. Because it was such a new sport, there weren't really coaches, so she was studying the "Pickleball channel" on YouTube.

Swimming had brought home several lessons.

The first was that you could possess, for a lifetime, what you thought was a basic understanding of some discipline and then discover you didn't really understand it at all. There are many ways to be a beginner. The second was that learning could come from anywhere; I learned by having good teachers analyze my behavior, but I also learned from being around others—people older than me, people younger than me. Third, I was reminded that once you'd started to learn something, once you'd taken a few tentative steps, your horizons seemed to dramatically expand. Before, I'd been flummoxed by simply doing laps in the sea. Suddenly I was investigating longer open-water swimming events that I could do with my wife and daughter. "You have to learn to walk before you can run," goes the old saying. Once you start to learn to walk, you get a sense of the things that might be beyond running.

The last, and most important, lesson was that it was never too late to be a beginner. Patricia was of an age, marked by experience and wisdom, when people tended to look backward. But she also had her eyes fixed on the future: the next swim trip, the next object of inquiry, the next thing in which to be an eager novice.

"It takes the whole of life," to quote Seneca once more, "to learn how to live."

LABORS OF LOVE: HAPPINESS IS IN YOUR HANDS

Ever since losing my second wedding ring—in the chilly winter surf at Malibu—I'd had it in mind to replace it. I missed the symbolism of it; I missed the weight. I could simply buy the same one, for the third time, but that seemed defeatist. Several friends suggested I just buy something supercheap off the internet, with an eye toward eventually losing *that* one. That struck me as too drably utilitarian. It wasn't an umbrella.

Motivated by the spirit of this book, I had another idea. I could *make* my own ring. Or, more feasibly, find an expert jeweler to help me make my own ring. I began looking around the internet and found that there was a flourishing practice of this in New York City.

The "IKEA effect," as it's been called, seems to lead people to place a higher value on things they'd had a hand in creating; we feel more attached to that bookcase we just struggled to assemble. So what better place to instill this value than in a wedding ring, this melding of aesthetic beauty and emotional resonance? If "labor leads to love," as the IKEA study described it, working on a wedding ring seemed a nice way to complete the circle.

As it turned out, I didn't need the internet, instead relying on an old-fashioned social network. One of my neighbors, David Alan, is a renowned custom jeweler, operating out of an atelier in midtown Manhattan, just adjacent to the Diamond District. I'd had years of elevator and lobby chats with him and his wife, Helena; we witnessed each other's daughters growing up. I'd once interviewed him for a story on synthetic diamonds and was intrigued by his vast repository of knowledge about an industry that was otherwise invisible to me. He had flowing, swept-back hair, was always casually but stylishly dressed, and had the air of a fast-talking raconteur.

To my surprise—given his often high-profile clientele—he was up for the challenge and invited me to his workshop one afternoon. After buzzing me through the "mantrap," a set of two interlocking doors installed as a security measure—there were, after all, hundreds of thousands of dollars of precious metals and gems on the premises—he led me to his desk. In the background, jewelers with head-mounted loupes hunched over benches, filing and twisting metal with pliers.

I remarked that the scene, these highly skilled craftsmen and craftswomen toiling high above the street below, seemed like a slice of old New York. "The trade of being a high-end bench jeweler is a dying trade," he said. "Nobody wants to spend the time on the side of the educator, and no one wants to take the time to properly apprentice." As if to underscore the point, his current jeweler, a genial Paraguayan named Max whom I'd soon be spending time alongside, had started making jewelry before I was born.

David was intrigued by the premise of my book, I think, because his whole career had begun with one of those after-work classes, taken at a community college, that are the beginner's natural habitat.

He'd actually had an early exposure to jewelry. His mother was in the business, and as a kid he'd sit with her and her partner and sift through product samples at their dining room table. But he never thought of it as a career option, drifting instead toward architecture, even interning with a firm during high school. In college, he decided to study philosophy. His father told him he needed to take a business class to "continue staying under our wing." So he picked up economics—more specifically, natural-resource economics. To his parents' mild chagrin, he eventually applied to be a forest ranger in Oregon.

And yet jewelry still glittered on the edge of his imagination. In that fallow first summer after the end of college, he took a class in what's known as the lost-wax casting process, an ancient method of jewelry making still practiced today that involves essentially crafting a wax sculpture from which a metal object will be cast. "I couldn't believe what I'd stumbled upon," he told me.

After a few more classes, he decided the only way to master the craft would be to apprentice with a master jeweler. Through a family connection, he secured an interview with a Frenchman named Jean. "I went to Forty-eighth Street and walked into this little smoke-filled dump of a shop," he said. "It was so filthy you couldn't see through the windows." At the center of it "was this angry little man; all you saw was his mustache and his hairline." This was Jean. "Do you know the Yiddish word *verbissen*?" David asked me. "It means 'pissed off.' Jean was the embodiment of *verbissen*." He showed Jean some pieces he'd made in the summer classes. "I'm looking at his workshop, with all this ultrafine work, thinking there's no way he's going to give me a shot. He's looking, he's looking, then he says, 'You start on Monday. You pay me fifty dollars a week.'"

In an age when interns at places like Google can make more than the average worker, it may seem strange to pay someone for the pleasure of working for them, but it wasn't an unheard-of practice in jewelry apprenticeship. "Back in the '90s, for a kid who had no job, fifty dollars a week was a lot," David told me. He took up bartending at night and, during the day, did whatever Jean needed him to do. "I didn't take a day off for three years." Early on, he mostly swept the floors and took care of the tools.

David was eventually given his first test, one that he'd later give his own apprentices. "Jean gave me a sheet of German silver," he said. "It's *not* silver; it's a combination of nasty materials that are very stiff and hard to work with. They tend to break tools and blades when you work with them."

From a one-millimeter sheet, he was instructed to cut a perfect three-by-three-centimeter square. He was then instructed to cut a one-by-one-centimeter hole in the center, and make another one-by-one-centimeter square piece of German silver that would fill the original hole in any direction. Jean gave him files and a digital measuring gauge precise down to the hundredths of a millimeter. The work required this level of precision, even if his apprentice didn't yet understand that. David toiled away on the squares and the hole, getting to where he thought it was perfect.

"I was so proud of myself," he said. "Jean holds it up to the light, measures, and says, 'This is shit!'" David was off by nearly imperceptible amounts. "His lesson was if your first move is off, everything gets worse from there."

Jean was a stern taskmaster. If David broke a saw blade, Jean would make him shorten his saw frame and continue to use the human-hair-thin cutting tool to where it barely had any teeth. "Why are you making me do this?

What do they cost?" David protested. "I used to make my *own* saw blades," his master thundered in response. "Make it shorter!" And yet Jean, for all his irascible bluster, was a phenomenal craftsman, one who'd take on elaborate projects—for example, gold-plated arachnids—that would stymie other jewelers. "He had such a delicate touch," David told me.

One day, retrieving something from Jean's safe, David came across a series of intensely complex enameled pieces, festooned with precious gems and fashioned with harlequins and fantastical figures.

"They must have been worth at least a hundred thousand dollars," he said. "I said, 'Jean, why don't you sell these?'"

"These are not for sale," Jean replied. "Because then they will *copy me*."

In his early career, David made any number of rookie mistakes. In the jewelry world, these tend to be expensive. He's had bad days, "twenty-five-thousand-dollar days." One time, a client—"a scary ex-military-something guy"—brought in a military graduation ring that he wanted "sized up," or enlarged. David cut through the bottom of the ring, then put it on the mandrel, a steel tool that expands a ring's diameter. He fashioned a piece of metal to solder into the gap. "I carefully forced it into place," he said. "It had perfect seams."

But he'd forgotten to anneal the gold, or, as he described it, "to give a regular, soft heat over the whole thing, to kind of push the molecules away from one another and remove any tension from the metal." Instead, the molecules, under a more intense heat, were rapidly separating from one another. The surface tension was too great. With a piercing, horrible clank, the ring snapped into two pieces. "I must have been white as paper," he said. "My employer says, 'You're dead. I'm not going to kill you. *He* is.'" The young jeweler was able to engineer a painstaking, time-consuming fix. Lesson learned.

Given that David had spent a year of his three-year apprenticeship before he was even allowed to touch a live piece of jewelry, it seemed deeply presumptuous of me to think I could come in and expect to create a piece of jewelry from scratch. His collection was filled with staggeringly detailed work, elaborate birdcage-like structures delicately interwoven around sparkling constellations of stones. But, he assured me, with a simpler men's wedding band, he could teach me enough of the process that I'd still feel as if my hand were involved.

In my mind's eye, I imagined the process would be something out of *The Lord of the Rings*, with some brilliantly gleaming sphere pounded out on a blackened forge while strains of Wagnerian music triumphantly swelled.

But the process that David began with, and worked in for many years—melting metal, pouring it into an ingot mold, hammering it out—had largely been eclipsed, at least with the simpler items, by the world of computer-aided design and manufacturing. Now, those pieces were typically drafted on a screen, using computer-aided design—or CAD, as it's called—and sent to a casting house, where printing machines would build the computer-modeled parts accurate to a hundredth of a millimeter. The resulting cast piece would then be finished in the workshop. The new technology allowed David to skip the first few steps that used to be done by a junior jeweler, and get right to the detail work. Old-school jewelers like Max occasionally grumbled. "It's killing the jewelry trade," he told me one afternoon.

I sympathized. But doing it the traditional way would take a lot longer and be costlier. In the end, David suggested, the ring wouldn't look any different. Unless, of course, I screwed it up, and with hand forging there were many more ways to do that. As much as I wanted to work on a ring, I didn't want to wear a ring that *looked* as if I'd done it.

Plus, I'd decided I wanted my ring to be made of platinum. For a novice, it wasn't an easy material to work with in the old-school way. "I've not poured platinum into an ingot mold in years," David told me. The melting point required of platinum could burn your retinas, if you weren't wearing the right protective eyewear—better to let a casting house do it. Safety aside, I didn't want to be old-school for the sake of it. I wanted to learn how to make a ring the way David was making rings, circa 2020.

But what ring? In our design meeting, which at times drifted into a seminar on metallurgy, we'd come up with rough parameters of size, shape, and material. But there was more to it, he insisted. "This can and should be about more than learning to make a physical object," he said. A wedding ring, he said, "is the only physical thing from your wedding, apart from photos, which we rarely look at." It was meant to be significant, he said, and it should be. "I get to be the guy who makes this thing that emblazons this very notion on thousands of people, every day, for the rest of their life," he said. "I might sound cheesy, but I'm fine with that!"

David's own ring, as he'd shown me, had a series of stones—diamonds, along with his and his family's birthstones—set on the interior surface. It was like secret symbolism, kept close to the skin.

I thought I too could do something beyond the standard simple metal band, something significant but not shouty. Thinking back to the thing that had launched this whole larger endeavor—the game of chess—I wondered aloud whether we could emboss the wood from chess pieces around the inner part of the ring. My wife, I thought to myself, could be queen, and I would be king. But what for my daughter? When I first presented the idea to her, she suggested, perhaps unsurprisingly, that *she* should be the queen.

David sprang to attention. "We could get a chess set from the year you were married? Cut the pieces and inlay them into the interior of the ring," he said. "If that's not something you feel up for doing, my lapidary guy could do it in a hot second."

As we kept talking, it suddenly occurred to me that he was thinking about a solid band of wood, made from chess pieces, circling the interior of the ring. "I see it as an inlaid track of pieces encircling the full interior of the band. It's a nice eternity track sort of thing," he said.

I told him I'd been thinking of having the forms of *individual* chess pieces carved into the interior. His eyes narrowed. "It'd be too small to see anything," he said. "If you want any detail from the chess piece, you'd never see it."

I had the sense that apart from seeming technically impossible, my idea to him seemed a bit overdetermined, even tacky. Maybe I thought so too. But simply having a track of repurposed wood chess pieces seemed too abstract. And I did like the inherent sculptural elegance of chess pieces.

The more we talked, the more he seemed to warm to the idea. We began playing around in a CAD program named Rhino. While jewelers relied heavily on Rhino these days, he felt their jewelry often looked computer generated. David felt that his many years on the bench gave him a deeper understanding of working with 3-D objects, so the jewelry keeps more of its old-world handcrafted feel.

On my suggestion, David took an image of a classic Staunton chess queen, outlined it in a skeletal series of points, and copied it. From this 2-D image, he executed what's called a "rail revolve," which spins a drawn line around a radius to create a 3-D representation. He compared it to a kid holding a bubble wand and spinning in a circle, trailing a halo of huge bubbles in the air.

He placed the 3-D queen in the ring's interior, hovering flat above the curves. His fingers dancing across the keyboard, his hand manipulating the mouse as steadily as a diamond setter, he twisted and torqued the queen, via a number of physics-based tools in Rhino, so that it conformed to the arc of the ring. Endless adjustments had to be made. To make the queen legible to the eye, the points of its crown couldn't just be copied; they had to be specially constructed. The indentations of the pieces had to be deep enough to be read, but not too deep to compromise the ring's structural integrity.

None of this was easy, and I fancied that David liked the challenge of doing something he hadn't quite done before. Helena, his wife and business partner, once asked him who the best jeweler he ever knew was. "Jean," he said. She asked David if he'd surpassed him. He felt he had. But he still needed to learn, still *wanted* to learn. There were new techniques, new tools, new clients with new requests.

When I asked him when he knew he was a master jeweler, he said, "It was when I got to the point that I knew I could do anything without having done it before." It might take some figuring out, but with enough time, and the proper mind-set, anything was possible.

Soon, the indentations, or "negative spaces," of three pieces—a king, a queen, and a bishop (the piece chosen by my daughter after careful deliberation)—were arrayed around the interior of the ring.

"To my mind it looks pretty cool," I ventured.

"It *does* look pretty cool," David said.

"Could we insert wood from pieces into those indentations?" I pressed.

"You're talking about tremendously precise work," he countered.

"Is there anything easier?"

"Enamel," he said. "It's a liquid that's inlaid and then cooked to stay on the surface. It turns to glass."

With a few keystrokes he rendered it on the screen. Suddenly the empty spaces of the half chess pieces glowed with a translucent sheen, as if they were little elaborately curved pools of water. "Bang!" he shouted. "Very cool."

"I'm glad you have more enthusiasm now."

"No, I love it!" he exclaimed. "Before CAD, we would never have done something like this."

And I could take a certain pride in that it was my naïve questions that had kicked the whole thing off. Here was the curious power of the beginner, mixed with expertise: I didn't know what could or couldn't be done; David, once presented with the idea, might not immediately know how to do it, but knew he could do it.

He pressed Send, and my ring, for now an ethereal assembly of pixels, was off to the casting house.

*

The object that came back—a dull, rough-textured, blunt-edged chunk of metal with a sharp, stubby chunk sticking out on one side—looked more like something you'd find in an old coffee can of nuts and bolts in someone's garage than a piece of fine jewelry. Peeping out from the interior, however, were the king, queen, and bishop, tiny but clearly legible.

The ring needed to be "finished," which involved successive rounds of ever-finer filing, buffing, sanding, and polishing. Now I was the apprentice, to be stationed at David's own jeweler's bench, just next to Max. It looked like an old-fashioned desk, its surface bristling with a vast array of obscure tools. Some weren't jeweler's tools per se, but things that had been adapted or repurposed; his buffers, for example, were housed in a caddy intended for dentist drills. This was part of the master craftsman's ethos: not simply mastering tools, but being able to come up with innovative solutions where standard tools failed.

The first step was to drop the ring into a "centrifugal magnetic finisher." It looked like a coffee bean grinder, its hopper filled not with beans but with a murky liquid. On the bottom, hidden, were scores of little steel pins and balls. Once activated, the machine would spin and the steel shrapnel would softly hammer the ring, including, David noted, "all the places we can't get to." The process would wipe out any "porosity," or pockets of air, that had been baked in during casting.

Then it was on to the bench. Sitting at David's bench felt like getting inside his head. He talked me through his carefully color-coded system, which was a safeguard against accidentally choosing a rougher-grit sandpaper when you wanted a finer-grit one. There was a blob of wax, jammed into a nook on the bench, that he used for lubricating tools. "I've had this piece of wax recycling on my desk for like twenty years," he said. Like a yeast starter in baking, it just kept evolving. "That's one of the tools on a diamond setter's bench that you never, *ever* touch."

There was another deeply personal object at the front of the bench: a small, somewhat battered wedge of wood, looking a bit like an angled doorstop, protruding outward. The bench pin, as it's called, is perhaps the single most important tool in a jeweler's life. It's used as a place to position and support one's hands as one works. Almost all labor happens upon it. David's had been subtly shaped with special cuts and angles over the years by his hands and his processes. I found I couldn't get comfortable with his, so he set up a standard one for me.

Over the coming days, my hands would begin to know the contours of that bench pin well. The first task was to remove the sprue, a bulge on the side of the ring left over from the casting process. Gripping the ring between a few nervous fingers, I needed to cut through the thick sprue with a thin hardened-steel saw blade easily capable of taking my finger off. To complicate things, I had to follow the curvature of the ring as I sawed, taking care not to saw into the ring itself. Last, I had to file down whatever metal was left, avoiding filing "flat spots" onto the surface or literally filing the ring away. "You will kill things if you're not careful here," David warned. I managed to remove the sprue with fingers intact, though not without breaking a few saw blades. Luckily, David was more generous than Jean had been, and he let me replace them at full size.

David had spotted some minor flaws in the ring—a nick here, a pockmark there—an almost inevitable by-product of casting. I could see these only when I looked through the jeweler's loupe. These would be laser welded out, via a big machine parked next to the jewelers' benches. Inside a shielded enclosure, you held the ring with one hand and with the other fed a bit of platinum wire into the cavity. You pressed a foot pedal and zap!—no more hole.

*

As it happened, I'd tried a bit of welding the previous summer, via a program called Metal Shop Fantasy Camp. It was run by Scott Behr, head of a Brooklyn-based company, Total Metal Resource, that specialized in custom-fabricated metal structures for high-end retail in the city.

He'd started the class on a bit of a whim, after he kept encountering people who seemed to be greatly intrigued by what he did for a living. He sensed there was a hunger among people to work with their hands, in a city where so few jobs called for that anymore. He came up with the idea of having students make a simple steel cube. "It's just a basic form," he told me. "If you can make that, you can make frames, windows, chairs." When he first described his plan to his girlfriend, she thought it was a terrible idea. "Nobody wants to make a cube," she said. He's since taught several thousand people, myself included, how to make that cube.

The fantasy camp is now a significant part of his overall business, and he still marvels at its success. "I've convinced people to come to my shop, work their ass off, and pay me," he joked. Sometimes, when he's on a deadline and shorthanded—finding skilled welders is not often easy—he offers to pay adept students to come in and help (I was tempted, but my steel cube was hardly a masterpiece). He suggested that the fantasy camp, beyond being fun, tapped into deep impulses. "I think we have this innate sense to make or use tools," he said, echoing Benjamin Franklin's assertion that "man is a tool-making animal." Tool use, it's been suggested, expanded our brain size and helped shape the hands we have today.

"People want to have an experience," Behr said, "rather than sit all day and just do this"—here he held up his phone. Welding at the shop was like an immersive theater of the senses, with acrid smoke and snapping, blinding light that still burned in my eyes the following day. Fire and metal—it seemed elemental. "We're breaking base metal apart at the molecular level," the instructor, a tall, jocular man named Alex, had told the class. Done correctly, he said, the bonds we were forging were stronger than the metals they joined.

Some alchemy may be going on in the brain as well. There's an argument, made by Kelly Lambert, who runs a neuroscience lab at the University of Richmond, that doing physical labor with your hands is a powerful, mood-enhancing way of activating what she terms "effort-driven rewards." We're "programmed," Lambert suggests, to "derive a deep sense of satisfaction and pleasure when our physical effort produces something tangible." And what's more tangible than a heavy steel cube? "It's a real immediate sense of satisfaction," Behr told me. "People are all smiles when they finish." Ordering lunch via a few soft pushes on a smartphone screen feels wonderfully easy—compared with all the procuring and chopping and stirring of cooking—but seems to short-circuit the old connection between "effort and consequence."

Back at David's bench, I was about to begin the process of filing away the fingerprint-like ridges that the printing and casting process had left on the ring's exterior. He ran through "the moves" a few times for me. With one hand pressing the ring firmly against the bench pin, his other began making strokes, smooth and long and delicate, at a diagonal angle across the ring's surface. With each file stroke, his other hand would minutely advance the ring. He'd also twist the ring, as well as the file, between his fingers, to ensure that he evenly followed its curvature. In between strokes, he would methodically tap the file on the bench pin. Like a metronome, it helped establish a rhythm. "If you're consistent in your movement," he told me, "you're going to have a consistent surface."

To practice the move, he gave me an inexpensive brass ring. "We are attentive here to the cubic hundredth of a millimeter," he told me. "These little things—one file stroke—could ruin a delicate piece." As I fumbled with the ring and the file, I had the sense that my brain was trying to teach my fingers what to do, but also that my fingers were trying to teach my brain what to do.

I filed for hours. My fingers hurt, and I was past the

point where I could see visible progress. I thought of a story David had told me about his last apprentice. He was a "good kid," he said, eager to learn the trade. He wanted to be a designer like David. But in the way that the master Mr. Miyagi doesn't let Daniel immediately start with actual karate moves in the movie *The Karate Kid*, David insisted his apprentice achieve mastery with filing—the precision of a surgeon, the fluidity of a concert violinist. One day, after a few months, his apprentice stepped out to use the bathroom. "He never came back," David said. "Five *hours* later, I get a text. He said, 'I just can't take any more filing.' "

He was still looking for a new apprentice, something that wasn't easy in a field where the number of skilled positions had declined, in a country where only a tiny number of young people train as apprentices.

I had a new appreciation for the idea that something like jewelry making, or welding, was as much a motor skill as surfing. Maybe even more so: Working with one's hands occupies more of the brain's motor cortex than much larger parts of our anatomy do, like our legs or our back. The tools seemed a part of David's hands, where mine struggled to accept these new appendages. "Don't hold your hand so tight," Max, David's jeweler, warned me. "You'll get tired and the tools will fight back." But as I struggled to learn the move, it was my brain that often gave out before my fingers.

I spent hours at the bench, filing or sanding endless strokes, pausing to peer at what I'd done through the loupe. I made mistakes, like filing too much in one direction and leaving telltale marks. As I worked, I'd chat with Max about our shared musical interests and his life in the jewelry trade. My fingers bled from the sandpaper, my back ached, and at night I could still smell the metallic tang on my hands. "You're a jeweler now," David joked.

At times I would slide my ring onto my finger, thinking it looked good enough to be worn as it was. Then
David would come by, squint through his loupe, and say,
"See these lines? It needs more sanding." Because I'd seen
it go from dull roughness to shining beauty, he said, I was
more willing to accept imperfections. When he hands a
piece off to a client, they wouldn't have this understanding. It needed to be perfect. The irony was that the ring
I was so painstakingly shepherding to perfection would,
as David noted, "get dinged up the first time you grab a
subway pole."

Through David's feedback and sheer repetition, I
slowly became more fluid in my motions. With each stroke
of the file, each scour of the sandpaper, each motor-driven
whir of the buffer, that ring was slowly taking shape. I
could start to see myself reflected in the surface luster and
think, "I did that." I could take pride in that my ring—the
idea of my ring, which I'd helped come up with—was now
joining their collection.

Effort and consequence. I'd be sure to not let this one
slip away.

IF YOU KNOW WHAT YOU'RE DOING,
YOU SHOULDN'T BE DOING IT:
THE ROAD TO SELF-RENEWAL

Beginners is not a tale of overnight success.

I didn't go on to win any big chess tournaments, surf
alongside Kelly Slater at Pipeline, or get chosen for *American Idol* (though, in all fairness, I didn't apply). I achieved
modest competency in a number of things to which I'd
long been attracted, from the outside. But doing these
things brought me an immense and almost forgotten kind
of pleasure.

I didn't go looking for happiness per se. I favor the assertion, made by the philosopher John Stuart Mill, that happiness is something that cannot be found as an end unto itself. The way to achieve it, he suggested, was to have one's mind "fixed on some object other than [one's] own happiness."

One of these objects, he noted, was some "art or pursuit." Don't ask if you are happy, he said. Do things that make you happy. Don't pursue happiness; find happiness in your pursuits. I might only add: Do not worry how *well* you're doing them.

My own learning continues beyond this book; it goes on ad infinitum. And, to be honest, I haven't taken to all these things with the same fervor. I loved the drawing classes, but haven't found myself haunted by an inconsolable desire to draw outside class. That's not me sketching furiously on that park bench. Perhaps if I had had that desire, I'd have expressed it long ago. This doesn't mean it holds no value. Drawing, for me, remains an immensely pleasurable (and sometimes intimidating) exercise, albeit one that I mostly need the structured environment—and time—of a class to engage with.

Is drawing a "passion"? I'm not sure. It may become one, the longer I work at it. The whole idea that there's some sole passion that's out there, or secretly within you, waiting to emerge and magically change your life is questionable.

As the psychologist Carol Dweck and colleagues have suggested, when people have a fixed notion that some passion is just out there waiting to be "found," they anticipate that it will "provide limitless motivation and that pursuing it will not be difficult." As if the would-be passion itself will do the work. But skill learning can be hard, and the moment that person encounters difficulty, they may feel it wasn't their passion after all.

A person with a growth mind-set, on the other hand, who believes that passions are "developed," knows it may not come easy at first—or ever. These people are likely to be more motivated to stick with the pursuit when challenges arise.

I know you would probably rather read how I conquered all these things in mere months, and learn the "secret" of how to do it yourself. We live in a frictionless age in which process is typically obscured by results. You press a few buttons on your phone, and a car or dinner comes to you, a moving blue dot on a map, hiding a whole range of human effort. An ancient art like meditation? There's an app for that! You search online for "how to sing," and what pops up in autocomplete? *In five minutes. In thirty days.* There are breathless reports of drugs and technologies, like transcranial direct-current stimulation, that will "speed" learning. And, believe me, there were moments, warbling off-key or getting checkmated, when I wished I could, like Keanu Reeves in *The Matrix*, wake up in wide-eyed wonder and declare, "I know kung fu."

But even more, I wanted effort. I wanted struggle. I wanted to be able to feel the little advances, the setbacks. This was a journey by foot, not airplane. To be a traveler, the writer Daniel Boorstin once observed, you need some *travail*—that's French for "painful or laborious effort." Otherwise you're just a tourist; someone else has done the legwork for you. You're watching the how-to video without getting your own hands dirty.

It's similar in learning: "If it's easy, you're not learning," goes the expression. And yet there have been plenty of times when it was hard and I *still* felt as if I were failing to learn. The surfer Laird Hamilton observed that when you're learning some new physical skill, you're "sore everywhere." When you get really good at it, you'll barely feel it. It's natural to want to avoid this pain, Hamilton says, to "indulge ourselves in our expertise." But as he noted, you can always go back to what you're good at. Learning those new things was like jumping off the safety boat into an ocean whose depths couldn't be predicted.

When I began road cycling in earnest a decade ago, I committed any number of beginner's mistakes. You might think that riding a bike is riding a bike, but there's a real skill to riding fast in groups or down mountains. There was no limit to this parade of embarrassment. I struggled to "clip in" to the pedals, falling over several times, typically at a stoplight with an audience. In my first big road race, I rode too close to someone, rubbed their wheel, and tumbled into a ditch—on the *very first mile*. Once, on a big multistate charity ride in the rainy chill of early spring, I opened my swag bag to find a jar of "embrocation," a term that was new to me. "Keeps your legs warm," my hotel roommate said as he stuffed wadded newspaper into his wet shoes. "Sounds good," I said, proceeding to apply it. It's a "borderline toxic" ointment meant to invigorate *bare* legs; I foolishly donned full-length thick Lycra winter leggings over it. I was more than warm: I had a fiery, six-hour skin peel that soon migrated to my nether regions.

All these episodes caused me embarrassment, even some pain. Would it have been better if I'd had some sage sensei who could have precisely shown me the way and prevented all these errors from occurring? Maybe. But I suspect the progress I made wouldn't have seemed as sweet.

What's curious is that all these errors I made loom much more vividly in my mind than any tangible moments of progress, which seems important: These were inflection points, moments when I was standing up against the edge of my knowledge and ability. Like the infants in Karen Adolph's lab in chapter 2, I was running an ongoing experiment, and mistakes gave me raw insight. Getting through them not only was useful for helping solve future problems, as they came up, but also made me more empathetic when I saw a novice making some of those same mistakes. *I've been there.*

Beginners was also never meant to be about unlocking some hidden talent, at least in a way that would bring about a major course correction in my life. I like what I do and want to keep doing it as long as I can. Neither I nor anyone else suspected I was a closet singer or artist harboring deep reserves of untapped potential. I just wanted to take a stab at some things and see what might result. I wanted to give myself permission to play around, the way we parents were constantly reminding ourselves our children needed to do. I wanted my daughter to see me struggle and to see me grow.

Beyond simply trying to get better at things, I was hoping to reawaken a desire to learn. And I quickly discovered that the act of trying new things could be infectious.

While working on these core pursuits, I had all sorts of weird *other* firsts. I ran my first marathon. I snowboarded. I dipped my toe into sailing and was dazzled, if intimidated, by its vast arsenal of terminology and equipment. Thanks to my daughter's enthusiasm, I seemed to be doing some strange new thing every week (indoor skydiving, rock climbing). I got back up on ice skates and a skateboard for the first time in decades. During her outdoor track season, I spent afternoons doing the long jump, something I hadn't thought much about since the days of long division (another skill I needed to quickly refresh).

The mathematician Richard Hamming once drew an interesting distinction between scientists and engineers. "In science," he wrote, "if you know what you are doing you should not be doing it." Meaning: Science was about probing beyond the edge of what we know. It was about experimentation and failure. There was no need to dabble in proven hypotheses.

In engineering, however, wrote Hamming, "if you do not know what you are doing you should not be doing it." Engineers are tasked with making sure things do not fail, with ensuring certain quantifiable levels of performance. No one wants to drive across an experimental bridge.

In our careers, we're largely engineers. We need to deliver reliable competence. In my work as a writer, when a publication asks me to write something, they expect something more or less in the house style, delivered at the proper length. They're not generally looking for radical experimentation or willful flights of fancy.

But we all, I think, also want to be scientists. We want to mess around, screw things up, push the boundaries just to see what might happen. We want to get in over our heads without worrying too much about the consequences. We want to see what other dimensions there might be to this self that presents every morning in the bathroom mirror. Those hidden selves become, arguably, even more important as you age and settle into a being that's ever more defined, by the outside world and by you. As the writer John Casey wrote, "My old teacher Kurt Vonnegut told me that to flatter a person it's more effective to praise their minor secret vanities than their major accomplishments." We don't always want to be known for that thing we're known for.

The disciplines and pursuits—call them hobbies, if you must—I've embarked upon here have been my science. Struggling to interpret what I saw while drawing, straining my body to try to hit an E5 note, and going out in the waves on a day it felt a little big for me were all moments when I did not know what I was doing. But I was doing them anyway.

Often, it was my brain holding me back. In singing,

people sometimes struggle to hit notes that they easily use in simple conversation. It's the *idea* of singing getting in the way more than the mechanics of the thing itself.

All this self-exploration, admittedly, has the whiff of indulgent self-absorption. But for all the inward focus, these activities actually brought me *outward*. One of the greatest joys in being a beginner, it turns out, is meeting other beginners. I met all sorts of people—ones I probably wouldn't have encountered in my everyday life—and we were united by our shared lack of skill, our willingness to expose our possible failings.

I met people I would now consider friends. This is important, because friendship, particularly among males, seems to decline in stature as we age, despite its many benefits. It sometimes seems, like singing or drawing, one of those things we cherished while young and is then expected to gradually retreat to the margins, until we're not quite sure how to get it back.

Lisa Wade, a sociologist at Occidental College, suggests that some of the stereotypical images of masculinity—competitiveness, self-reliance, a reluctance to display insecurities—often get in the way of forming friendships. Being a beginner is precisely about putting your status aside, about being willing to listen to and learn from others, about revealing your insecurities.

It's probably not accidental that, as in the group of swimmers, I so often tended to find myself in groups dominated by women. They just seemed more open to trying new things, to putting themselves out there, being more supportive companions to their fellow beginners. "Learning," as *The Journal of Positive Psychology* put it, "requires the humility to realize one has something to learn."

For me, it was being a parent that knocked me out of my mid-career comfort zone. It puts you in a curious position: You are at once teacher and learner. Almost every day, it seemed as if I were trying to teach my daughter something: how to dribble a basketball, light a match, throw a football (a hardly intuitive thing). Most of these I learned, as you probably did, a long time ago and no longer thought much about. And then one day she's bringing home algebra problems and I'm suddenly a re-learner, dusting off something I wrongly assumed I knew how to do with ease.

You're seeing all these experiences through your children's eyes, but often through *your* eyes as well. My local ice-skating rink is filled with children and parents shuffling along on about the same footing (because the parents probably haven't skated so much since they were their children's age). You're amazed that you can still do something from so long ago; skills are like memories contained by the body.

Even better is when parent and child are learning something new—rappelling at the climbing gym, making cookies, playing some new game—together. That's when you realize that you and your child's growth need not be competing entities in some zero-sum game, or that your child's learning is something that must be managed only from afar, and that this thing that you're so fetishizing in your child—learning—does not have to end at childhood.

My own little experiment, all these little boats I've pushed out, continues. I haven't learned any of these skills; I'm learning them.

Now that we've ended, it's time for you to begin.

ACKNOWLEDGMENTS

Most of the people who helped me along the way, with research, or teaching, or just being a good sport, are already mentioned in the text, so I won't duplicate my inherent gratitude to them here. But there are a few whose contributions I wasn't able to note.

Special thanks are due to Gabriella Cantarero, Firas Mawase, and Manuel Anaya at the Human Brain Physiology and Stimulation Laboratory at the Johns Hopkins Medical Institute; as well as Ryan Roemmich at the Center for Movement Studies at Hopkins' Kennedy Krieger Institute. In Alabama, Destin Sandlin and Barney Dalton tried to talk me through how to ride a backward bicycle, and were rewarded by my staggering and humorous incompetence. In Crested Butte, Dusty Dyer took time to talk over the finer points of ski instruction. In Dallas, Sarah Festini and Xi Chen, among others at the University of Texas' Center for Vital Longevity, helped me understand the aging brain. Lucy Norcliffe-Kaufmann at New York University's Langone Health Center guided me through the intricacies of the vagus nerve. Rob Gray at the University of Arizona answered my queries, and his "Perception-Action Podcast" was an invaluable resource in learning about motor skills. Adam Cross at the New York Academy of Art patiently led me through drawing and painting, while Heather Petruzelli did the same for voice.

With Alfred A. Knopf, I've had the pleasure of publishing three books with a first-rate, and largely unchanged, team. My editor, Andrew Miller, as always, provided sage counsel, while Maris Dyer unflaggingly kept things on track. Gabrielle Brooks has been helping to get the word out since day one. Thanks also to Sarah Nisbet, Ingrid Sterner, Maria Massey, Tyler Comrie, and Soonyoung Kwon. And let me pay tribute here to the legendary Sonny Mehta, a true literary lion—I'm proud, and humbled, to have been part of his editorial legacy. Thanks as well to my longtime agent and friend, Zöe Pagnamenta, and her colleagues at the Zöe Pagnamenta Agency: Jess Hoare and Alison Lewis. In the U.K., thanks to Sally Holloway at Felicity Brian, and Mike Harpley at Atlantic Books. Thanks are also due to some of the editors I most enjoy working with in between book projects: Michael Roberts at *Outside*, Flora Stubbs and Maura Egan at *Travel and Leisure*, and Simon Willis at *The Economist*, among others.

Lastly, thanks to my daughter, Sylvie, a willing companion, research subject, and inspiration; and to my wife, Jancee Dunn, always ready to consider another draft, in writing as in life.

NOTES

PROLOGUE

THE OPENING GAMBIT

4 "I like the moment": Larry Evans, "Dick Cavett's View of Bobby Fischer," *Chess Daily News*, Aug. 24, 2008, web.chessdailynews.com.

5 Keens Chophouse: See Frank Brady, "The Marshall Chess Club Turns 100," *Chess Life*, Sept. 2015, 2–7.

6 children can acquire a proficiency: This idea is mentioned in Wolfgang Schneider et al., "Chess Expertise and Memory for Chess Positions in Children and Adults," *Journal of Experimental Child Psychology* 56, no. 3 (1993): 328–49.

6 innocently skin you alive: "What is particularly striking," observes an article in *Applied Cognitive Psychology*, "is that children—not normally known for their rationality—can compete with adults on an even basis in chess tournaments." Dianne D. Horgan and David Morgan, "Chess Expertise in Children," *Applied Cognitive Psychology* 4, no. 2 (1990): 109–28.

11 It learned as it went: See James Somers, "How Artificial-Intelligence Program AlphaZero Mastered Its Games," *New Yorker*, Dec. 3, 2018.

11 aid of a coach: This point was made by the DeepMind researcher Matthew Lai in Matthew Sadler and Natasha Regan, *Game Changer* (Alkmaar, Neth.: New in Chess, 2019), 92.

11 "If you want to improve": Anders Ericsson and Robert Pool, *Peak: Secrets from the New Science of Expertise* (Boston: Houghton Mifflin Harcourt, 2016).

12 The studies were typically small: For a comprehensive overview of the literature, see Fernand Gobet and Guillermo Campitelli, "Educational Benefits of Chess Instruction: A Critical Review," in *Chess and Education: Selected Essays from the Koltanowski Conference*, ed. T. Redman (Richardson: Chess Program at the University of Texas at Dallas, 2006), 124–43.

12 "direction of causality" problem: See, for example, Merim Bilalić and Peter McLeod, "How Intellectual Is Chess—a Reply to Howard," *Journal of Biosocial Science* 38, no. 3 (2006): 419–21.

12 tangible positives: Maybe chess was just a sort of placebo whose benefits could be obtained by other activities in which kids were spurred on by closely watching adults. Giovanni Sala and Fernand Gobet make this suggestion in their article "Do the Benefits of Chess Instruction Transfer to Academic and Cognitive Skills? A Meta-analysis," *Educational Research Review* 18 (May 2016): 46–57.

12 "as a way to teach thinking": Dianne Horgan, "Chess as a Way to Teach Thinking," Article No. 11 (1987), United States Chess Federation Scholastic Department.

13 Male players' ratings: See, for example, Lisa Zyga, "Why Men Rank Higher Than Women at Chess (It's Not Biological)," Phys Org.com, Jan. 12, 2009, phys.org.

13 *"Girls lose to boys"*: See Hank Rothgerber and Katie Wolsiefer, "A Naturalistic Study of Stereotype Threat in Young Female Chess Players," *Group Processes and Intergroup Relations* 17, no. 1 (2014): 79–90.

CHAPTER ONE

A BEGINNER'S GUIDE TO BEING A BEGINNER

17 "Perhaps you think that you can know": L. A. Paul, "What You Can't Expect When You Are Expecting," *Res Philosophica* 92, no. 2 (2015): 149–70.

18 novice parents shown a sample: Joanna Gaines and David C. Schwebel, "Recognition of Home Injury Risks by Novice Parents," *Accident Analysis and Prevention* 41, no. 5 (2009): 1070–74.

18 the way you speak to your young child: Parents who were coached, in one study, how to speak better "parentese"—not baby talk, but real words, more effortfully articulated—had more verbally proficient babies than those who didn't get the training. See Naja Ferjan Ramírez et al., "Parent Coaching at 6 and 10 Months Improves Language Outcomes at 14 Months: A Randomized Controlled Trial," *Developmental Science* (2018): e12762, doi:10.1111/desc/12762.

18 "errorless learning": For a good summary, see Janet Metcalfe, "Learning from Errors," *Annual Review of Psychology* 68 (2017): 465–89.

19 "As adults," write the authors: Alison Gopnik, Andrew Meltzoff, and Patricia Kuhl, *The Scientist in the Crib* (New York: Harper Perennial, 1996), 196.

21 "micromastery": See Robert Twigger's enjoyable *Micromastery: Learn Small, Learn Fast, and Unlock Your Potential to Achieve Anything* (New York: TarcherPerigree, 2017).

23 "life résumé": I got this phrase from Jesse Itzler.

23 "symbolic self-completion theory": For a discussion, see Eddie Brummelman, "My Child Redeems My Broken Dreams: On Parents Transferring Their Unfulfilled Ambitions onto Their Child," *PLOS One*, June 19, 2013, doi.org/10.1371/journal.poe.0065360.

23 In one fascinating experiment: Julia A. Leonard et al., "Infants Make More Attempts to Achieve a Goal When They See Adults Persist," *Science*, Sept. 22, 2017, 1290–94.

24 Beginner archers grip the bow: See "These Archery Mistakes Are Ruining Your Accuracy," Archery Answers, archeryanswers.com, and "9 Common Archery Mistakes and How to Fix Them," The Archery Guide, Nov. 30, 2018, thearcheryguide.com.

24 Beginner auto mechanics spill oil: "5 Annoying Things Beginner Mechanics Do," Agradetools.com, agradetools.com.

25 "how much deep and shallow water": This example is taken from Larry MacDonald, "Learn from Others' Boating Mistakes," *Ensign*, theensign.org.

25 It's the rookies getting woozy: R. L. Hughson et al., "Heat Injuries in Canadian Mass Participation Runs," *Canadian Medical Association Journal* 122, no. 1 (1980): 1141–42.

25 In snowboarding, the majority of injuries: Christopher Bladin et al., "Australian Snowboard Injury Data Base Study: A Four-Year Prospective Study," *American Journal of Sports Medicine* 21, no. 5 (1993): 701–4.

25 In equestrian sports, novices: John C. Mayberry et al., "Equestrian Injury Prevention Efforts Need More Attention to Novice Riders," *Journal of Trauma: Injury, Infection, and Critical Care* 62, no. 3 (2007): 735–39.

25 beginner jumpers are up to twelve times: See Anton Westman and Ulf Björnstig, "Injuries in Swedish Skydiving," *British Journal of Sports Medicine* 41, no. 6 (2007): 356–64.

25 "extreme neurobiological state": See Krishna G. Seshadri, "The Neuroendocrinology of Love," *Indian Journal of Endocrinology and Metabolism* 20, no. 4 (2016): 558–63.

25 Our language often reverts: Meredith L. Bombar and Lawrence W. Littig Jr., "Babytalk as a Communication of Intimate Attachment: An Initial Study in Adult Romances and Friendships," *Personal Relationships* 3, issue 2 (June 1996): https://onlinelibrary.wiley.com/doi/abs/10.1111/j.1475-6811.1996.tb00108.x.

26 dubbed prediction errors: So-called prediction errors are a key element in motor learning. Put most simply, an error briefly suppresses the release of dopamine in the brain; it does not reward itself for doing the wrong thing. Errors in particular command the attention of the brain and are central to learning. For a good discussion, see R. D. Seidler et al., "Neurocognitive Mechanisms of Error-Based Motor Learning," in *Progress in Motor Control: Neural, Computational, and Dynamic Approaches,* ed. Michael J. Richardson, Michael A. Riley, and Kevin Shockley (New York: Springer, 2013).

26 "In the beginner's mind": See Shunryu Suzuki, *Zen Mind, Beginner's Mind: Informal Talks on Zen Meditation and Practice* (Boston: Shambhala, 2011), 1.

26 a journey of not knowing: These thoughts are drawn from an interesting talk, "Cultivate Beginner's Mind," by Myogen Steve Stucky, the former abbot of the San Francisco Zen Center. Talk accessed at sfzc.org.

26 "You never intend to go": See Norman Rush, *Mating* (New York: Vintage Books, 1992), 337.

27 "steep learning curve": For an interesting discussion of the evolution of the phrase, see Ben Zimmer, "A Steep 'Learning Curve' for 'Downton Abbey,'" *Vocabulary.com Blog,* Feb. 8, 2013, www .vocabulary.com.

29 "unskilled and unaware of it": J. Kruger and D. Dunning, "Unskilled and Unaware of It," *Journal of Personality and Social Psychology* 77, no. 6 (1999): 1121–34.

29 additional research later showed: Dunning and Carmen Sanchez crafted an experiment in which people had to diagnose victims of a zombie outbreak. "We were confident that this would be a new scenario to all our participants," they wrote, "allowing them all to start as total novices." The hypothetical patients were suffering from one of "two strains of zombie disease," which had similar symptoms, and subjects had to figure out which. After each diagnosis, they were given feedback on whether they'd made the correct choice. During the study, people gradually got better as they diagnosed more patients.

But what grew faster than their success rate was their *estimation* of their success rate. Emboldened by the flush of first success, they were in an advanced beginner's bubble of overconfidence. See David Dunning and Carmen Sanchez, "Research: Learning a Little About Something Makes Us Overconfident," *Harvard Business Review,* March 29, 2018.

29 speed chess players: B. D. Burns, "The Effects of Speed on Skilled Chess Performance," *Psychological Science* 15 (July 2004): 442–47.

29 Chess experts can become so entranced: In one study, grandmasters were presented with chess positions and asked to find the quickest way to win. There was a familiar, longer way to win, and a shorter, more novel way. Even though the players told researchers they were scanning the entire board, eye-tracking software revealed the truth: *They could not take their eyes off the familiar move.* M. Bialić et al., "Why Good Thoughts Block Better Ones: The Mechanism of the Pernicious Einstellung (Set) Effect," *Cognition* 108, no. 3 (2008): 652–61.

29 Or consider an experiment: See Katherine Woollett and Eleanor A. Maguire, "The Effect of Navigational Expertise on Wayfinding in New Environments," *Journal of Environmental Psychology* 30, no. 4 (2010): 565–73.

30 the "overlearned" London: In a similar way, studies of memory recall have shown that older adults do less well in incorporating new memories when the information is linked to memories they have "overlearned." Older participants asked to recall a new version of the "Little Red Riding Hood" fairy tale were more likely than younger participants to "confabulate" elements of the original fairy tale. See Gianfranco Dallas Barba et al., "Confabulation in Healthy Aging Is Related to Interference of Overlearned, Semantically Similar Information on Episodic Memory Recall," *Journal of Clinical and Experimental Neuropsychology* 32, no. 6 (2010): 655–60.

30 They see the world with fresher eyes: One area of cognitive testing where older adults outperformed younger adults was in the retrieval of "semantic-memory" general-information questions (for example, "In which ancient city were the Hanging Gardens located?"), particularly when the questions and answers were based on *facts*, rather than novel experimental paradigms, or as the researchers put it, "irrelevant mumbo jumbo." Older adults, it is suggested, "are capable of rallying their attentional resources as well as, and sometimes better than, young adults . . . they will engage their attention and effort to learn the truth." See Janet Metcalfe et al., "On Teaching Old Dogs New Tricks," *Psychological Science* 26, no. 12 (2015): 1833–42.

30 adults might discard as irrelevant: See J. N. Blanco and V. M. Sloutsky, "Adaptive Flexibility in Category Learning? Young Children Exhibit Smaller Costs of Selective Attention Than Adults," *Developmental Psychology* 55, no. 10 (2019).

30 less concerned with being wrong: See, for instance, Christopher G. Lucas et al., "When Children Are Better (or at Least More Open-Minded) Learners Than Adults: Developmental

Differences in Learning the Forms of Causal Relationships," *Cognition* 131, no. 2 (2014): 284–99.

30 Take the curious case: Michael Wilson, "After a Funeral and Cremation, a Shock: The Woman in the Coffin Wasn't Mom," *New York Times*, March 21, 2016.

31 "Before you make your move": See "Play Like a Beginner!," Chess.com, April 3, 2016, www.chess.com.

33 "At five years old": Adam Thompson, "Magnus Carlsen, an Unlikely Chess Master," *Financial Times*, Nov. 28, 2014.

33 "probabilistic sequence learning": See K. Janacsek et al., "The Best Time to Acquire New Skills: Age-Related Differences in Implicit Sequence Learning Across Human Life Span," *Developmental Science* 15, no. 4 (2012): 496–505.

34 "neural systems are particularly responsive": Virginia B. Penhune, "Sensitive Periods in Human Development: Evidence from Musical Training," *Cortex* 47, no. 9 (2011): 1126–37.

34 my brain may be so "tuned": See Amy S. Finn et al., "Learning Language with the Wrong Neural Scaffolding: The Cost of Neural Commitment to Sounds," *Frontiers in Systems Neuroscience*, Nov. 12, 2013.

34 "less is more hypothesis": See J. S. Johnson and E. L. Newport, "Critical Period Effects in Second Language Learning: The Influence of Maturational State on the Acquisition of English as a Second Language," *Cognitive Psychology* 21, no. 1 (1989): 60–99.

34 The skill of having perfect pitch: Stephen C. Van Hedger et al., "Auditory Working Memory Predicts Individual Differences in Absolute Pitch Learning," *Cognition* 140 (July 2015): 95–110.

35 with a "synaptic density": P. R. Huttenlocher, "Synaptic Density in Human Frontal Cortex—Developmental Changes and Effects of Aging," *Brain Research* 162, no. 2 (1979): 195–205.

36 My brain volume was atrophying: See, for example, Lindsay Oberman and Alvaro Pascual-Leone, "Change in Plasticity Across the Lifespan: Cause of Disease and Target for Intervention," in *Changing Brains: Applying Brain Plasticity to Advance and Recover Human Ability*, ed. Michael M. Merzenich, Mor Nahum, and Thomas M. Van Vleet (Boston: Elsevier, 2013), 92.

36 we lose about one neuron: See David A. Drachman, "Do We Have Brain to Spare?," *Neurology* 64, no. 12 (2005): 2004–5.

36 Using more brain means: See Marc Roig et al., "Aging Increases the Susceptibility to Motor Memory Interference and Reduces Off-Line Gains in Motor Skill Learning," *Neurobiology of Aging* 35, no. 8 (2014): 1892–900.

36 age-related declines: Timothy Salthouse, "What and When of Cognitive Aging," *Current Directions in Psychological Science* 13, no. 4 (2004): 140–44.

37 This general pattern is replicated: Tiffany Jastrzembski, Neil Charness, and Catherine Vasyukova, "Expertise and Age Effects on Knowledge Activation in Chess," *Psychology and Aging* 21, no. 2 (2006): 401–5.

38 practice a golf swing: See L. Bezzola et al., "The Effect of Leisure Activity Golf Practice on Motor Imagery: An fMRI Study in Middle Adulthood," *Frontiers in Human Neuroscience* 6, no. 67 (2012).

38 "fluid" and "crystallized" intelligence: See Joshua K. Hartshorne and Laura T. Germine, "When Does Cognitive Functioning Peak? The Asynchronous Rise and Fall of Different Cognitive Abilities Across the Life Span," *Psychological Science* 26, no. 4 (2015).

38 When children play chess: Experts, curiously, make similarly rapid intuitive judgments, yet they are also able to draw upon a vast body of knowledge. Magnus Carlsen, for example, has described how he often makes a move quickly in his head, then spends a great amount of time verifying it is the correct one.

39 a function of learning: See Michael Ramscar et al., "Learning Is Not Decline," *Mental Lexicon* 8, no. 3 (2013): 450–81.

40 "transfer" in the learning of chess: See Sala and Gobet, "Do the Benefits of Chess Instruction Transfer to Academic and Cognitive Skills?"

40 learning becomes a "stress buffer": See Chen Zhang, Christopher G. Myers, and David Mayer, "To Cope with Stress, Try Learning Something New," *Harvard Business Review*, Sept. 4, 2018.

41 students who studied both science and arts: See Carl Gombrich, "Polymathy, New Generalism, and the Future of Work: A Little Theory and Some Practice from UCL's Arts and Sciences BASc Degree," in *Experiences in Liberal Arts and Science Education from America, Europe, and Asia: A Dialog Across Continents*, ed. William C. Kirby and Marijk van der Wende (London: Palgrave Macmillan, 2016), 75–89. I was alerted to the research by Robert Twigger's book *Micromastery*.

41 "are at least twenty-two times": This is via the work of Robert Root-Bernstein et al. See David Epstein, *Range: Why Generalists Triumph in a Specialized World* (New York: Riverhead, 2019), 33.

41 "Time and time again": See Jimmy Soni, "10,000 Hours with Claude Shannon: How a Genius Thinks, Works, and Lives," *Medium*, July 20, 2017, medium.com.

41 "perpetual novices": This phrase comes from Dineh M. Davis, "The Perpetual Novice: An Undervalued Resource in the Age of Experts," *Mind, Culture, and Activity* 4, no. 1 (1997): 42–52. The author uses the phrase in the context of the introduction of personal computers into American households and describes the perpetual novice as "one who has been thoroughly entrenched in this technology for years without having ever lost the edge we associate with beginners."

42 "You have to learn to learn": This comes from an interview between Kumar and Knowledge@Wharton, "Want a Job in the Future? Be a Student for Life," Knowledge@Wharton, July 2, 2019, knowledge.wharton.upenn.edu.

42 "novelty-seeking machine": See Winifred Gallagher, *New: Understanding Our Need for Novelty and Change* (New York: Penguin, 2013).

42 that is the brain: See, for example, Denise Park et al., "The Impact of Sustained Engagement on Cognitive Function in Older Adults: The Synapse Project," *Psychological Science* 25, no. 1 (2014): 103–12. See also Jan Oltmanns et al., "Don't Lose Your Brain at Work—the Role of Recurrent Novelty at Work in Cognitive and Brain Aging," *Frontiers in Psychology* 8, no. 117 (2017), doi:10.3389/fpsyg.2017.00117.

42 novelty itself seems to trigger learning: See, for example, J. Schomaker, "Unexplored Territory: Beneficial Effects of Novelty on Memory," *Neurobiology of Learning and Memory* 161 (May 2019): 46–50.

42 A study that had adults: The study, it should be noted, had a very small control group. See Shirley Leanos et al., "The Impact of Learning Multiple Real-World Skills on Cognitive Abilities and Functional Independence in Healthy Older Adults," *Journals of Gerontology: Series B* (2019), doi:10.1093/geronb/gbz084.

42 swimming lessons: See Robyn Jorgensen, "Early-Years Swimming: Adding Capital to Young Australians," Aug. 2013, docs.wixstatic.com.

43 Research suggests that couples: See A. Aron et al., "Couples' Shared Participation in Novel and Arousing Activities and Experienced Relationship Quality," *Journal of Personal and Social Psychology* 78 no. 2 (Feb. 2000): 273–84.

44 "cognitive and behavioral flexibility": See Benjamin Chapman et al., "Personality and Longevity: Knowns, Unknowns, and Implications for Public Health and Personalized Medicine," *Journal of Aging Research* (2011), doi:10.4061/2011/759170.

44 "More than any other animal": Alison Gopnik, "A Manifesto Against 'Parenting,'" *Wall Street Journal*, July 8, 2016.

45 As the art historian Bruce Redford: See Redford's fascinating study, *Dilettanti: The Antic and the Antique in Eighteenth-Century England* (Los Angeles: Getty Center, 2008).

45 "the long arm of the job": I took the phrase, which comes from Martin Meissner, from Steven M. Gelber's valuable study, *Hobbies: Leisure and the Culture of Work in America* (New York: Columbia University Press, 1999).

45 "What is admired is success": Mihaly Csikszentmihalyi, *Flow* (New York: Harper Perennial, 2008), 236.

46 What if we just want to enjoy them?: In *Peak*, Ericsson describes a study in which two groups of choral singers, professionals and amateurs, were interviewed before and after their rehearsals. The amateurs reported feeling elated. The professionals did not. They'd simply focused on getting the job done, on intensely honing their technique. Because it was a *job*. They were paid to be at the top of their game. That doesn't mean everyone has to be. Imagine you were going to start singing tomorrow. Would you want an experience that left you feeling elated, or would you desire a sober slog toward technical perfection? Unless you were actually aiming at Carnegie Hall, I'm guessing you'd shoot for the elation. See Ericsson, *Peak*, 151. And for an interesting discussion of the distinctions between music professionals and amateurs, see Susana Juniu et al., "Leisure or Work? Amateur and Professional Musicians' Perception of Rehearsal and Performance," *Journal of Leisure Research* 28, no. 1 (1996): 44–56. For more on amateurs, see Robert A. Stebbins, "The Amateur: Two Sociological Definitions," *Pacific Sociological Review* 20, no. 4 (1977): 582–606.

46 "who loves the rituals": See George Leonard, *Mastery* (New York: Plume, 1992), 19–20.

46 self-reported perfectionism: See Thomas Curran and Andrew P. Hill, "Perfectionism Is Increasing over Time: A Meta-analysis of Birth Cohort Differences from 1989 to 2016," *Psychological Bulletin* 145, no. 4 (2019): 410–29, dx.doi.org/10.1037/bul0000138.

46 We "overvalue performance": See D. E. Hamachek, "Psychodynamics of Normal and Neurotic Perfectionism," *Psychology* 15, no. 1 (1978): 27–33.

46 just okay at things: As the legal scholar and writer Tim Wu has argued, we have so internalized the endgame of results, in our "intensely public, performative age," that our leisure pursuits "have become too serious, too demanding, too much an occasion to become anxious about whether you are really the person you claim to be." We can't just try art; we are meant to become, in an

all-consuming way, an *artist*. See Tim Wu, "In Praise of Mediocrity," *New York Times*, Sept. 19, 2018.

46 "to do what you like": George Orwell, "England Your England," in *The Orwell Reader: Fiction, Essays, and Reportage* (New York: Houghton Mifflin Harcourt, 1956), 256.

48 "the heaviness of being successful": Shellie Karabell, "Steve Jobs: The Incredible Lightness of Beginning Again," *Forbes*, Dec. 10, 2014, www.forbes.com.

48 "It may well be": Winston S. Churchill, *Painting as a Pastime* (London: Unicorn Press, 2013), 15.

48 had to be *one* passion: This raises the question of where passions come from. An interesting piece of research suggests that when people think that passions are inherent, they are more likely to give them up when they become challenging. When people think that passions must be developed, they seem more likely to stick with them. See Paul O'Keefe et al., "Implicit Theories of Interest: Finding Your Passion or Developing It?," *Association of Psychological Science* 29, no. 10 (2018): 1653–64.

49 "it would have been impossible": See Lauren Sosniak, "From Tyro to Virtuoso: A Long-Term Commitment to Learning," in *Music and Child Development: Proceedings of the 1987 Denver Conference*, ed. Frank L. Wilson and Franz L. Roehmann (St. Louis: MMB Music, 1990).

49 Children's participation in sports: Michael S. Rosenwald, "Are Parents Ruining Youth Sports?," *Washington Post*, Oct. 4, 2015; Peter Witt and Tek Dangi, "Why Children/Youth Drop Out of Sports," *Journal of Park and Recreation Administration* 36, no. 3 (2018): 191–99.

50 players' chess ratings: See R. W. Howard, "Searching the Real World for Signs of Rising Population Intelligence," *Personality and Individual Differences* 30, no. 6 (2001): 1039–58.

51 "Pretty close to anything": KSNV, "Fake Doctor, Rick Van Thiel, Says He Learned Surgical Procedures on YouTube," News 3 Las Vegas, Oct. 7, 2015, news3lv.com.

51 transmission of techniques: Maxwell Strachan, "Rubik's Cube Champion on Whether Puzzles and Intelligence Are Linked," *HuffPost*, July 23, 2015, www.huffingtonpost.com.

52 Time-use data show: See, for instance, Jonathan Gershuny and Oriel Sullivan, *Where Does It All Go? What We Really Do All Day: Insights from the Center for Time Use Research* (London: Pelican, 2019).

53 increase your perceptual abilities: The work of Daphné Bavelier and colleagues is most instructive here. See, for example, Daphné

Bavelier et al., "Altering Perception: The Case of Action Video Gaming," *Current Opinion in Psychology* 29 (March 2019): 168–73.

54 Fathers spend less time: See, for example, Shelly Lundberg, "Sons, Daughters, and Parental Behavior," *Oxford Review of Economic Policy* 21, no. 3 (2005): 340–56; and Kristin Mammen, "Fathers' Time Investments in Children: Do Sons Get More?," *Journal of Population Economics* 24, no. 3 (2011): 839–71.

54 "I still insist that I can get better": John Marchese, "Tony Bennett at 90: 'I Just Love What I'm Doing,'" *New York Times*, Dec. 14, 2016.

55 "fixed and immutable": See, for example, Tobias Rees, "Being Neurologically Human Today," *American Ethnologist* 37, no. 1 (2010).

55 the "creative aging" movement: For a good summary, see the report "The Summit on Creativity and Aging in America," National Endowment for the Arts, Jan. 2016.

CHAPTER TWO
LEARNING HOW TO LEARN

58 more than the average *adult* in America: According to a recent study, the average adult in the United States takes 4,774 steps per day. See Tim Althoff et al., "Large-Scale Physical Activity Data Reveal Worldwide Activity Inequality," *Nature*, July 20, 2017, 336–39.

59 some 160 separate "bouts": See Whitney G. Cole, Scott R. Robinson, and Karen E. Adolph, "Bouts of Steps: The Organization of Infant Exploration," *Developmental Psychobiology* 58, no. 3 (2016): 341–54.

59 new walkers will often carry things: See Lana B. Karasik et al., "Carry On: Spontaneous Object Carrying in 13-Month-Old Crawling and Walking Infants," *Developmental Psychology* 48, no. 2 (2012): 389–97.

59 crawl in all manner of ways: As the developmental psychologist Myrtle McGraw noted, "No other neuromuscular function of the growing infant exhibits greater variations in pattern." Myrtle McGraw, *The Neuromuscular Maturation of the Human Infant* (New York: Columbia University Press, 1945).

59 Eye-tracking software reveals: J. Hoch, J. Rachwani, and K. Adolph, "Where Infants Go: Real-Time Dynamics of Locomotor Exploration in Crawling and Walking Infants," *Child Development* (in press).

59 Mobility seems its own reward: As Adolph wrote, "The promise of unexplored space is sufficiently alluring to instigate locomotion."

She calls it the "peragration hypothesis," which is another way of saying that infants move less for specific goals than for the goal of moving itself. See Justine E. Hoch, Sinclaire M. O'Grady, and Karen E. Adolph, "It's the Journey, Not the Destination: Locomotor Exploration in Infants," *Developmental Science*, Aug. 7, 2018, doi:10.1111/desc.12740.

59 reach "adultlike" fluency: See Karen E. Adolph and Scott R. Robinson, "The Road to Walking: What Learning to Walk Tells Us About Development," in *The Oxford Handbook of Developmental Psychology*, ed. P. Zelazo (New York: Oxford University Press, 2013), 15.

59 *seventy* times in one hour: See Karen E. Adolph et al., "How Do You Learn to Walk? Thousands and Steps and Dozens of Falls per Day," *Psychological Science* 23, no. 11 (2012): 1387–94.

60 Sitting requires many weeks: This is harder than it seems. As Adolph notes, "Upright balance involves several non-obvious components, including control of the torso, attainment of a stable position, compensatory postural sway, and perhaps most important, behavioral flexibility." See Jaya Rachwani, Kasey C. Soska, and Karen E. Adolph, "Behavioral Flexibility in Learning to Sit," *Developmental Psychobiology* 59, no. 8 (2017).

60 Infants are learning machines: Studies have shown, for instance, that infants prefer to interact with people who they think will, as one scholar put it, "provide them with learning activities." See Katarina Begus, Teodora Gliga, and Victoria Southgate, "Infants Choose Optimal Teachers," *Proceedings of the National Academy of Sciences* 113, no. 44 (2016): 12397–402, doi:10.1073/pnas.1603261113.

61 the rise of "adult parkour": As one instructor said, being afraid of falling "puts you at higher risk of falling." Christopher F. Schuetze, "Afraid of Falling? For Older Adults, the Dutch Have a Cure," *New York Times*, Jan. 2, 2018.

61 "Why would expert crawlers": See Adolph et al., "How Do You Learn to Walk?"

62 It allows them to see more: See K. S. Kretch et al., "Crawling and Walking Infants See the World Differently," *Child Development* 85, no. 4 (2014): 1503–18.

62 "social agency": See Adolph and Robinson, "Road to Walking," 23.

62 It gives them a measure of control: As Adolph notes, this is in itself rewarding. See Karen E. Adolph et al., "Gibson's Theory of Perceptual Learning," in *International Encyclopedia of the Social & Behavioral Sciences*, ed. James D. Wright (Boston: Elsevier, 2015), 10:132.

62 the word "no" more often: See Joseph J. Campos et al., "Travel Broadens the Mind," *Infancy* 1, no. 2 (2000): 149–219.

62 infants who propel themselves: See Adolph and Robinson, "Road to Walking," 23.

62 "Perceptual information doesn't come": Walking is a vehicle for learning about the world in all sorts of ways, including how we can actually move through it. "The body has to instruct the brain," as the prominent developmental theorist Esther Thelen put it. See Esther Thelen, "The Improvising Infant: Learning About Learning to Move," in *The Developmental Psychologists: Research Adventures Across the Life Span*, ed. M. R. Merrens and G. G. Brannigan (New York: McGraw-Hill, 1996), 31.

63 a stage of "neuromuscular adaptation": Esther Thelen, a bit sarcastically, summed up this view as "a little clock inside the baby." She argued that it was the challenge of the task, not this "clock," that propelled development. See ibid., 37.

63 But babies *learn* to walk: See Jane Clark, "On Becoming Skillful: Patterns and Constraints," *Research Quarterly for Exercise and Sport* 66, no. 3 (1995): 173–83.

64 kids who hit motor-skills milestones early: See, for example, Oskar G. Jenni et al., "Infant Motor Milestones: Poor Predictive Value for Outcome of Healthy Children," *Acta Paediatrica* 102, no. 4 (2013): e181, doi:10.1111/apa.12129. See also Emma Sumner and Elisabeth Hill, "Are Children Who Walk and Talk Early Geniuses in the Making?," *Conversation*, Feb. 4, 2016.

65 they've been reported to wake up: See Michelle Lampl, "Evidence of Saltatory Growth in Infancy," *American Journal of Human Biology* 5, no. 5 (1993): 641–52.

66 "the process is no faster": See Adolph and Robinson, "Road to Walking," 8.

67 variable practice: For more on memory and variable practice, see Shailesh S. Kantak et al., "Neural Substrates of Motor Memory Consolidation Depend on Practice Structure," *Nature Neuroscience* 13, no. 8 (2010), doi:10.1038/nn.2596.

68 the same walk twice: In an experiment, Adolph and colleagues paired a team of soccer-playing robots trained using infant walking paths against a team trained on less varied paths. The "infants" won. See Ori Ossmy et al., "Variety Wins: Soccer-Playing Robots and Infant Walking," *Frontiers in Neurorobotics* 12, no. 19 (2018).

68 *variability* is the key: For more on "motor variability" and its effects on learning, see Howard G. Wu et al., "Temporal Structure of Motor Variability Is Dynamically Regulated and Predicts Motor Learning Ability," *Nature Neuroscience* 17, no. 2 (2014): 312–21.

68 Progress is often "U shaped": See Lisa Gershkoff-Stowe and Esther Thelen, "U-Shaped Changes in Behavior: A Dynamic Sys-

tems Perspective," *Journal of Cognition and Development* 5, no. 1 (2006): 11–36.

68 Skills rarely "transfer": For a good review of transfer in motor learning, see Richard A. Schmidt and Douglas E. Young, "Transfer of Movement Control in Motor Skill Learning," Research Note 86-37, U.S. Army Research Institute for the Behavioral and Social Sciences, April 1986.

68 rarely gives you an automatic leg up: As one researcher put it, "Even the most skilled experts cannot skip the essential process of dynamic organization with a new task." See Zheng Yan and Kurt Fischer, "Always Under Construction," *Human Development* 45 (2002): 141–60.

69 "beyond Jell-O cubes": See Thelen, "Improvising Infant," 39.

CHAPTER THREE

UNLEARNING TO SING

70 "Driving with background music": Warren Brodsky, *Driving with Music* (London: Ashgate, 2015), xiv.

71 children "forcefully requesting" a parent: See Lisa Huisman Koops, "Songs from the Car Seat: Exploring the Early Childhood Music-Making Place of the Family Vehicle," *Journal of Research in Music Education* 62, no. 1 (2014): 52–65.

71 "Car-aoke" is so endemic: To summarize the findings: Singing doesn't seem to hurt driving too much, though singing tends to suffer when driving gets more hectic. See Warren Brodsky, "A Performance Analysis of In-Car Music Engagement as an Indication of Driver Distraction and Risk," *Transportation Research Part F* 55 (May 2018): 201–18.

71 "are so compulsively drawn": Steven Mithen, "The Music Instinct: The Evolutionary Basis of Musicality," *Annals of the New York Academy of Sciences* 1169 (July 2009): 3–12.

71 Singing *is* good for us: Jing Kang et al., "A Review of the Physiological Effects and Mechanisms of Singing," *Journal of Voice* 32, no. 4 (2018): 390–95.

71 By activating the crucial bundle of fibers: I was talked through the complexities of the vagus nerve by Dr. Lucy Norcliffe-Kaufmann, a professor of neurology at New York University.

72 before they speak their first word: See Helmut Moog, *The Musical Experience of the Pre-school Child* (London: Schott, 1976), 62.

72 one study of "infant-directed singing": Sandra E. Trehub, Anna M. Unyk, and Laurel J. Trainor, "Adults Identify Infant-Directed Music Across Cultures," *Infant Behavior and Development* 16, no. 2

(1993): 193–211. In another study, babies *themselves* showed a preference for recordings in which they had been present while their mother sang. See Laurel J. Trainor, "Infant Preferences for Infant-Directed Versus Noninfant-Directed Playsongs and Lullabies," *Infant Behavior and Development* 19, no. 1 (1996): 83–92.

72 Simply raising the voice of a *stranger:* M. Patterson et al., "Infant Sensitivity to Perturbations in Adult Infant-Directed Speech During Social Interactions with Mother and Stranger" (poster presented at the Society for Research in Child Development).

72 raise our pitch by smiling: See John J. Ohala, "The Acoustic Origin of the Smile" (revised version of paper delivered at the hundredth meeting of the Acoustical Society of America, Los Angeles, Nov. 19, 1980). Smiling, one theory goes, evolved in humans not as a way to show teeth—which might be deemed aggressive—but to allow us to speak higher, which generally signifies friendliness and cooperation. See V. C. Tartter, "Happy Talk: Perceptual and Acoustic Effects of Smiling on Speech," *Perceptual Psychophysics* 27, no. 1 (1980): 24–27. Another way we can lift our pitch is by raising our eyebrows, which makes our faces look more welcoming by making our eyes seem bigger, like those of infants, and thus friendlier. Indeed, when people sing on a higher pitch, their faces have been judged as more friendly compared with when they sing on a low pitch. See David Huron and Daniel Shanahan, "Eyebrow Movements and Vocal Pitch Height: Evidence Consistent with an Ethological Signal," *Journal of the Acoustical Society of America* 133, no. 5 (2013): 2947–52. As Huron and Shanahan note, "[John Ohala] suggested that raised eyebrows encourage retraction of the eyelids and draw attention to the eyes—effectively increasing the apparent eye-size-to-head ratio."

72 Infants prefer mothers' singing: Takayuki Nakata and Sandra E. Trehub, "Infants' Responsiveness to Maternal Speech and Singing," *Infant Behavior and Development* 27, no. 4 (2004): 455–64.

72 infants actually preferred the dads' tunes: See Colleen T. O'Neill et al., "Infants' Responsiveness to Fathers' Singing," *Music Perception* 18, no. 4 (2001): 409–25.

75 "androgynously sweet tenor": See James Gavin's authoritative, if hardly adulatory, biography, *Deep in a Dream: The Long Night of Chet Baker* (New York: Alfred A. Knopf, 2002), 87.

75 "an anemic voice": Ibid., 85.

75 "Eighty percent of singing": Thanks to Ingo Titze for this comment.

76 vocal pedagogy relies heavily: One researcher identified, in talking to six vocal instructors, some 260 metaphors and expressions used

to describe desired singing techniques. See Jennifer Aileen Jest-ley, "Metaphorical and Non-metaphorical Imagery Use in Vocal Pedagogy: An Investigation of Underlying Cognitive Organisa-tional Constructs" (Ph.D. diss., University of British Columbia, 2011). In contrast to some criticisms of the use of imagery and metaphor in vocal training, Jestley argued, "Importantly, the study showed that the expressions were not arbitrarily or randomly employed as a result of temporary ad hoc categorization processes but rather were shown to be constrained by underlying image-schematic structures arising out of our embodied experiences. . . . Contrary to the criticisms levelled in Chapters 1 and 2 which vari-ously described the metaphoric and imagistic language used in the voice studio as mumbo jumbo, mythological, opaque, and overly subjective, I did not find the expressions offered in this study at all confusing or illogical."

79 a slow, palpable decline: When a researcher in Canada interviewed a group of women a few decades ago about the role of singing in their lives, she found "the widespread practice of singing in social and family groups around the piano ended in the 1950s, singing in social groups with the guitar was prevalent in the 1960s and 1970s, and singing with social groups happened rarely in the 1980s and 1990s." Katharine Smithrim, "Still Singing for Our Lives: Sing-ing in the Everyday Lives of Women Through This Century," in *Sharing the Voices: The Phenomenon of Singing*, ed. B. Roberts (St. John's: Memorial University of Newfoundland, 1998), 224.

79 Music went from "lean in" to "lean back": Thanks to the Smule CEO, Jeff Smith, for this idea.

79 "Our culture of performance": Cathy Lynn Grossman, "Many Church Choirs Are Dying. Here's Why," Religion News Service, Sept. 17, 2014.

79 "considerable embarrassment reaction": Jason Bardi, "UCSF Team Describes Neurological Basis for Embarrassment," news release, April 15, 2011, University of California at San Francisco, www.ucsf.edu.

80 "We mythologize and romanticize": Tracey Thorn, *Naked at the Albert Hall* (London: Virago, 2015), vii.

80 The title of one paper: The study in question actually distin-guished between singing that was *inaccurate* (that is, relating to "the average difference between sung and target pitches") and *imprecise* (that is, "the consistency of repeated attempts to produce a pitch"). "Poor-pitch singing," the authors wrote, "is associated with a tendency to sing both inaccurately and imprecisely." See

Peter Q. Pfordresher et al., "Imprecise Singing Is Widespread," *Journal of the Acoustical Society of America* 128, no. 4 (2010).

80 "Listening to any gathering": Karen J. Wise and John A. Sloboda, "Establishing an Empirical Profile of Self-Defined 'Tone Deafness': Perception, Singing Performance, and Self-Assessment," *Musicae Scientiae* 12, no. 1 (2008): 3–26.

80 sing it too quickly: Graham Welch brings up this idea in his fascinating lecture, "The Benefits of Singing in a Choir" (delivered July 8, 2015, at Gresham College).

81 that particular ditty: Interestingly, a more recently discovered version of the original composition depicts a narrower range of notes. See Tara Anderson, "An Unnoticed 'Happy Birthday' Draft Gives Singers a Simpler Tune," NPR, Sept. 6, 2015, www.npr.org.

82 People often don't sing as accurately: See Y. Minami, "Some Observations on the Pitch Characteristics of Children's Singing," in *Onchi and Singing Development: A Cross-Cultural Perspective*, ed. Graham Welch and Tadahiro Murao (London: David Fulton, 1994), 18–24.

82 When your voice is out there: This idea comes from Steven Connor, in his excellent book *Dumbstruck: A Cultural History of Ventriloquism* (Oxford: Oxford University Press, 2001).

83 "You hear your voice": Taken from the transcript of a TEDxBeaconStreet talk, Rébecca Kleinberger, "Why You Don't Like the Sound of Your Own Voice."

84 When we really do listen: In his fascinating book *Dumbstruck*, Steven Connor makes an interesting suggestion: "Perhaps we cannot enjoy the sound of a voice without the sound having begun to offer the prospect of this quasi-tactile self-caress." In other words, the voice we hear from without ourselves not only sounds better; it *feels* better. See *Dumbstruck*, 10.

84 When we have this "voice confrontation": See Philip S. Holzman and Clyde Rousey, "The Voice as a Percept," *Journal of Personality and Social Psychology* 4, no. 1 (1966): 79–86.

84 "the highest ratio of nerve fibers": Ibid., 85.

84 our desirability as a mate: For a brief summary, see Susan M. Hughes and Marissa A. Harrison, "I Like My Voice Better: Self-Enhancement Bias in Perceptions of Voice Attractiveness," *Perception* 42, no. 9 (2013): 941–49.

84 fleeting utterance of the word: See P. McAleer, A. Todorov, and P. Belin, "How Do You Say 'Hello'? Personality Impressions from Brief Novel Voices," *PLOS One* 9, no. 3 (2014), journals.plos.org.

84 voice students had a higher average IQ: See E. Glenn Schellen-
berg, "Music Lessons Enhance IQ," *Psychological Science* 15, no. 8
(2004), doi.org/10.1111/j.0956-7976.2004.00711.x.

87 The key word here is "think": See Steven M. Demorest et al.,
"Singing Ability, Musical Self-Concept, and Future Music Participation," *Journal of Research in Music Education* 64, no. 4 (2017):
405–20.

87 "Disbelief in one's capabilities": See Albert Bandura, "Self-
Efficacy," in *Encyclopedia of Human Behavior*, ed. V. S. Ramachan-
dran (San Diego: Academic Press, 1998), 71–81.

87 a function of innate talent: See S. O'Neill, "The Self-Identity
of Young Musicians," in *Musical Identities*, ed. R. MacDonald,
D. Hargreaves, and D. Miell (New York: Oxford University Press,
2002).

88 We are musical, or not: This point is helpfully made by Graham
Welch, "We Are Musical," *International Journal of Music Education*
23, no. 117 (2005): 117–20.

88 In fact, congenital amusia: See Julie Ayotte, Isabelle Peretz, and
Krista Hyde, "Congenital Amusia: A Group Study of Adults Afflicted
with a Music-Specific Disorder," *Brain* 125 (Feb. 2002): 238–51.

88 *perceiving* correct notes: For a good discussion on William Hung,
see Vance Lehmkuhl, "The William Hung Challenge," *Philadel-
phia Inquirer*, May 4, 2011, www.philly.com.

89 We lose our voice: Ingo Titze, a former aerospace engineer
who turned his attention to the equally intricate wind dynamics
inside our throats, and directs the National Center for Voice and
Speech, notes that when we don't stretch for higher pitches or
louder sounds, our vocal mechanism can start to atrophy. This
"use it or lose it" dynamic, he suggests, may be occurring on a
larger scale. Our overwhelming reliance these days on speaking at
low-frequencies at short range, our speech boosted by electronics,
means we're barely tapping into what our vocal systems can do.
"Adaptation of the mammalian larynx for long-range unamplified
vocal communication," he writes, "could eventually be reversed."
Ingo R. Titze, "Human Speech: A Restricted Use of the Mammalian Larynx," *Journal of Voice* 31, no. 2 (2017): 135–41.

90 *1,400* times per second: This idea comes from M. Echternach
et al., "Vocal Fold Vibrations at High Soprano Fundamental Frequencies," *Journal of the Acoustical Society of America* 133, no. 2
(2013): 82–87.

90 Weirdly, whispering usually puts: See Adam Rubin et al., "Laryn-
geal Hyperfunction During Whispering: Reality or Myth?," *Journal of Voice* 20, no. 1 (2006): 121–27.

90 The bulk of that air: My interview with Ingo Titze.

90 We can usually *whistle:* See Michael Belyk et al., "Poor Neuro-motor Tuning of the Human Larynx: A Comparison of Sung and Whistled Pitch Imitation," *Royal Society Open Science*, April 1, 2018.

90 than we can sing: Even expert singers cannot hit notes as precisely as instrumentalists can. See P. Q. Pfordresher and S. Brown, "Vocal Mistuning Reveals the Origin of Musical Scales," *Journal of Cognitive Psychology* 29, no. 1 (2017): 35–52. Curiously, we expect this. When we listen to a slightly out-of-tune human and a slightly out-of-tune musical instrument, Hutchins has found, we don't notice the human as much. He calls it the "vocal generosity effect." See Sean Hutchins, Catherine Roquet, and Isabelle Peretz, "The Vocal Generosity Effect: How Bad Can Your Singing Be?," *Music Perception* 20, no. 2 (2012): 147–59.

91 "start new ones": W. Timothy Gallwey, *The Inner Game of Tennis* (New York: Random House, 1997), 74.

92 "the worst enemy of the singer": See Dena Murry, *Vocal Technique: A Guide to Finding Your Real Voice* (New York: Musicians Institute Press, 2002), 20.

92 according to research: For a good summary, see Martin S. Remland, *Nonverbal Communication in Everyday Life* (New York: Sage Books, 2016).

92 bring my speaking voice into singing: The goal was to move the most air, most efficiently, without interference, and without really thinking about it. "In speaking," wrote the bel canto teacher Giovanni Battista Lamperti, "momentum is constantly arrested; in singing, never." Giovanni Battista Lamperti, *Vocal Wisdom* (New York: Taplinger, 1931), 47.

92 "The vowel is the voice": William D. Leyerle, *Vocal Development Through Organic Imagery* (Geneseo, N.Y.: Leyerle, 1986), 75.

92 In English-language speech: See "Whisper, Talk, Sing: How the Voice Works," Kindermusik, April 28, 2016, www.kindermusik .com.

93 We drop some sixteen thousand words daily: See Matthias R. Mehl et al., "Are Women Really More Talkative Than Men?," *Science,* July 6, 2007, 82.

97 activates many more regions: See Daniel E. Callan et al., "Song and Speech: Brain Regions Involved with Perception and Covert Production," *NeuroImage* 31, no. 3 (2006): 1327–42.

99 Our jaws are immensely powerful: In one early study, people asked to bite down on a measuring device gave up only because their teeth began to hurt. See "The Power of the Human Jaw," *Scientific American*, Dec. 2, 1911.

99 but our closing muscles: See T. M. G. J. Van Eijden, J. A. M. Kor-
fage, and P. Brugman, "Architecture of the Human Jaw-Closing
and Jaw-Opening Muscles," *Anatomical Record* 248, no. 3 (1997):
464–74.

100 "tended to pull back the head": See Michael Bloch, *F.M.: The Life
of Frederick Matthias Alexander* (New York: Little, Brown, 2004), 34.

100 "When you are asked not to do something": See F. Matthias Alexander, *The Alexander Technique: The Essential Writings of F. Matthias
Alexander* (New York: Lyle Stuart, 1980), 4.

100 "action slips": For an excellent discussion of "technique change"
in the realm of motor skills, see Rob Gray's *Perception Action* podcast, episode 14, 2015, perceptionaction.com/14-2.

102 pregame hitting practice: For a good account of the various critiques, see Jeff Sullivan, "Batting Practice Is Probably a Waste of
Everyone's Time," *The Hardball Times*, tht.fangraphs.com.

102 straw phonation, as it's known: For more on straw phonation, see
Ingo Titze, "Voice Training and Therapy with a Semi-occluded
Vocal Tract: Rationale and Scientific Underpinnings," *Journal of
Speech, Language, and Hearing Research* 49, no. 2 (2006): 448–59.

103 partially hold our breath to talk: I came across this idea in Anne
Kapf's wonderful book *The Human Voice* (New York: Simon &
Schuster, 2006).

103 "The singer has two languages": Hollis Dann, "Some Essentials of
Choral Singing," *Music Educators Journal* 24, no. 1 (1937): 27.

104 "life is governed by phlegm": Ian Bostridge, *A Singer's Notebook*
(London: Faber and Faber, 2012).

CHAPTER FOUR

I DON'T KNOW WHAT I'M DOING,

BUT I'M DOING IT ANYWAY

108 "It's as if all of our inner ions": Alice Parker, interview by Krista
Tippett, "Singing Is the Most Companionable of Arts," *On Being*,
Dec. 6, 2016, onbeing.org.

108 "In a cognitive sense": For a good survey of the acoustical qualities of choirs, see Sten Ternström, "Physical and Acoustic Factors That Interact with the Singer to Produce the Choral Sound,"
Journal of Voice 5, no. 2 (1991): 128–43.

110 choir singers report experiencing: Charlene Ryan, "An Investigation into the Choral Singer's Experience of Music Performance
Anxiety," *Journal of Research in Music Education* 57, no. 2 (2009):
108–26.

115	an analysis of high school choirs: The study notes, "The research literature has not settled on a commonly accepted cause for the 'missing males' in choral music." See K. Elpus, "National Estimates of Male and Female Enrolment in American High School Choirs, Bands, and Orchestras," *Music Education Research* 17, no. 1 (2015): 88–102.

117	"Social facilitation": For a good roundup, see Charles F. Bond et al., "Social Facilitation: A Meta-analysis of 241 Studies," *Psychological Bulletin* 94, no. 2 (1983): 265–92.

117	"Social loafing": See S. J. Karau, "Social Loafing (and Facilitation)," in *Encyclopedia of Human Behavior* (Amsterdam: Elsevier, 2012), 486–92.

117	"more Americans engage": See Cindy Bell, "Update on Community Choirs and Singing in the United States," *International Journal of Research in Choral Singing* 2, no. 1 (2004).

118	"all-time high": See "Number of UK Choirs at All-Time High," *M*, July 13, 2017, www.m-magazine.co.uk.

118	A rise in attendance: See "Sing and They Will Come," *Economist*, March 4, 2014.

118	Choirs in Australia: See Ali Colvin, "Community Choirs Growing as Members Reap Health Benefits," ABC News, June 17, 2016, www.abc.net.au.

118	"national pastime": See www.skane.com/en/choirs-a-national-pastime.

118	Singing with someone else: See L. M. Parsons et al., "Simultaneous Dual-fMRI, Sparse Temporal Scanning of Human Duetters at 1.5 and 3 Tesla." Conference paper presented at the Annual Meeting of the Society for Neuroscience, Jan. 2009.

118	stress hormone cortisol: See Gunter Kreutz, "Does Singing Facilitate Social Bonding?," *Music and Medicine* 6, no. 2 (2014).

118	people suffering from a stress-related: See R. N. Christina Grape et al., "Choir Singing and Fibrinogen: VEGF, Cholecystokinin, and Motilin in IBS Patients," *Medical Hypotheses* 72, no. 2 (2009): 223–55.

119	post-Katrina "Hurricane Choir": A psychologist who worked on a special post-Katrina "Hurricane Choir" project told me it was "one of the most genuine engagements with a community in my history."

119	more powerful human impulse: For example, a study by Eiluned Pearce and colleagues found that participants taking singing and other types of classes all reported greater well-being after seven months; it did not seem to matter what the activity was *as long as it was social*. The more social bonding they felt, the greater the reported increase in well-being. See Eiluned Pearce et al., "Is Group Singing Special? Health, Well-Being, and Social Bonds in Community-Based Adult Education Classes," *Journal of Community Applied Psychology* 26, no. 6 (2016): 518–33.

119 making music together: For this idea, I drew upon a paper by Daniel Weinstein et al., "Singing and Social Bonding: Changes in Connectivity and Pain Threshold as a Function of Group Size," *Evolution and Human Behavior* 37, no. 2 (2016): 152–58.

119 "experienced much faster bonding": See Eiluned Pearce et al., "The Ice-Breaker Effect: Singing Mediates Fast Social Bonding," *Royal Society Open Science*, Sept. 29, 2015. One caveat of this study is the people in the other newly formed activity groups (craft and creative writing) were working on *individual* projects; as the authors note, "This means that this study did not distinguish between the group-bonding effects of the physical act of singing *per se* and the existence of a shared group motivation to create a piece of music together."

120 heartbeats of choral singers: See Björn Vickhoff et al., "Music Structure Determines Heart Rate Variability of Singers," *Frontiers in Psychology* 4, no. 334 (2013).

129 it's often "preserved" in the face: One study, for example, found that in twenty-four patients with Broca's aphasia twenty-one had the "capacity to sing in some degree." See A. Yamadori et al., "Preservation of Singing in Broca's Aphasia," *Journal of Neurology, Neurosurgery, and Psychiatry* 40, no. 3 (1977): 221–24.

129 As Oliver Sacks suggests: Oliver Sacks, *Musicophilia* (New York: Vintage Books, 2007), 240.

130 kick-start the flow of speech: See Benjamin Stahl, "Facing the Music: Three Issues in Current Research on Singing and Aphasia," *Frontiers in Psychology*, Sept. 23, 2014.

132 "Lombard effect": See Steven Tonkinson, "The Lombard Effect in Choral Singing," *Journal of Voice* 8, no. 1 (1994): 24–29.

132 "Choral directors are from Mars": See Sharon Hansen et al., "On the Voice: Choral Directors Are from Mars and Voice Teachers Are from Venus," *Choral Journal* 52, no. 9 (2012): 51–58.

132 *bad* for the "solo voice": See, for example, Dallas Draper, "The Solo Voice as Applied to Choral Singing," *Choral Journal* 12, no. 9 (1972).

133 Novices like me, it turns out: See Michael J. Bonshor, "Confidence and Choral Configuration: The Affective Impact of Situational and Acoustic Factors in Amateur Choirs," *Psychology of Music* 45, no. 5 (2017), doi.org/10.1177/0305735616669996.

SURFING THE U-SHAPED WAVE

139 "more cocky and judgmental": I got this quotation from Jamail Yogis, *Saltwater Buddha: A Surfer's Quest to Find Zen on the Sea* (New York: Simon & Schuster, 2009), 128.

144 In the "novice" stage: Hubert Dreyfus and Stuart Dreyfus, *Mind over Machine* (New York: Free Press, 1988), 21.

146 "life path": Peter Heller, *Kook* (New York: Free Press, 2010), 268.

147 "Seahab," the writer and surfer: Allan Weisbecker, *In Search of Captain Zero* (New York: TarcherPerigree, 2002), 3.

147 I don't know if you need science: See, for example, Ryan Pittsinger et al., "The Effect of a Single Bout of Surfing on Exercise-Induced Affect," *International Journal of Exercise Science* 10, no. 7 (2017): 989–99, as well as Jamie Marshall et al., "'When I Go There, I Feel Like I Can Be Myself': Exploring Programme Theory Within the Wave Project Surf Therapy Intervention," *International Journal of Environmental Research in Public Health* 16, no. 12 (2019).

147 therapeutic instrument: See Amitha Kalaichandran, "Catching Waves for Well-Being," *New York Times*, Aug. 8, 2019.

148 As one analysis of a surf competition: See A. Mendez-Villanueva et al., "Activity Profile of World-Class Professional Surfers During Competition: A Case Study," *Journal of Strength Conditioning Research* 20, no. 3 (2006).

150 "Focus on *process*, not *product*": See Barbara Oakley, *A Mind for Numbers: How to Excel at Math and Science* (New York: Penguin, 2014), 101.

151 Too *much* feedback can hinder learning: See Chak Fu Lam et al., "The Impact of Feedback Frequency on Learning and Task Performance: Challenging the 'More Is Better' Assumption," *Organizational Behavior and Human Decision Processes* 116, no. 2 (2011): 217–28. For a good discussion of the effects of feedback on learning and performance, see Richard A. Schmidt, "Frequent Augmented Feedback Can Degrade Learning: Evidence and Intrepretations," in *Tutorials in Motor Neuroscience*, ed. J. Requin and G. E. Stelmach, NATO ASI Series (Series D: Behavioral and Social Sciences), Vol. 62 (Dordrecht: Springer, 1991).

151 "People who tried to start": William Finnegan, *Barbarian Days: A Surfing Life* (New York: Penguin Press, 2015), 123.

156 at least one acute injury: See Andrew Nathanson et al., "Surfing Injuries," *American Journal of Emergency Medicine* 20, no. 3 (2002): 155–60.

168 average break in an hour: The figure comes from Matt Warshaw, *The History of Surfing* (New York: Chronicle Books, 2011), 477.
168 "surfer's dilemma": Robert Rider makes this point in a paper that treats surfing as a "common-pool resource problem," and suggests that simple surf etiquette helps mitigate the problem. See Robert Rider, "Hangin' Ten: The Common-Pool Resource Problem of Surfing," *Public Choice* 97, no. 1–2 (1998): 49–64.
168 "mixed-motive game": For a discussion, see Daniel Nazer, "The Tragedy of the Surfers' Commons," *Deakin Law Review* 9, no. 2 (2004): 655–713.
169 This attentional focus was key: Knowing where, and how long, to look seems to be crucial in elite sports, according to a theory called the quiet eye. First proposed by the movement scientist Joan Vickers several decades ago, the idea behind quiet eye is simple: The best performers fixate sooner, and longer, on a key target during their task. In basketball, the better free throw shooters looked earlier and longer at the net than less successful players. Vickers has suggested that vision helps explain the success of superstar athletes like Wayne Gretzky and Lionel Messi whose gifts may not be otherwise explained by their size or speed. The quiet eye phenomenon is still something of a mystery, but it seems to stimulate an increase in brain activity that helps exert "top-down control on the visuomotor networks controlling movements." Your eyes, in other words, orchestrate your body's movements. See Joan N. Vickers et al., "Quiet Eye Training Improves Accuracy in Basketball Field Goal Shooting," *Progress in Brain Research* 234 (Jan. 2017): 1–12.
169 In wave-pool experiments: See "Using Eye Tracking to Analyze Surfers' Gaze Patterns," Tobii Pro, www.tobiipro.com.
171 "touch the elemental magma": Warshaw, *History of Surfing*, 13.
177 "gender socializing agents": See Lisa Kindelberg Hagan et al., "Mothers' and Fathers' Socialization of Preschoolers' Physical Risk Taking," *Journal of Applied Developmental Psychology* 28, no. 1 (2007): 2–14.
178 "Complacent type" in tennis: David Foster Wallace, *Infinite Jest* (New York: Back Bay Books, 2006), 116.
179 "capricious and tenacious enthusiasms": James Dickey, *Deliverance* (New York: Delta Books, 2004), 5.

CHAPTER SIX

HOW WE LEARN TO DO THINGS

180 "learning curve": See Edgar James Swift, "Studies in the Psychology and Physiology of Learning," *American Journal of Psychology*

14, no. 2 (1903): 201–51. Swift himself refers to a similar, earlier study, on telegraphy; see William Bryan and Noble Harter, "Studies in the Physiology and Psychology of the Telegraphic Language," *Psychological Review* 4, no. 1 (1897): 27–53.

183 One way to improve learning: In one study, golfers were asked to putt the ball to a hole that was surrounded by large holes (making it look smaller), or to a hole that was surrounded by small holes (making the target hole look larger). Golfers putting to the hole that seemed bigger did better, as you might expect. But in later trials, in which all golfers used a regular hole, the big hole golfers *again* did better than the small hole golfers. They had learned better on the easier-seeming hole. See Guillaume Chauvel et al., "Visual Illusions Can Facilitate Sport Skill Learning," *Psychonomic Bulletin and Review* 22, no. 3 (2015): 717–21. And when people successfully complete a golf putt, it turns out, they think the hole was bigger than it really was. An enlarged target boosts confidence; a confident performance boosts the size of the target.

184 "Almost everyone can ride": David Jones, "The Stability of the Bicycle," *Physics Today*, Sept. 2006, 51–56.

184 As bike geeks from Wilbur Wright: Wright wrote, "I have asked dozens of bicycle riders how they turn to the left. I have never found a single person who stated all the facts correctly when first asked." Quotation comes via Kark J. Åström et al., "Bicycle Dynamics and Control," *IEEE Control Systems Magazine*, Aug. 2005.

184 This is why written instructions: As the philosopher Gilbert Ryle puts it, "Knowledge-how cannot be built up by accumulation of pieces of knowledge-that." From Gilbert Ryle's influential lecture, "Knowing How and Knowing That" (delivered to the Aristotelian Society at the University of London Club, Nov. 1945), www.jstor.org. An interesting response to Ryle's famous theory comes in Jason Stanley and John W. Krakauer, "Motor Skill Depends on Knowledge of Facts," *Frontiers in Human Neuroscience*, Aug. 29, 2013. The authors argue that Ryle's division between declarative and implicit is not as absolute as some have made it. To take a very simple example, one could implicitly learn how to hammer a nail, but the task will be done more effectively if one is told beforehand which is the proper side to use. Work by Daniel Wolpert and colleagues also shows that when manipulating novel tools, people seem to learn to use a virtual hammer better when they can see, and not simply feel, how it works. See Mohsen Sadeghi et al., "The Visual Geometry of a Tool Modulates Generalization During Adaptation," *Nature Scientific Reports*, Feb. 25, 2019.

184 "Knowledge helps": Jerome Bruner, *The Culture of Education* (Cambridge, Mass.: Harvard University Press, 1996), 152.

184 theory of "reinvestment": The theory is credited to the movement scientist Rich Masters. See, for example, R. S. W. Masters et al., "'Reinvestment': A Dimension of Personality Implicated in Skill Breakdown Under Pressure," *Personality and Individual Differences* 14, no. 5 (1993): 655–66.

185 "The trick," as Masters: This quotation comes from a talk by Rich Masters, "The Epic Story of Implicit Motor Learning," Sept. 24, 2015, www.youtube.com. One way to help stroke patients relearn to walk is to put them on a "split-belt treadmill," an unusual device in which one leg moves faster than the other. Walking in this strange fashion, stroke patients subconsciously learn to counteract their limp *off* the treadmill. I saw this in action one morning at Johns Hopkins University's Human Brain Physiology and Stimulation Lab at the Kennedy Krieger Institute in Baltimore. As Ryan Roemmich, a human movement scientist at the university's Center for Movement Studies, told me, patients are put on the split-belt treadmill and told simply to walk. He invited me to do the same. To try to walk when one leg wants to go three times faster than the other is not easy, but after a while I began to adapt to it, albeit with a pronounced limp. "When patients get off the treadmill," Roemmich said, "the limp produced by the treadmill counteracts their baseline limp, so they can now walk more symmetrically." The treadmill is helping to speed the relearning process. As a patient walks, Roemmich said, his brain, "at some conscious level—and at a very large subconscious level—begins to predict what's happening on the treadmill." When a patient gets off the treadmill, "you know you're no longer on the treadmill, but your brain is still predicting that you need to walk in this particular way. That's the real benefit for rehab. It lasts when you get off the treadmill."

185 look for explanations: Researchers call this process "credit assignment": Was the error your fault or something in the environment?

185 Our cerebellum has "canceled": See Sarah-Jayne Blakemore, Daniel Wolpert, and Chris Firth, "Central Cancellation of Self-Produced Tickle Sensation," *Nature Neuroscience* 1 (Nov. 1998): 635–40.

186 Jugglers look to the *apex:* See A. A. M. Van Santvoord and Peter J. Beek, "Phasing and the Pickup of Optical Information in Cascade Juggling," *Ecological Psychology* 6, no. 4 (1994): 239–63.

187 I rushed the fourth throw: This is a common occurrence with novices. As one study noted, "The novice is not giving him or herself adequate time to sustain the structure of the pattern." See Pamela S. Haibach et al., "Coordination Changes in the Early Stages

of Learning to Cascade Juggle," *Human Movement Science* 23, no. 2 (2004): 185–206.

187 juggling would come to seem slower: But why? One theory suggests that in the same way that people felt that targets were smaller after they had completed a successful golf putt or football field goal, a good performance might alter one's *temporal* sense. In one study, some people playing a version of *Pong* were given a bigger paddle. Not surprisingly, they did better. But because they did better, the argument goes, they also reported that the ball seemed slower. Perhaps after I successfully juggled, the balls seemed slower in retrospect. Jessica K. Witt and Mila Sugovic, "Performance and Goal Influence Perceived Speed," *Perception* 39, no. 10 (2010): 1341–53.

187 novices pay attention to everything: A study that looked at novice and expert shooters, for instance, found that novices focused their attention constantly on the target through the aiming process, whereas experts honed their attention much closer to the time they actually pulled the trigger. As the authors note, "Experts are better able to allocate cortical resources in time." See M. Doppelmayr et al., "Frontal Midline Theta in the Pre-shot Phase of Rifle Shooting: Differences Between Experts and Novices," *Neuropsychologia* 46, no. 5 (2008): 1463–67.

188 You have a better sense: One line of thinking is that preparing for some motor action prompts the brain to essentially "maximize the capacity of sensory information-acquisition prior to executing a movement." This makes it easier to adapt the movement if something changes in the external environment and might also promote the sensation of having more time. See Nobuhiro Hagura et al., "Ready Steady Slow: Action Preparation Slows the Subjective Passage of Time," *Proceedings of the Royal Society B* 279, no. 1746 (2012): 4399–406.

188 A throw that was just a few degrees off: See Peter J. Beek and Arthur Lewbel, "The Science of Juggling," *Scientific American*, Nov. 1995, 94.

188 twenty-six different degrees of freedom: See William H. Edwards, *Motor Learning and Control* (New York: Cengage Learning, 2010), 48.

188 hundred billion neurons: This figure comes from Clark, "On Becoming Skillful."

189 Pick any skill: See Cláudia Tarragô Candotti et al., "Cocontraction and Economy of Triathletes and Cyclists at Different Cadences During Cycling Motion," *Journal of Electromyography and Kinesiology* 19, no. 5 (2009): 915–21.

189 This means "inhibiting" muscles: For a discussion, see Julie Duque et al., "Physiological Markers of Motor Inhibition During Human Behavior," *Trends in Neuroscience* 40, no. 4 (2017): 219–36.

190 The physical part of juggling: As MIT's Howard Austin argued, juggling "has nothing to do with muscles, neural pathways in the usual sense, or feedback." See Howard Austin, "A Computational View of the Skill of Juggling," *Artificial Intelligence Memo No. 330*, LOGO Memo No. 17, 1974, 8.

190 huge version of your signature: Thanks to UCLA professor of psychology Jesse Rissman for a version of this idea.

191 running out of unfamiliar mistakes: See Jonathan Rowson, *The Moves That Matter: A Chess Grandmaster on the Game of Life* (New York: Bloomsbury, 2019), 109.

192 "action-observation network": For a review, see Daniel M. Smith, "Neurophysiology of Action Anticipation in Athletes: A Systematic Review," *Neuroscience and Biobehavioral Reviews* 60 (Jan. 2016): 115–20.

192 "motor repertoire": According to one study, the action observation network requires a "motor representation" of an observed activity, not simply a "visual representation," in order to be stimulated. As the authors write, "We show that the brain's response to seeing an action depends not only on previous visual knowledge and experience of seeing the action, but also on previous motor experience of performing the action." See Beatriz Calvo-Merino et al., "Seeing or Doing? Influence of Visual Motor Familiarity in Action Observation," *Current Biology* 16, no. 19 (2006), doi .org/10.1016/j.cub.2006.07.065.

192 watching a dog bark: This example comes from Giacomo Rizzolatti and Corrado Sinigaglia, "Curious Book on Mirror Neurons and Their Myth," review of *The Myth of Mirror Neurons: The Real Neuroscience of Communication and Cognition*, by Gregory Hickock, *American Journal of Psychology* 128, no. 4 (2015).

192 fully engage one's motor cortex: Maxime Trempe et al., "Observation Learning Versus Physical Practice Leads to Different Consolidation Outcomes in a Movement Timing Task," *Experimental Brain Research* 209, no. 2 (2011): 181–92.

192 The more curious you are: See Matthias J. Gruber et al., "States of Curiosity Modulate Hippocampus-Dependent Learning via the Dopaminergic Circuit," *Neuron* 84, no. 2 (2014), doi:doi.org /10.1016/j.neuron.2014.08.060. The study showed, interestingly, that people who expressed higher curiosity about an answer to a question were also better at remembering "incidental" material presented during that "curious state" than during less curious states.

192 People who believe they will need to *teach:* See Marcos Daou, Keith R. Lohse, and Matthew W. Miller, "Expecting to Teach Enhances Motor Learning and Information Processing During Practice," *Human Movement Science* 49 (Oct. 2016): 336–45. As Daou, Lohse, and Miller note in another paper, the exact mechanism for this is unknown. Being expected to teach something, for example, did not result in different EEG results from subjects who were not expected to teach. Perhaps, they speculated, expecting to teach may activate the brain in ways not captured by EEG. "Expecting to teach may increase a learner's interest in skill acquisition, which could increase connectivity between midbrain and hippocampal regions." See Marcos Daou, Keith R. Lohse, and Matthew W. Miller, "Does Practicing a Skill with the Expectation of Teaching Alter Motor Preparatory Cortical Dynamics?" *International Journal of Psychophysiology* 127 (Feb. 2018): 1–19.

192 Curiously, we seem to learn better: Hassan Rohbanfard and Luc Proteau, "Learning Through Observation: A Combination of Expert and Novice Models Favor Learning," *Experimental Brain Research* 215, no. 3–4 (2011): 183–97.

192 When we watch the flawless performance: Daniel R. Lametti and Kate E. Watkins, "Cognitive Neuroscience: The Neural Basis of Motor Learning by Observing," *Current Biology* 26, no. 7 (2016): R288–R290.

193 three-ball cascade juggling: See Spencer J. Hayes, Derek Ashford, and Simon J. Bennett, "Goal-Directed Imitation: The Means to an End," *Acta Psychologica* 127, no. 2 (2008): 407–15.

193 boosts learners' confidence: See Rokhsareh Badami et al., "Feedback About More Accurate Versus Less Accurate Trials: Differential Effects on Self-Confidence and Activation," *Research Quarterly for Exercise and Sport* 83, no. 2 (2012): 196–203.

195 "airborne seizure": Richard Hoffer, *Something in the Air: American Passion and Defiance in the 1968 Mexico City Olympics* (New York: Free Press, 2009), 74.

195 "activation-dependent structural brain plasticity": See Joenna Driemeyer et al., "Changes in Gray Matter Induced by Learning— Revisited," *PLOS One* 3, no. 7 (2008), journals.plos.org.

196 white matter: See Jan Scholz et al., "Training Induces Changes in White Matter Architecture," *Nature Neuroscience* 12, no. 11 (2009): 1370–71. The researchers noted, "Despite the close spatial proximity of gray matter and white matter regions showing training-related changes, we did not find any correlation between the magnitude of gray matter and white matter changes across subjects." They speculated that this implies whatever processes are

behind the white and gray matter changes, they are independent. See also Bimal Lakhani et al., "Motor Skill Acquisition Promotes Human Brain Myelin Plasticity," *Neural Plasticity*, April 2016, 1–7.

196 bind it all together: Metaphor courtesy of "Intelligence in Men and Women Is a Gray and White Matter," *ScienceDaily*, Jan. 22, 2005, www.sciencedaily.com.

196 When we learn to do something: In animal experiments, learning has been found to provoke "synaptogenesis," the growth of new neural connections, whereas simply repeating well-practiced movements promotes "angiogenesis," or the formation of new blood vessels in the brain, to help handle the "metabolic load." See James E. Black et al., "Learning Causes Synaptogenesis, Whereas Motor Activity Causes Angiogenesis, in Cerebellar Cortex of Adult Rats," *Proceedings of the National Academy of Sciences* 87, no. 14 (1990): 5568–72.

196 brain's size or weight: This point is made in Driemeyer et al., "Changes in Gray Matter Induced by Learning—Revisited."

196 internal reshuffling: As for exactly how this reshuffling happens, or by how much, the process is still not entirely clear. For a comprehensive review of training-induced plasticity studies, see Cibu Thomas and Chris Baker, "Teaching an Adult Brain New Tricks: A Critical Review of Evidence for Training-Dependent Plasticity in Humans," *NeuroImage* 73 (June 2013): 225–36.

196 we're *always* learning something: For a good discussion of plasticity in the face of skills learning, see Elisabeth Wenger et al., "Expansion and Renormalization of Human Brain Structure During Skill Acquisition," *Trends in Cognitive Sciences* 21, no. 12 (2017): 930–39.

197 research has shown that sleep: See Yuko Morita et al., "Napping After Complex Motor Learning Enhances Juggling Performance," *Sleep Science* 9, no. 2 (2016): 112–16.

197 even just a short rest: See, for example, Marlene Bönstrup et al., "A Rapid Form of Offline Consolidation in Skill Learning," *Current Biology* 29, no. 8 (2019): 1346–51.

197 "The brain wants to be puzzled": See Jessica Hamzelou, "Learning to Juggle Grows Brain Networks for Good," *New Scientist*, Oct. 11, 2009.

199 "It was something he could not master": Jon Gertner, quoted in Jimmy Soni and Rob Goodman, *A Mind at Play: How Claude Shannon Invented the Information Age* (New York: Simon & Schuster, 2017), 249.

200 "As people age": Janina Boyke et al., "Training-Induced Brain Structure Changes in the Elderly," *Journal of Neuroscience* 28, no. 28 (2008): 7031–35.

200 The more learning older adults: See, for instance, Rachael D. Seidler, "Older Adults Can Learn to Learn New Motor Skills," *Behavioral Brain Research* 183, no. 1 (2007): 118–22.

CHAPTER SEVEN
MEDITATION WITH BENEFITS

201 "Everybody ought to be taught": Quoted in Aymer Vallance, *William Morris, His Art, His Writings, and His Public Life: A Record* (London: George Bell & Sons, 1897), 251.

201 In 2017, Google released a list: See Annalisa Merelli, "Google's Most-Searched 'How-To' Questions Capture All the Magic and Struggle of Being Human," *Quartz*, Sept. 2, 2017, qz.com.

202 In one study: Jessica Davis, "Drawing's Demise: U-Shaped Development in Graphic Symbolization," Harvard Project Zero, Harvard Graduate School of Education (paper presented at SRCD Biennial Meeting, New Orleans, March 1993).

203 "the doldrums of *literalism*": Howard Gardner, *Artful Scribbles: The Significance of Children's Drawings* (New York: Basic Books, 1980), 148.

203 "technical challenges of representing space": Angela Anning, "Learning to Draw and Drawing to Learn," *International Journal of Art and Design Education* 18, no. 2 (1999): 163–72.

203 "is at once more carefully wrought": Gardner, *Artful Scribbles*, 143.

203 strictly vocational exercise: Maureen Cox notes that drawing, in the earlier part of the twentieth century, appeared "as a timetabled subject in the school curriculum, although it was actually available mainly to boys while girls were doing needlework." Not surprisingly, boys were often found to be better drawers. See Cox, *Children's Drawings of the Human Figure* (New York: Psychology Press, 1993), 3.

204 "highly important" skills: Baldassare Castiglione, *The Book of the Courtier* (London: Penguin Books, 2004), 97.

204 "social practice": Ann Bermingham, *Learning to Draw: Studies in the Cultural History of a Polite and Useful Art* (London: Paul Mellon Centre for British Art, 2000), ix.

204 another layer of memory encoding: See Myra A. Fernandes et al., "The Surprisingly Powerful Influence of Drawing on Memory," *Current Directions in Psychological Science* 27, no. 5 (2018): 302–8.

204 "ordinary daily round": Churchill, *Painting as a Pastime*, 25.

208 "guide and promote insight": Betty Edwards, *Drawing on the Right Side of the Brain* (New York: TarcherPerigree, 2012), xiv.

208 The right hemisphere, meanwhile: See M. S. Gazzaniga, J. E. Bogen, and R. W. Sperry, "Observations on Visual Perception After Disconnexion of the Cerebral Hemispheres in Man," *Brain* 88, pt. 2 (June 1965): 221–36.

209 stretched the neuroscience: In *Left Brain, Right Brain*, Sally Springer and Georg Deutsch note that no cognitive task involves just one hemisphere, and there's little reason to believe "that the left hemisphere interferes with the right hemisphere as it engages in drawing." The left hemisphere, the authors suggest, often implicated in activities like the identification of details, may even be *more* involved in the upside-down drawing exercise than the right hemisphere. Sally P. Springer and Georg Deutsch, *Left Brain, Right Brain: Perspectives from Cognitive Neuroscience* (New York: W. H. Freeman, 1997), 301.

209 "the idea that many people": Chris McManus, *Right Hand, Left Hand: The Origins of Asymmetry in Brains, Bodies, Atoms, and Cultures* (Cambridge, Mass.: Harvard University Press, 2004), 298.

209 Despite being widely disseminated: See, for example, Jared Nielsen et al., "An Evaluation of the Left-Brain vs. Right-Brain Hypothesis with Resting State Functional Connectivity Magnetic Resource Imaging," *PLOS One* 8, no. 8 (2013), doi.org/10.1371/journal.pone.0071275. On learning styles, see Paul A. Kirschner, "Stop Propagating the Learning Styles Myth," *Computers and Education* 106 (March 2017): 166–71.

209 right hemisphere is more "creative": For a good review, see Dahlia W. Zaidel, "Split-Brain, the Right Hemisphere, and Art: Fact and Fiction," *Progress in Brain Research* 204 (2013): 3–17.

209 "run wild": R. W. Sperry, "Some Effects of Disconnecting the Cerebral Hemispheres," *Science* 217 (Sept. 1982): 1223–26.

209 "perpetuates outmoded dichotomies": E. I. Schiferl, "Both Sides Now: Visualizing and Drawing with the Right and Left Hemispheres of the Brain," *Studies in Art Education* 50, no. 1 (2008): 67–82.

210 depicting them honestly: In his classic 1917 book, *The Practice and Science of Drawing*, for instance, Harold Speed suggested, as Edwards would later, that when we draw, we rely less on sight than on "the mental idea of the objective world." Harold Speed, *The Practice and Science of Drawing* (New York: Dover, 1972), 47.

210 "the innocent eye": People have debated whether an "innocent eye"—another way, really, of saying "beginner's mind"—is actually possible, whether some concept always intrudes. For a discussion, see Erik Forrest, "The 'Innocent Eye' and Recent Changes in Art Education," *Journal of Aesthetic Education* 19, no. 4 (1985): 103–14.

210 "childish perception": John Ruskin, *The Elements of Drawing* (New York: Dover, 1971), 27.

210 "When you go out and paint": Quotation retrieved from National Gallery of Art, www.nga.gov.

210 In a well-known study: See L. Carmichael et al., "An Experimental Study of the Effect of Language on the Reproduction of Visually Perceived Form," *Journal of Experimental Psychology* 15, no. 1 (1932): 73–86.

210 replicated elsewhere: See, for example, Justin Ostrofsky, Heather Nehl, and Kelly Mannion, "The Effect of Object Interpretation on the Appearance of Drawings of Ambiguous Figures," *Psychology of Aesthetics, Creativity, and the Arts* 11, no. 1 (2017): 99–108.

210 "These symbols actually seem": Edwards, *Drawing on the Right Side of the Brain*, 169.

213 "false beliefs that are held": Dale J. Cohen and Susan Bennett, "Why Can't Most People Draw What They See?," *Journal of Experimental Psychology: Human Perception and Performance* 23, no. 3 (1997): 609–21.

213 copy a series of angled lines: Monica Lee, "When Is an Object Not an Object? The Effect of 'Meaning' upon the Copying of Line Drawings," *British Journal of Psychology* 80, no. 1 (1989): 15–37.

215 "Meditation in a state of activity": Quoted in Frederick Frank, *Zen Seeing, Zen Drawing* (New York: Bantam Books, 1993), 114.

216 "Most drawings are failures": Peter Steinhart, *The Undressed Art* (New York: Vintage Books, 2004), 55.

217 "Never graduate from drawing": John Sloan, *John Sloan on Drawing and Painting: The Gist of Art* (New York: Dover, 2010), 110.

217 art schools were sending graduates: For an excellent account of what the painter David Hockney called the "destruction of drawing" in modern art schools, see Jacob Will, "What Happened to Art Schools?," *Politeia* (2018), www.politeia.co.uk.

218 "lots of students painting people": Jacob Bernstein, "Downtown Art School That Warhol Started Raises Its Celebrity Profile," *New York Times*, April 26, 2017.

218 "For some reason it felt important": Jeremy Deller, *Iggy Pop Life Class* (London: Heni, 2016), 12.

219 95 percent of nonartist subjects: See Justin Ostrofsky et al., "Why Do Non-artists Draw Eyes too Far up the Head? How Vertical Eye Drawing Errors Relate to Schematic Knowledge, Pseudoneglect, and Context-Based Perceptual Biases," *Psychology of Aesthetics, Creativity, and the Arts* 10, no. 3 (2016): 332–43. The authors note that "despite its prevalence, the basis of this bias is currently not well understood." One partial factor that has been noted is

that when drawings of people include depictions of hair, the scalp line is often implicitly taken as the top of the head. When research subjects drew bald people, the error, while still present, was not as great.

221 Artists tend to look at their subjects: See Dale J. Cohen, "Look Little, Look Often: The Influence of Gaze Frequency on Drawing Accuracy," *Perception and Psychophysics* 67, no. 6 (2005): 997–1009.

CHAPTER EIGHT

THE APPRENTICE

229 one long-term study found: See Nancy L. Chase, Xuemei Sui, and Steven N. Blair, "Swimming and All-Cause Mortality Risk Compared with Running, Walking, and Sedentary Habits in Men," *International Journal of Aquatic Research and Education* 2, no. 3 (2008): 213–23.

229 For actual clinical proof: See Weina Liu et al., "Swimming Exercise Reverses CUMS-Induced Changes in Depression-Like Behaviors and Hippocampal Plasticity-Related Proteins," *Journal of Affective Disorders* 227 (Feb. 2018): 126–35.

230 how not to drown: This idea was popularized by Terry Laughlin in his influential book, *Total Immersion: The Revolutionary Way to Swim Better, Faster, and Easier* (New York: Simon & Schuster, 2004), 2.

231 "One of the major differences": Terry McLaughlin, "Inside-Out Breathing," *CrossFit Journal*, Dec. 1, 2005, journal.crossfit.com.

235 "feeble old men": Seneca, *On the Shortness of Life* (New York: Penguin Books, 2005), 16.

236 Fitness gets you only so far: Studies have shown that, on average, technique is more important than strength in terms of swimming velocity. See R. Havriluk, "Performance Level Differences in Swimming: Relative Contributions of Strength and Technique," in *Biomechanics in Swimming XI*, ed. Per-Ludvik Kjendiie, Robert Keig Stallman, and Jan Cabri (Oslo: Norwegian School of Sport Science, 2010).

238 "A good, efficient swimming stroke": Laughlin, *Total Immersion*, 17.

239 "IKEA effect": See Michael Norton et al., "The IKEA Effect: When Labor Leads to Love," *Journal of Consumer Psychology* 22, no. 3 (2012): 453–60.

251 expanded our brain size: In his excellent book *Hands*, John Napier writes, "S. L. Washburn of Berkeley has emphasized that increase in brain size (a somewhat crude but useful method of estimating the overall capability of the brain in terms of motor and tactile functions, skill, memory, and foresight—all of which take up brain

space) is more likely to have followed than preceded tool-making, so that a positive feed-back became established." See John Napier, *Hands* (Princeton, N.J.: Princeton University Press, 1980), 101.

251 helped shape the hands: The anthropologist Mary Marzke is particularly associated with this line of argument. See, for example, Mary W. Marzke, "Tool Making, Hand Morphology, and Fossil Hominins," *Philosophical Transactions of the Royal Society B: Biological Sciences* 368, no. 1630 (2013): 1–8. Also see Sara Reardon, "Stone Tools Helped Shape Human Hands," *New Scientist*, April 10, 2013.

252 "derive a deep sense": See Kelly Lambert, *Lifting Depression* (New York: Basic Books, 2010), 28. See also Kelly G. Lambert, "Rising Rates of Depression in Today's Society: Consideration of the Roles of Effort-Based Rewards and Enhanced Resilience in Day-to-Day Functioning," *Neuroscience and Biobehavioral Reviews* 30, no. 4 (2006): 497–510.

253 train as apprentices: By one account, less than 5 percent of young people in the United States were in an apprentice program. See Tamar Jacoby, "Why Germany Is So Much Better at Training Its Workers," *Atlantic*, Oct. 16, 2014.

253 Working with one's hands: See Kelly Lambert, "Depressingly Easy," *Scientific American Mind*, Aug. 2009.

255 "provide limitless motivation": See Paul A. O'Keefe et al., "Implicit Theories of Interest: Finding Your Passion or Developing It?," *Association for Psychological Science* 29, no. 10 (2018): 1653–64.

256 To be a traveler: See Daniel J. Boorstin, *The Image* (New York: Vintage Books, 1992), 85.

257 "indulge ourselves in our expertise": "Laird Hamilton on Being a Beginner and Mixing Things Up," The Mullet, Oct. 5, 2015, www.distressedmullet.com.

257 "borderline toxic": This useful descriptor is courtesy of Jeff Stewart, "The Dos and Don'ts of Embrocation," Competitive Cyclist, April 21, 2014, www.competitivecyclist.com.

258 "In science," he wrote: See Richard Hamming, *The Art of Doing Science and Engineering* (Amsterdam: Gordon and Breach, 2005), 5.

259 "My old teacher Kurt Vonnegut": John Casey, *Room for Improvement: A Life in Sport* (New York: Vintage, 2012), 177.

260 "Learning," as *The Journal*: See Elizabeth J. Krumrei-Mancuso et al., "Links Between Intellectual Humility and Acquiring Knowledge," *Journal of Positive Psychology*, Feb. 14, 2019.

A NOTE ABOUT THE AUTHOR

Tom Vanderbilt is author of *You May Also Like: Taste in an Age of Endless Choice*, *Traffic: Why We Drive the Way We Do (and What It Says About Us)*, and *Survival City: Adventures Among the Ruins of Atomic America*. He lives in Brooklyn, New York.

A NOTE ON THE TYPE

This book was set in Janson, a typeface long thought to have been made by the Dutchman Anton Janson, who was a practicing typefounder in Leipzig during the years 1668–1687. However, it has been conclusively demonstrated that these types are actually the work of Nicholas Kis (1650–1702), a Hungarian, who most probably learned his trade from the master Dutch typefounder Dirk Voskens. The type is an excellent example of the influential and sturdy Dutch types that prevailed in England up to the time William Caslon (1692–1766) developed his own incomparable designs from them.

Composed by Westchester Publishing Services,
Danbury, Connecticut

Printed and bound by LSC Communications,
Kendallville, Indiana

Designed by Soonyoung Kwon